SOCIOLOGY OF SOCIAL STRATIFICATION

SOCIOLOGY OF SOCIAL STRATIFICATION

Dr. Bindeshwari Pd. Mandal

CENTRUM PRESS
NEW DELHI-110002 (INDIA)

CENTRUM PRESS
H.O.: 4360/4, Ansari Road, Daryaganj,
New Delhi-110002 (India)
Tel: 23278000, 23261597, 23255577, 23286875
B.O.: No. 1015, Ist Main Road, BSK IIIrd Stage,
IIIrd Phase, IIIrd Block, Bangalore-560085 (INDIA)
Tel: 080-41723429
Email: centrumpress@gmail.com
Visit us at: www.centrumpress.com

Sociology of Social Stratification

First Edition, 2011

ISBN 978-93-80921-55-6

PRINTED IN INDIA

Printed at Tarun Offset Printers, Delhi-110053

Contents

Preface

Social inequality is a universal phenomenon in all societies. It can exist either in form of a hierarchy of groups or individuals or it may exist without the creation of a hierarchy. In the former case it is called social hierarchy. While in the latter case it is known as social differentiation for in almost all societies men and women are treated unequally. If social inequality manifests itself in the form of a hierarchy involving ranking of groups then it is known as social stratification, thus social stratification is a particular case of the social inequality. Social stratification is essentially a group phenomena. According to Ogburn and Nimkoff the process by which individuals and groups are ranked in a more or less enduring hierarchy of status is known as stratification. Melvin Tumin defines social stratification as an arrangement of any social group or society into a hierarchy of positions that are unequal with regard to power, property, social evaluation and psychic gratification. According to Lundberg a stratified society is one marked by inequality by differences among people that are evaluated by them as being lower and higher.

In modern Western societies, stratification is broadly organized into three main layers: upper class, middle class, and lower class. Each class may be further subdivided into smaller classes (e.g. occupational). These categories are particular to state-based societies as distinguished from, for instance, feudal societies composed of nobility-to-peasant relations. Stratification may also be defined by kinship ties or castes. For Max Weber, social class pertaining broadly to material wealth is distinguished from status class which is based on such variables as honour, prestige and religious affiliation. It is debatable whether the earliest hunter-gatherer groups may be defined as 'stratified', or if such differentials began with agriculture and broad acts of exchange between groups. One of the ongoing issues in determining social stratification arises from the point that status inequalities between individuals are common, so it becomes a quantitative issue to determine how much inequality qualifies as stratification.

The concept of social stratification is interpreted differently by the various theoretical perspectives of sociology. Proponents of structural-functionalism have suggested that since social stratification is commonly found in developed societies, hierarchy may be necessary in order to stabilize social structure. Talcott Parsons, an American sociologist, asserted that stability and social order are achieved by means of a universal value consensus, satisfying the functional prerequisites of a society. By contrast, conflict theories, such as Marxism, point to the inaccessibility of resources and lack of social mobility found in stratified societies. Many sociological theorists have criticized the extent to which the working classes are unlikely to advance socioeconomically; the wealthy tend to hold political power which they use to exploit the proletariat intergenerationally. Theorists such as Ralf Dahrendorf, however, have noted the tendency toward an enlarged middle-class in modern Western societies due to the necessity of an educated workforce in technological and service economies. Various social and political perspectives concerning globalization, such as dependency theory, suggest that these effects are due to the shift of workers to the third world.

The present publication has been designed to approach this subject in a simple and lucid style. The method of presentation is very clear and lucid, which can be easily followed by the students.

1

Introduction

A society or a human society is (1) a group of people related to each other through persistent relations such as social status, roles and social networks. (2) A large social grouping that shares the same geographical territory and is subject to the same political authority and dominant cultural expectations. Human societies are characterized by patterns of relationships between individuals sharing a distinctive culture and institutions. Without an article, the term refers either to the entirety of humanity or a contextually specific subset of people.

Used in the sense of an association, a society is a body of individuals outlined by the bounds of functional interdependence, possibly comprising characteristics such as national or cultural identity, social solidarity, language or hierarchical organization.

Like other groupings, a society allows its members to achieve needs or wishes they could not fulfil alone; the social fact can be identified, understood or specified within a circumstance that certain resources, objectives, requirements or results, are needed and utilized in an individual manner and for individual ends, although they can't be achieved, gotten or fulfilled in an individual manner as well, but, on the contrary, they can be gotten only in a collective, collaborative manner; namely, team work becomes the valid functional means, to individual ends which an individual would need to have but isn't able to get.

More broadly, a society is an economic, social or industrial infrastructure, made up of a varied collection of individuals. Members of a society may be from different ethnic groups. A society may be a particular ethnic group, such as the Saxons; a nation state, such as Bhutan; a broader cultural group, such as a Western society. The word *society* may also refer to an organized voluntary association of people for religious, benevolent, cultural, scientific, political, patriotic, or other purposes. A "society" may even, though more by means of metaphor, refer to a social organism such as an ant colony or any cooperative aggregate such as for example in some formulations of artificial intelligence.

Conceptions of "Society"

Society, in general, addresses the fact that an individual has rather limited means as an autonomous unit. The Great apes have always been more (*Bonobo. Homo, Pan*) or less (*Gorilla, Pongo*) social animals so Robinson Crusoe like situations are either fictions or unusual corner cases to the ubiquity of social context for humans who fall between presocial and eusocial in the spectrum of animal ethology.

Anthropology

Human societies are most often organized according to their primary means of subsistence. Social scientists have identified hunter-gatherer societies, nomadic pastoral societies, horticulturalist or simple farming societies, and intensive agricultural societies, also called civilizations. Some consider industrial and post-industrial societies to be qualitatively different from traditional agricultural societies.

Today, anthropologists and many social scientists vigorously oppose the notion of cultural evolution and rigid "stages" such as these. In fact, much anthropological data has suggested that complexity (civilization, population growth and density, specialization, etc.) does not always take the form of hierarchical social organization or stratification.

Also, cultural relativism as a widespread approach/ethic has largely replaced notions of "primitive," better/worse, or "progress" in relation to cultures (including their material culture/technology and social organization).

According to anthropologist Maurice Godelier, one critical novelty in human society, in contrast to humanity's closest biological relatives (chimpanzees and bonobo), is the parental role assumed by the males, which supposedly would be absent in our nearest relatives for whom paternity is not in general determinable.

Political Science

Societies may also be organized according to their political structure. In order of increasing size and complexity, there are bands, tribes, chiefdoms, and state societies. These structures may have varying degrees of political power, depending on the cultural geographical, and historical environments that these societies must contend with. Thus, a more isolated society with the same level of technology and culture as other societies is more likely to survive than one in closer proximity to others that may encroach on their resources. A society that is unable to offer an effective response to other societies it competes with will usually be subsumed into the culture of the competing society.

Sociology

Sociologist Gerhard Lenski differentiates societies based on their level of technology, communication and economy: 1) hunters and gatherers, 2) simple agricultural, 3) advanced agricultural, 4) industrial, and 5) special (e.g. fishing societies or maritime societies). This is somewhat similar to the system earlier developed by anthropologists Morton H. Fried, a conflict theorist, and Elman Service, an integration theorist, who have produced a system of classification for societies in all human cultures based on the evolution of social inequality and the role of the state. This system of classification contains four categories:

Hunter-gatherer bands (categorization on duties and responsibilities.)

Tribal societies in which there are some limited instances of social rank and prestige.

Stratified structures led by chieftains.

Civilizations, with complex social hierarchies and organized, institutional governments.

In addition to this there are:

- Humanity, mankind, that upon which rest all the elements of society, including society's beliefs.

- Virtual society is a society based on online identity, which is evolving in the information age.

Over time, some cultures have progressed toward more-complex forms of organization and control. This cultural evolution has a profound effect on patterns of community. Hunter-gatherer tribes settled around seasonal food stocks to become agrarian villages. Villages grew to become towns and cities. Cities turned into city-states and nation-states.

Many societies will distribute largess, at the behest of some individual or some larger group of people. This type of *generosity* can be seen in all known cultures; typically, prestige accrues to the generous individual or group. Conversely, members of a society may also shun or scapegoat members of the society who violate its norms. Mechanisms such as gift-giving and scapegoating, which may be seen in various types of human groupings, tend to be institutionalized within a society. Social evolution as a phenomenon carries with itself certain elements that could be detrimental to the population it serves.

Some societies will bestow status on an individual or group of people, when that individual or group performs an admired or desired action. This type of recognition is bestowed by members of that society on the individual or group in the form of a name, title, manner of dress, or monetary reward. Adult male/female status, in many societies, is subject to a ritual or process of this type. Altruistic action in the interests of the larger group is seen in virtually all societies. The phenomena of community action, shunning, scapegoating, generosity, shared risk and reward are common to many forms of society.

Contemporary Usage

The term *society* is currently used to cover both a number of political and scientific connotations as well as a variety of associations.

Western Society or Western World

The development of the Western world has brought with it the emerging concepts of Western culture, politics and ideas, often referred to simply as *Western society*. Geographically, it covers at the very least the countries of Western Europe, North America, Australia and New Zealand and sometimes also includes South America and Israel. The cultures and lifestyles of all of these stem from Western Europe. They all enjoy relatively strong economies and stable governments, allow freedom of religion, have chosen democracy as a form of governance, favor capitalism and international trade, are heavily influenced by Judeo-Christian values, and have some form of political and military alliance or cooperation. The Western world, also known as the West and the Occident, is a term that can have multiple meanings depending on its context (e.g., the time period, the region or social situation). Accordingly, the basic definition of what constitutes "the West" varies, expanding and contracting over time, in relation to various historical circumstances.

The concept of the Western world has its roots in Greco-Roman civilization in Europe, the advent of Christianity, and the Great Schism in the 11th Century which divided the religion into Eastern and Western halves. In the modern era, Western culture has been heavily influenced by the traditions of The Renaissance and The Enlightenment, and shaped by expansive colonialism in the 18th-19th Century. Its political usage was temporarily informed by mutual antagonism with the Soviet bloc during the Cold War in the mid to late 20th Century. In the contemporary political and cultural context, the Western World generally refers to the nations of the Americas, Europe, Australia, New Zealand, Israel, and South Africa.

The consensus is that the West originated with ancient Greece and ancient Rome. Over time, their associated empires grew first to the east and south, conquering and absorbing many older great civilizations of the ancient Near East; later, they grew to the north and west to include Western Europe.

Other historians, such as Carroll Quigley (*Evolution of Civilizations*), contend that Western Civilization was born around 400 AD, after the total collapse of the Western Roman Empire, leaving a vacuum for new ideas to flourish that were impossible in Classical societies. In either view, between the fall of the Western Roman Empire and the Renaissance, the West experienced a period of considerable decline, known as the Middle Ages, which include the Dark Ages and the Crusades. The knowledge of the ancient Western world was partly preserved during this period due to the survival of the Eastern

Roman Empire; it was also greatly expanded by the Arab World, and mostly by the concurrent ascendency of the Islamic Golden Age. The Arab importation of both the Ancient and new technology from the Middle East and the Orient to Renaissance Europe represented "one of the largest technology transfers in world history."

Since the Renaissance, the West evolved beyond the influence of the ancient Greeks, Romans and Muslims due to the Commercial, Scientific, and Industrial Revolutions, and the expansion of the Christian peoples of Western European empires, and particularly the globe-spanning empires of the eighteenth and nineteenth centuries. Since the Age of Discovery and Columbus, the notion of the West expanded to include the Americas, though much of the Americas have considerable pre-Western cultural influence. Australia, New Zealand and most countries of Latin America are considered part of Western culture due to their former status as settler colonies of Western Christian nations. Generally speaking, the current consensus would locate the West, at the very least, in the cultures and peoples of Europe, North America (namely Canada, U.S., and Mexico), Australia, New Zealand and most countries in South America. There is debate among some as to whether Eastern Europe is in a category of its own. Culturally Eastern Europe is usually more or less accepted into the 'West', mainly because of its geographic location in what is mostly Europe (and cultural ties). However, it does not fill the traditional economic and living-standard criteria typically associated with "The West".

When referring to current events, the term "Western World" often includes developed countries in Asia, such as Japan, Singapore, Taiwan, and South Korea, that have strong economic, political and military ties to Western Europe, NATO or the United States. While these countries also have substantial Western influence and similarities in their cultures, they nonetheless maintain largely different and distinctive cultures, religions (although Christianity is a major religion in South Korea), languages, customs, and worldviews that are products of their own indigenous development, rather than Western influences.

Japan and South Korea, in particular, are the only Asian members of the Organisation for Economic Cooperation and

Development (OECD) and the two leading full democracies in Asia, having a high standard of living and a high level of human development. All of these are amongst the generally accepted political or economic characteristics of Western nations.

Western Culture

The term "Western culture" is used very broadly to refer to a heritage of social norms, ethical values, traditional customs, religious beliefs, political systems, and specific artifacts and technologies.

Specifically, Western culture may imply:

- a Biblical-Christian cultural influence in spiritual thinking, customs and either ethic or moral traditions, around Post-Classical Era.
- European cultural influences concerning artistic, musical, folkloric, ethic and oral traditions, whose themes have been further developed by Romanticism.
- a Graeco-Roman Classical and Renaissance cultural influence, concerning artistic, philosophic, literary, and legal themes and traditions, the cultural social effects of migration period and the heritages of Celtic and Germanic and other ethnic groups, as well as a tradition of rationalism in various spheres of life, developed by Hellenistic philosophy, Scholasticism, Humanisms, the Scientific Revolution and Enlightenment, and including, in political thought, widespread rational arguments in favour of freethought, human rights, equality and democratic values averse to irrationality and theocracy.

The concept of Western culture is generally linked to the classical definition of the Western world. In this definition, Western culture is the set of literary, scientific, political, artistic and philosophical principles that set it apart from other civilizations. Much of this set of traditions and knowledge is collected in the Western canon. The term has come to apply to countries whose history is strongly marked by Western European immigration or settlement, such as the Americas, and Australasia, and is not restricted to Western Europe.

Some tendencies that define modern Western societies are the existence of political pluralism, prominent subcultures or countercultures (such as New Age movements), increasing cultural syncretism resulting from globalization and human migration.

Historical Divisions

The geopolitical divisions in Europe that created a concept of *East* and *West* originated in the Roman Empire. The Eastern Mediterranean was home to the highly urbanized cultures that had Greek as their common language (owing to the older empire of Alexander the Great), whereas the West was much more rural in its character and more readily adopted Latin as its common language. After the fall of the Western Roman Empire, Western Europe was substantially cut off from the East where *Byzantine* Greek culture and Eastern Christianity became founding influences in the Arab/Muslim world and among the Slavic peoples. Roman Catholic western Europe, as such, maintained a distinct identity particularly as it began to redevelop during the Renaissance. Even following the Protestant Reformation, Protestant Europe continued to see itself as more tied to Roman Catholic Europe than other parts of the *civilized* world.

Use of the term *West* as a specific cultural and geopolitical term developed over the course of the Age of Exploration as Western Europe spread its culture to other parts of the world. In the past two centuries the term *western world* has sometimes been used synonymously with *Christian world* because of the numerical dominance of Roman Catholicism and Protestantism compared to other Christian traditions, though this dominance is somewhat recent. As secularism rose in Europe and elsewhere during the 19th and 20th centuries, the term *West* came to take on less religious connotations and more political connotations, especially during the Cold War. Additionally, closer contacts between the *West* and Asia and other parts of the world in recent times have continued to cloud the use and meaning of the term.

Hellenic

The Hellenic division between the barbarians and the Greeks contrasted in many societies the Greek-speaking culture of the Greek settlements around the Mediterranean to the surrounding non-Greek cultures. Herodotus considered the Persian Wars of the early 5th century BC a conflict of Europa versus Asia (which he considered to be all land north and east of the Sea of Marmara, respectively). The terms "West" and "East" were not used by any Greek author to describe that conflict. The anachronistic application of those terms to that division entails a stark logical contradiction, given that, when the term "West" appeared, it was used in opposition to the Greeks and Greek-speaking culture.

Western society traces its cultural origins to both Greek thought and Christian religion, thus following an evolution that began in ancient Greece, continued through the Roman Empire and, with the coming of Christianity (which has its origins in the Middle East), spread throughout Europe. The inherently "Greek" classical ideas of history (which one might easily say they invented) and art may, however, be considered almost inviolate in the West, as their original spread of influence survived the Hellenic period of Roman classical antiquity, The Dark Ages, its resurgence during the western Renaissance, and has managed somehow to keep and exert its pervasive influence down into the present age, with every expectation of it continuing to dominate any secular Western cultural developments.

However, the conquest of the western parts of the Roman Empire by Germanic peoples and the subsequent dominance by the Western Christian Papacy (which held combined political and spiritual authority, a state of affairs absent from Greek civilization in all its stages), resulted in a rupture of the previously existing ties between the Latin West and Greek thought, including Christian Greek thought. The Great Schism and the Fourth Crusade confirmed this deviation.

Hence, the Medieval West is limited to Western Christendom only, as the Greeks and other European peoples not under the authority of the Papacy are not included in it. The clearly Greek-influenced form of Christianity, Orthodoxy, is more linked to Eastern than Western Europe. On the other hand, the Modern West, emerging after the Renaissance as a new civilization, has been influenced by (its own interpretation of) Greek thought, which was preserved in the Roman Empire and the medieval Islamic world during the Medieval West's

Dark Ages and transmitted from there by emigration of Greek scholars, courtly marriages, and Latin translations. The Renaissance in the West emerged partly from currents within the Roman (Byzantine) Empire. Moreover, European peoples not included in Western Christendom, such as the Greeks, have redefined their relationship to this new, secular, variant of Western civilization, and have increasingly participated in it since then.

Thus, the idea of Western society being influenced from (but not being the single evolution of) ancient Greek thought makes sense only for the post-Renaissance period of Western history.

The Roman Empire

That grew from a city-state founded on the Italian Peninsula about the 9th century BC to a massive empire straddling the Mediterranean Sea. In its 12-century existence, Roman civilization shifted from a monarchy, to a republic, to an autocratic empire. It came to dominate Western Europe, the Balkans and the entire area surrounding the Mediterranean Sea through conquest using the Roman legions and then through cultural assimilation by giving Roman privileges and eventually citizenship to the whole empire. Nonetheless, despite its great legacy, a number of factors led to the eventual decline of the Roman Empire.

The Western Roman Empire eventually broke into several kingdoms in the 5th century due to civil wars, corruption, and devastating Germanic invasions from such tribes as the Goths, the Franks and the Vandals.

The Eastern Roman Empire, governed from Constantinople, is usually referred to as the Byzantine Empire after 476, the traditional date for the "fall of the Western Roman Empire" and for the subsequent onset of the Early Middle Ages. The Eastern Roman Empire survived the fall of the West, and protected Roman legal and cultural traditions, combining them with Greek and Christian elements, for another thousand years.

The Roman Empire succeeded the about 500 year-old Roman Republic (510 BC - 1st century BC), which had been weakened by the conflict between Gaius Marius and Sulla and the civil war of Julius Caesar against Pompey and Marcus Brutus.

During these struggles hundreds of senators were killed, and the Roman Senate had been refilled with loyalists of the First Triumvirate and later those of the Second Triumvirate.

Several dates are commonly proposed to mark the transition from Republic to Empire, including the date of Julius Caesar's appointment as perpetual roman dictator (44 BC), the victory of Caesar's heir Octavian at the Battle of Actium (September 2, 31 BC), and the Roman Senate's granting to Octavian the honorific *Augustus.* (January 16, 27 BC). Octavian/Augustus officially proclaimed that he had saved the Roman Republic and carefully disguised his power under republican forms: Consuls continued to be elected, tribunes of the plebeians continued to offer legislation, and senators still debated in the Roman Curia. However, it was Octavian who influenced everything and controlled the final decisions, and in final analysis, had the legions to back him up, if it became necessary.

Roman expansion began long before the state was changed into an empire and reached its zenith under emperor Trajan with the conquest of Dacia in AD 106. During this territorial peak, the Roman Empire controlled about 5 900 000 km^2 (2,300,000 sq.mi.) of land surface and had a population of 100 million. From the time of Caesar to the Fall of the Western Empire, Rome dominated Western Eurasia and the Mediterranean, comprising the majority of its population. Ancient Rome has contributed greatly to the development of law, war, art, literature, architecture, technology and language in the Western world, and its history continues to have a major influence on the world today. The Roman Empire is where the idea of the "West" began to emerge. Due to Rome's central location at the heart of the Empire, "West" and "East" were terms used to denote provinces west and east of the capital itself. Therefore, Iberia (Portugal and Spain), Gaul (France), Africa (Tunisia, Algeria, and Morocco) and Britannia were all part of the "West", while Greece, Anatolia, Syria, and Egypt were part of the "East." Italy itself was considered central, until the reforms of Diocletian, when the idea of formally dividing the Empire into true Eastern and Western halves was introduced.

In 395, the Roman Empire formally split into a Western Roman Empire and an Eastern one, each with their own emperors, capitals, and governments, although ostensibly they still belonged to one formal Empire. The dissolution of the Western half (nominally in 476, but in truth a long process that ended by 500) left only the Eastern Empire alive. For centuries, the East continued to call themselves Eastern Romans, while the West began to think in terms of Latins (those living in the old Western Empire) and Greeks (those inside the Roman remnant to the east).

Christian Schism

In the early 4th century, the Roman Emperor Constantine the Great established the city of Constantinople as the capital of the Eastern Roman Empire. The Eastern Empire included lands east of the Adriatic Sea and bordering on the Eastern Mediterranean and parts of the Black Sea. These two divisions of the Eastern and Western Empires were reflected in the administration of the Christian Church, with Rome and Constantinople debating and arguing over whether either city was the capital of Christianity.

As the eastern and western churches spread their influence, the line between "East" and "West" can be described as moving. But it generally followed a cultural divide that was defined by the existence of the Byzantine empire and the fluctuating power and influence of the church in Rome.

Some people, including Huntington, theorized that this cultural division still existed during the Cold War as the approximate western boundary of those countries that were allied with the Soviet Union. Others have criticized these views on the basis that they confuse the Eastern Roman Empire with Russia, especially considering the fact that the country that had the most historical roots in Byzantium, Greece, was allied with the West during the Cold War.

Under Charlemagne, the Franks established an empire that was recognized as the Holy Roman Empire by the Pope in Rome, offending the Roman Emperor in Constantinople. The crowning of the Emperor by the Pope led to the assumption that the highest power was the papal hierarchy, establishing, until the Protestant Reformation, the civilization of Western Christendom. The Latin Rite Christian Church of western and central Europe headed by the Pope split with the eastern,

Greek-speaking Patriarchates during the Great Schism. Meanwhile, the extent of each expanded, as Scandinavia, Germany, Britain, and the other non-Christian lands of the northwest were converted by the Western Church, while Russia and some of Eastern Europe were converted by the Eastern Church.

In this context, the Protestant reformation may be viewed as a schism within the Latin Church. Martin Luther, in the wake of precursors, broke with the pope and with the emperor, backed by many of the German princes. These changes were adopted by the Scandinavian kings. Later, the commoner Jean Cauvin (John Calvin) assumed the religio-political leadership in Geneva, a former ecclesiastical city whose prior ruler had been the bishop. The English King later improvised on the Lutheran model, but subsequently many Calvinist doctrines were adopted by popular dissenters, leading to the English Civil War. Both royalists and dissenters colonized North America, eventually resulting in an independent United States of America.

The Colonial "West"

The Reformation, and consequent dissolution of Western Christendom as even a theoretical unitary political body, resulted in the Thirty Years War. The war ended in the Peace of Westphalia, which enshrined the concept of the nation-state and the principle of absolute national sovereignty in international law.

These concepts of a world of nation-states, coupled with the ideologies of the Enlightenment, the coming of modernity, the Scientific Revolution, and the Industrial Revolution, produced powerful political and economic institutions that have come to influence (or been imposed upon) most nations of the world today. Historians agree that the Industrial Revolution was one of the most important events in history.

This process of influence (and imposition) began with the voyages of discovery, colonization, conquest, and exploitation of Spain and Portugal; it continued with the rise of the Dutch East India Company, and the creation and expansion of the British and French colonial empires. Due to the reach of these empires, Western institutions expanded throughout the world.

Even after demands for self-determination from subject peoples within Western empires were met with decolonization, these institutions persisted. One specific example was the requirement that post-colonial societies were made to form nation-states (in the Western tradition), which often created arbitrary boundaries and borders that did not necessarily represent a whole nation, people, or culture, and are often the cause of international conflicts and friction even to this day. Though the overt colonial era has passed, Western nations, as comparatively rich, well-armed, and culturally powerful states, still wield a large degree of influence throughout the world.

Palestinian-American literary critic Edward Said uses the term occident in his discussion of orientalism. According to his binary, the West, or Occident, created a romanticized vision of the East, or Orient, in order to justify colonial and imperialist intentions. This Occident-Orient binary is focused on the Western vision of the East instead of any truths about the East. His theories are rooted in Hegel's Master-slave dialectic: The Occident would not exist without the Orient and vice versa. Further, Western writers created this irrational, feminine, weak "Other" to contrast with the rational, masculine, strong West because of a need to create a difference between the two that would justify imperialist ambitions, said influenced Indian-American theorist Homi K. Bhabha.

The Cold War

During the Cold War, a new definition emerged. The Earth was divided into three "worlds". The First World, analogous in this context to what was called *the West*, was composed of NATO members and other countries aligned with the United States. The Second World was the Eastern bloc in the Soviet sphere of influence, including the Soviet Union and Warsaw Pact countries. It included some Central European countries (like The German Democratic Republic, Czechoslovakia, Hungary and Poland) which had a Western type culture.

The Third World consisted of countries unaligned with either, and important members included India and Yugoslavia; some include the People's Republic of China, though this is disputed, as the People's Republic of China is communist, had friendly relations—at certain times—with the Soviet bloc, and had a significant degree of importance in global geopolitics. There were a number of countries which did not fit comfortably into this neat definition of partition, including Switzerland, Sweden, Austria and Ireland, which chose to be neutral. Finland was under the *Soviet Union's* military sphere of influence but remained neutral, was not communist, nor was it a member of the Warsaw Pact or Comecon but a member of the EFTA since 1986, and was west of the Iron Curtain. In 1955, when Austria again became a fully independent republic, it did so under the condition that it remain neutral, but as a country to the west of the Iron Curtain, it was in the *United States* sphere of influence. Spain did not join NATO until 1982, towards the end of the Cold War and after the death of the authoritarian Franco.

Modern Definitions

The exact scope of the Western world is somewhat subjective in nature, depending on whether cultural, economic, spiritual or political criteria are employed. But these definitions almost always include the countries of Western Europe, the United States, Canada, Australia and New Zealand. These are Western European or Western European-derived nations which enjoy relatively strong economies and stable governments, allow freedom of religion, have chosen democracy as a form of governance, favor capitalism and international trade, are heavily influenced by Judeo-Christian values, and have some form of political and military alliance or cooperation. Many anthropologists, sociologists and historians oppose "the West and the Rest" in a categorical manner. The same has been done by Malthusian demographers with a sharp distinction between European and non-European family systems. Among anthropologists, this includes Durkheim, Dumont and Lévi-Strauss. As the term "Western world" does not have a strict international definition, governments do not use the term in legislation of international treaties and instead rely on other definitions.

Cultural

From a cultural and sociological approach the Western world is defined as including all cultures that are directly derived from European cultures, i.e. Europe, the Americas

(North and South America), Israel, Australia and New Zealand. Together these countries constitute Western society

In the 20th century, Christianity declined in influence in many western countries, in Western Europe and elsewhere. Secularism (separating religion from politics and science) increased. However, while church attendance is in decline, most Westerners nominally identify themselves as Christians (e.g. 70% in the UK) and occasionally attend church on major occasions. In the United States, Christianity continues to play an important societal role, thus helping to maintain Christianity's important role in Western culture.

The official religion of the United Kingdom and some Nordic countries is Christianity, even though the majority of European countries have no official religion. Despite this, Christianity, in its different forms, remains the largest faith in most Western countries. Thus another definition of *Occident* would include reference to this majority Christian content within the culture.

Modern Political

Countries of the Western world are generally considered to share certain fundamental political ideologies, including those of liberal democracy, the rule of law, human rights and a high degree of gender equality (although there are notable exceptions, especially in foreign policy). Additionally countries with strong political and/or military ties to Western Europe, NATO and/or the United States, such as Japan, Israel, and South Korea can be said to be Western in a political sense at least.

As such, this definition of the term "Western" is not necessarily tied to the geographic sense of the word. A geographically Western nation such as Cuba is sometimes not considered politically Western due to its general rejection of liberal democracy, freedom of the press, and personal liberty.

Conversely, some Eastern nations, for example, Japan, India, Israel, Taiwan, and South Korea, could be considered politically Western, due to their adoption of indigenous liberal democratic political institutions similar in structure to those of the traditionally Western nations.

Economic

Though the Cold War has ended, and some members of the former Eastern Bloc are making a general movement towards liberal democracy and other values held in common by the traditionally Western states, some former Soviet republics are not considered Western because of the small presence of social and political reform, as well as their obvious cultural, economic and political differences to what is known today as described by the term "the West" (Western Europe, North America, Israel, Australia and New Zealand).

These include the three Transcaucasian republics (Azerbaijan, Georgia, Armenia), as well as Kazakhstan, Tajikistan, Turkmenistan, Uzbekistan, Kyrgyzstan, Russia, Belarus and Ukraine. Central Europe is currently a separate entity occupying an in-between economic position.

Although it is inaccurate to do so, the term "Western world" is often interchangeable with the term First World stressing the difference between First World and the Third World or developing countries. The term "The North" has in some contexts replaced earlier usage of the term "the West", particularly in the critical sense, as a more robust demarcation than the terms "West" and "East". The North provides some absolute geographical indicators for the location of wealthy countries, most of which are physically situated in the Northern Hemisphere, although, as most countries are located in the northern hemisphere in general, some have considered this distinction to be equally unhelpful.

The thirty countries in the Organisation for Economic Cooperation and Development (OECD), which include: the EU, Norway, Iceland, Switzerland, Canada, the United States, Australia, New Zealand, South Korea and Japan, generally include what used to be called the "first world" or the "developed world", although the OECD includes a few countries, namely Mexico and Turkey, that are not yet fully industrial countries, but newly industrialized countries. The existence of "The North" implies the existence of "The South", and the socio-economic divide between North and South. Although Singapore, Taiwan and Hong Kong are not members of the OECD, they might also be regarded as "western" or "northern" countries or regions, because their high living standards and their social, economical and political structure are quite similar to those of the OECD member countries.

Other Views

A series of scholars of civilization, including Arnold J. Toynbee, Alfred Kroeber and Carroll Quigley have identified and analyzed "Western civilization" as one of the civilizations that have historically existed and still exist today. Toynbee entered into quite an expansive mode, including as candidates those countries or cultures who became so heavily influenced by the West as to adopt these borrowings into their very self-identity; carried to its limit, this would in practice include almost everyone within the West, in one way or another. In particular, Toynbee refers to the *intelligentsia* formed among the educated elite of countries impacted by the European expansion of centuries past. While often pointedly nationalist, these cultural and political leaders interacted within the West to such an extent as to change both themselves and the West.

Yet more recently, Samuel P. Huntington has taken a far more restricted approach, forging a political science hypothesis he labelled the "The Clash of Civilizations?" in a *Foreign Affairs* article and a book. According to Huntington's hypothesis, what he calls "conflicts between civilizations" will be the primary tensions of the 21st century world. In this hypothesis, the West is based on religion, as the countries of Western and Central Europe were historically influenced by the two forms of Western Christianity, namely Catholicism and Protestantism. Also, many Anglophone countries share these traits, e.g. Australia and New Zealand, as well as the more heterogeneous United States and Canada. Of course, so does Latin America.

Huntington's thesis, while influential, was by no means universally accepted; its supporters say that it explains modern conflicts, such as those in the former Yugoslavia. The thesis's detractors fear that by equating values like democracy with the concept of "Western civilization", it reinforces stereotypes that some perceive as being common within the West about non-traditionally Western societies that some may consider racist or xenophobic. Others believe that Huntington ignores the existence of non-Western democracies such as the East Asian and South-Central Asian democracies. As such, these detractors believe that it will serve to provoke and amplify conflict rather than illuminating a way to find an accommodating world order, or in particular cases a commonly agreed solution.

In Huntington's narrow thesis, the historically Eastern Orthodox nations of southeastern and Eastern Europe constitute a distinct "Euro-Asiatic civilization"; although European and mainly Christian (as well as notable Muslim influence and populations, particularly in the Balkans and southern/central Russia), these nations were not, in Huntington's view, shaped by the cultural influences of the Renaissance. The Renaissance did not affect Orthodox Eastern Europe due in part to the proximity of Ottoman domination, despite the decisive influence of Greek emigre scholars on the Renaissance.

Other views might be made regarding Eastern Europe.

A controversial theory of Huntington is that he considered the possibility of South America being a separate civilization from the West, but also mused that it might become a third part (the first two being North America and Europe) of the West in the future.

The theologian and paleontologist Pierre Teilhard de Chardin conceived of the West as the set of civilizations descended from the Nile Valley Civilization of Egypt.

The term the "West" may also be used pejoratively by certain tendencies especially critical of the influence of the traditional West, due to the history of most of the members of the traditional West being previously involved, at one time or another, in outright imperialism and colonialism. Some of these critics also claim that the traditional West has continued to engage in what might be viewed as modern implementations of imperialism and colonialism, such as neoliberalism and globalization. (It should be noted that many Westerners who subscribe to a positive view of the traditional West are also very critical of neoliberalism and globalization, for their allegedly negative effects on both the developed and developing world.)

Allegedly, definitions of the term "Western world" that some may consider "ethnocentric" are considered by some to be "constructed" around one or another Western culture. The British writer Rudyard Kipling wrote about this contrast: *East is East and West is West and never the twain shall meet,* expressing his belief that somebody from the West "can never understand the Asian cultures" as the latter "differ too much" from the Western cultures. Some may view this alleged incompatibility as a precursor to Huntington's "clash of civilizations" theory.

Paradoxically, today Asia and Africa to varying degrees may be considered quasi-Western. Many East Asians and South Asians and Africans and others associate or even identify with the cosmopolitan cultures and international societies referred to sometimes as Western. Likewise, many in the West identify with a transcultural humanity, a notion often found in visions of the sacred.

From a very different perspective, it has also been argued that the idea of the West is, in part, a non-Western invention, deployed in the non-West to shape and define non-Western pathways through or against modernity.

Eastern Society or Eastern World

The term Eastern world refers very broadly to the various cultures or social structures and philosophical systems of "the East" or geographically the Eastern Culture. These are namely Asia: the Indian subcontinent, the Far East, the Middle East/ Near East, and Central Asia sometimes including many Orthodox Christian regions like Russia, Eastern European countries, although these are considered more of zone which is both Eastern and Western depending upon the context of discussion.

The division between "East" and "West" is a product of European cultural history, and of the distinction between European Christendom and the alien cultures beyond it to the East. Before the discovery of the Americas and the exploration of Sub-Saharan Africa by the Europeans, only North Africa and other Islamic countries to the East were known in detail, though India and China were vaguely known of. With the European colonization of the Americas the East/West distinction became global. The concept of an Eastern, "Indian" (Indies) or "Oriental" sphere was emphasized by ideas of racial as well as religious and cultural differences. Such distinctions were articulated by Westerners in the scholarly tradition known as Orientalism and Indology. People from the East are known by certain regions in the West as "Oriental". During the Cold War, the term "Eastern world" was sometimes used as an extension of Eastern bloc, connoting the Soviet Union, China and their communist allies, while the term "Western world" often connoted the United States and its NATO allies such as the United Kingdom. The concept is often another term for the Far East—a region that bears considerable cultural and religious commonality. Eastern philosophy, art, literature, and other traditions, are often found throughout the region in places of high importance, such as popular culture, architecture and traditional literature. The spread of Buddhism and Hindu Yoga is partly responsible for this.

Eastern Culture

Eastern culture has developed many themes and traditions. Some important ones are:

- Eastern religion, Eastern philosophy
  - Far Eastern religions
    - Confucianism—social hierarchy where position is based upon merit as determined through the imperial examination system. This social hierarchy promoted respect for elders and authority, and valued harmony within family.
    - Far Eastern Buddhism
    - Shinto
    - Taoism—concepts of good and bad energy, the connectedness of mind and body and nature, etc.
  - Indian religions
    - Buddhism—path of liberation attained through insight into the ultimate nature of reality
    - Hinduism- an umbrella term for religious sects native to India
    - Jainism
    - Sikhism—A religion that developed in the warring plains of Punjab in an atmosphere of

ideological clash between Islam and Hinduism. Its followers retain spiritual as well as martial qualities.

- o The Middle East, today largely coterminous with the Islamic world
    - * Christianity — like other Abrahamic religions like Judaism and Islam, originates in the Middle East, where it is now a small minority religion.
    - * Islam—the majority of the world Muslim population have always lived in Asia, due to Islam conquering and becoming the dominant religion of these areas.
    - * Judaism — although not as much of a presence as it once was, Judaism still exists in Asia.
    - * Zoroastrianism, the monotheistic of Sassanid Persia

- Oriental medicine
    - o Ayurveda
    - o Chinese medicine
    - o Traditional Tibetan medicine
    - o Traditional Korean Medicine.

Information Society

Although the concept of information society has been under discussion since the 1930s, in the modern world it is almost always applied to the manner in which information technologies have impacted society and culture. It therefore covers the effects of computers and telecommunications on the home, the workplace, schools, government and various communities and organizations, as well as the emergence of new social forms in cyberspace.

One of the European Union's areas of interest is the Information Society. Here policies are directed towards promoting an open and competitive digital economy, research into information and communication technologies, as well as their application to improve social inclusion, public services and quality of life.

The International Telecommunications Union's World Summit on the Information Society in Geneva and Tunis (2003/2005) has led to a number of policy and application areas where action is required. These include:

- promotion of ICTs for development;
- information and communication infrastructure;
- access to information and knowledge;
- capacity building;
- building confidence and security in the use of ICTs;
- enabling environment;
- ICT applications in the areas of government, business, learning, health, employment, environment, agriculture and science;
- cultural and linguistic diversity and local content;
- media;
- ethical dimensions of the Information Society;
- international and regional cooperation.

Knowledge Society

As access to electronic information resources increased at the beginning of the 21st century, special attention was extended from the Information Society to the knowledge society.

In the words of an Irish governmental analysis, "The capacity to manipulate, store and transmit large quantities of information cheaply has increased at a staggering rate over recent years. The digitisation of information and the associated pervasiveness of the Internet are facilitating a new intensity in the application of knowledge to economic activity, to the extent that it has become the predominant factor in the creation of wealth. As much as 70 to 80 percent of economic growth is now said to be due to new and better knowledge."

The Second World Summit on the Knowledge Society, held in Chania, Crete, in September 2009, gave special attention to the following topics:

- business and enterprise computing;
- technology-enhanced learning;
- social and humanistic computing;

- culture, tourism and technology;
- e-government and e-democracy;
- innovation, sustainable development and strategic management;
- service science, management and engineering;
- intellectual and human capital development;
- ICTs for ecology and the Green Economy;
- future prospects for the Knowledge Society;
- technologies and business models for the creative industries.

Other Uses

People of many nations united by common political and cultural traditions, beliefs, or values are sometimes also said to be a society (such as Judeo-Christian, Eastern, and Western). When used in this context, the term is employed as a means of contrasting two or more "societies" whose members represent alternative conflicting and competing worldviews.

Some academic, professional and scientific associations describe themselves as *societies* (for example, the American Mathematical Society, American Society of Civil Engineers, or the Royal Society).

In some countries (for example the United States, France and Latin America), the term "society" is used in commerce to denote a partnership between investors or the start of a business. In the United Kingdom, partnerships are not called societies, but cooperatives or mutuals are often known as societies (such as friendly societies and building societies).

2

Social Stratification in Social System

In sociology and other social sciences, social stratification refers to the hierarchical arrangement of individuals into divisions of power and wealth within a society. *Stratification* derives from the geological concept of *strata* - rock layers created by natural processes. The term most commonly relates to the socio-economic concept of class, involving the "classification of persons into groups based on shared socio-economic conditions... a relational set of inequalities with economic, social, political and ideological dimensions."

In modern Western societies, stratification is broadly organized into three main layers: upper class, middle class, and lower class. Each class may be further subdivided into smaller classes (e.g. occupational). These categories are particular to state-level societies as distinguished from, for instance, feudal societies composed of nobility-to-peasant relations. Stratification may also be defined by kinship ties or castes. For Max Weber, social class pertaining broadly to material wealth is distinguished from status class which is based on such variables as honour, prestige and religious affiliation. It is debatable whether the earliest hunter-gatherer groups may be defined as 'stratified', or if such differentials began with agriculture and broad acts of exchange between groups. One of the ongoing issues in determining social stratification arises from the point that status inequalities between individuals are common, so it becomes a quantitative issue to determine how much inequality qualifies as stratification.

Sociological Overview

The concept of social stratification is interpreted differently by the various theoretical perspectives of sociology. Proponents of structural-functionalism have suggested that since social stratification is commonly found in developed societies, hierarchy may be necessary in order to stabilize social structure. Talcott Parsons, an American sociologist, asserted that stability and social order are achieved by means of a universal value consensus, satisfying the functional prerequisites of a society. By contrast, conflict theories, such as Marxism, point to the inaccessibility of resources and lack of social mobility found in stratified societies. Many sociological theorists have criticized the extent to which the working classes are unlikely to advance socioeconomically; the wealthy tend to hold political power which they use to exploit the proletariat intergenerationally. Theorists such as Ralf Dahrendorf, however, have noted the tendency toward an enlarged middle-class in modern Western societies due to the necessity of an educated workforce in technological and service economies. Various social and political perspectives concerning globalization, such as dependency theory, suggest that these effects are due to the shift of workers to the third world.

Karl Marx

In Marxist theory, the capitalist mode of production consists of two main economic parts: the Base and the Superstructure. The base comprehends the relations of production — employer-employee work conditions, the technical division of labour, and property relations — into which people enter to produce the necessities and amenities of life. In the capitalist system, the ruling classes own the means of production, which essentially includes the working class itself as they only have their own labour power ('wage labour') to offer in order to survive. These relations fundamentally determine the ideas and philosophies of a society, constituting the superstructure. A temporary status quo is achieved by various methods of social control employed, consciously or unconsciously, by the bourgeoisie in the course of various aspects of social life. Through the ideology of the ruling class, false consciousness is promoted both through ostensibly political and non-political institutions, but also through the arts and other elements of culture. Marx believed the capitalist mode would eventually give way, through its own internal conflict, to revolutionary consciousness and the development of egalitarian communist society.

According to Marvin Harris and Tim Ingold, Lewis Henry Morgan's accounts of egalitarian hunter-gatherers formed part of Karl Marx and Engels's inspiration for communism. Morgan spoke of a situation in which people living in the same community pooled their efforts and shared the rewards of those efforts fairly equally. He called this "communism in living." But when Marx expanded on these ideas, he still emphasized an economically-oriented culture, with property defining the fundamental relationships between people. Yet, issues of ownership and property are arguably less emphasized in hunter-gatherer societies. This, combined with the very different social and economic situations of hunter-gatherers may account for many of the difficulties encountered when implementing communism in industrialized states. As Ingold points out: "The notion of communism, removed from the context of domesticity and harnessed to support a project of social engineering for large-scale, industrialized states with populations of millions, eventually came to mean something quite different from what Morgan had intended: namely, a principle of redistribution that would override all ties of a personal or familial nature, and cancel out their effects."

Max Weber

Max Weber was strongly influenced by Marx's ideas, but rejected the possibility of effective communism, arguing that it would require an even greater level of detrimental social control and bureaucratization than capitalist society. Moreover, Weber criticized the dialectical presumption of proletariat revolt, believing it to be unlikely. Instead, he developed the three-component theory of stratification and the concept of life chances. Weber supposed there were more class divisions than Marx suggested, taking different concepts from both functionalist and Marxist theories to create his own system. He emphasized the difference between class, status, and party, and treated these as separate but related sources of power, each with different effects on social action. Working around half a century later than Marx, Weber claimed there to be in fact four main classes: the upper class, the white collar workers, the petite bourgeoisie, and the manual working class. Weber's theory more-closely resembles modern Western class structures, although economic status does not seem to depend strictly on earnings in the way Weber envisioned.

Weber derived many of his key concepts on social stratification by examining the social structure of Germany. He noted that contrary to Marx's theories, stratification was based on more than simply ownership of capital. Weber examined how many members of the aristocracy lacked economic wealth yet had strong political power. Many wealthy families lacked prestige and power, for example, because they were Jewish. Weber introduced three independent factors that form his theory of stratification hierarchy; class, status, and power:

- Class: A person's economic position in a society. Weber differs from Marx in that he does not see this as the supreme factor in stratification. Weber noted how managers of corporations or industries control firms they do not own; Marx would have placed such a person in the proletariat.
- Status: A person's prestige, social honour, or popularity in a society. Weber noted that political power was not rooted in capital value solely, but also in one's individual status. Poets or saints, for example, can possess immense influence on society with often little economic worth.
- Power: A person's ability to get their way despite the resistance of others. For example, individuals in state jobs, such as an employee of the Federal Bureau of Investigation, or a member of the United States Congress, may hold little property or status but they still hold immense power.

Three-component Theory of Stratification

The three-component theory of stratification, more widely known as Weberian Stratification or Three Class System, was developed by German sociologist Max Weber with class, status and party as distinct ideal types. Weber developed a multidimensional approach to Social stratification that reflects the interplay among wealth, prestige and power.. "Weber argued that power can take a variety of forms. A person's power can be shown in the social order through their status, in the economic order through their class, and in the political order through their party. Thus, class, status and party are each aspects of the distribution of power within a community." (Hurst, 202) Class, Status and party have a great deal of effect not only within their individual areas but also have a great deal of influence over the other areas as well.

- Wealth: includes property such as buildings, lands, farms, houses, factories and as well as other assets - Economic situation
- Prestige: the respect with which a person or status position is regarded by others - Status Situation
- Power: the ability of people or groups to achieve their goals despite opposition from others - Parties

There are two basic dimensions of power: The possession of power and the exercising of power.

The Possession of Power

According to Weber, the ability to possess power derives from the individual's ability to control various "social resources." "The mode of distribution gives to the propertied a monopoly on the possibility of transferring property from the sphere of use as "wealth" to the sphere of "capital," that is, it gives them the entrepreneurial function and all chances to share directly or indirectly in returns on capital." These resources can be anything and everything and might include things like land, capital, social respect, physical strength, intellectual knowledge, etc.

The Exercising of Power

The ability to exercise power takes a number of different forms, but all involve the idea that it means the ability to get your own way with others, regardless of their ability to resist you." For example, if we think about an individual's chances of realizing their own will against someone else, it is reasonable to believe that the person's social prestige, class position, and membership in a political group will have an effect on these chances." In terms of understanding the relationship between power and social stratification, Weber theorized the various ways in which societies are organized in hierarchical systems of domination and subordination using the several major concepts.

Class Power

"Class, at its core, is an economic concept; it is the position of individuals in the market that determines their class position. And it is how one is situated in the marketplace that directly affects one's life chances." This was theorized by Weber on the basis of "unequal access to material resources." For example, if someone possesses something that you want or need then this makes him potentially more powerful than you. He is in a dominant position and you are in a subordinate position because he controls access to a desired social resource. A classic illustration here is the relationship between an employer and employee.

Social Power (Status)

"The existence of status groups most often shows itself in the form of:

1. endogamy or the restricted pattern of social intercourse,
2. sharing of food and other benefits within groups,
3. status conventions or traditions, and
4. monopolistic acquisition of certain economic opportunities or the avoidance of certain kinds of acquisitions.

If you respect someone or view him as your social superior, then he will potentially be able to exercise power over you (since you will respond positively to his instructions/commands). In this respect, social status is a social resource simply because he may have it while you may not.. "Not all power, however entails social honour: The Typical American Boss, as well as the typical big speculator, deliberately relinquishes social honour. Quite generally, "mere economic" power, and especially "naked" money power, is by no means a recognized basis or social honour."

Political Power (Party)

Parties are associations that aim at securing "power within an organization [or the state] for its leaders in order to attain ideal or material advantages for its active members." This form of power can be related to the way in which the State is organized in modern social systems (involving the ability to make laws, for example). If you can influence this process of law creation then you will be in a potentially powerful position. Thus, by your ability to influence a decision-making process you possess power, even though you may not directly exercise that power personally. Political parties are the organizational means to possess power through the mechanism of the State and they include not just formally organized parties, but any group that is organized to influence the way in which power is exercised legitimately through the machinery of the State. "Since parties aim at such goals as getting their programs developed or accepted and getting positions of influence within organizations, it is clear that they operate only within a rational order within which these goals are possible to attain and only when there is a struggle for power".

Social Action

Social action is in direct relation to "Political or Party Power" in combination with the class situation. The influence of laws is based on the social action of members of the classes. "The direction of interests may vary according to whether or not social action of a larger or smaller portion of those commonly affected by the class situation, or even an association among them, e.g., a trade union, has grown out of the class situation, from which the individual may expect promising results for himself." "The degree in which "social action" and possibly associations emerge from the mass behaviour of the members of a class is linked to general cultural conditions, especially to those of an intellectual sort. It is also liked to the extent of the contrasts that have already evolved." We can also see this in another quote "Class-conscious action is most likely if, first, "the connection between the causes and consequences of the 'class situation'" are transparent, or clear. If individuals can plainly see that there is a connection between the structure of the economic system and what happens to them in terms of life chances, class action is more likely" The greater the numbers within these class positions will increase the chance that they will rise up in action.

Mobility

The greater the numbers within these class positions will increase the chance that they will rise up in action.

"It is noncontroversial that the class situation in which each individual finds himself represents a limitation on his scope, tends to keep him within the class. It acts as an obstacle to any rise into a higher class, and as a pair of water wings with respect to the classes below...Class type, relations with class fellows, power over outward resources adapted to the class situation, and so on." The capitalist society movement between classes is a possibility. Hence the use of the term "The American Dream" to show the ability of people to ascend to a higher class through hard work and ingenuity. "Class composition is forever changing, to the point where there may be a completely new set of families." He saw four classes - the propertied class, non-propertied class, petit bourgeoisie and the manual labourer class.

Tripartite Classification of Authority

Max Weber distinguished three ideal types of legitimate political leadership, domination and authority:

1. charismatic authority (*familial and religious*),
2. traditional authority (*patriarchs, patrimonalism, feudalism*) and
3. legal authority (*modern law and state, bureaucracy*).

These three types are ideal pure types and rarely appear in their pure form.

According to Weber, authority is power accepted as legitimate by those subjected to it. These three forms of authority are said to appear in an "hierarchical development order". States progress from *charismatic authority*, to *traditional authority*, and finally reach the *state of rational-legal authority* which is characteristic of a modern liberal democracy.

Charismatic Domination

Charismatic authority grows out of the personal charm or the strength of an individual personality. It was described by Weber in a lecture as "the authority of the extraordinary and personal gift of grace (charisma)"; he distinguished it from the other forms of authority by stating "Men do not obey him [the charismatic ruler] by virtue of tradition or statute, but because they believe in him." Thus the actual power or capabilities of the leader are irrelevant, as long as the followers believe that such power exists. Thus, according to Weber, it is particularly difficult for charismatic leaders to maintain their authority because the followers must continue to legitimize the authority of the leader.

Charismatic domination is insofar different from legal-rational and tradition power as it does not develop from established tradition but rather from the belief the followers have in the leader.

According to Weber, once the leader loses his charisma or dies, systems based on charismatic authority tend to transform into traditional or legal-rational systems.

Traditional Domination

In traditional authority, the legitimacy of the authority comes from tradition or custom; Weber described it as "the authority of the eternal yesterday" and identified it as the source of authority for monarchies. In this type of domination, the traditional rights of a powerful individual or group are accepted by the subordinate, or at least not challenged. The dominant individual could be a clan leader, eldest, the head of a family, a patriarchal figure or dominant elite. Historically this has been the most common type of government.

According to Weber inequalities are created and preserved by traditional authority. Should this authority not be challenged, the dominant leader or group will stay in power. For Weber, traditional power blocked the development of rational-legal authority.

Legal Domination

Legal authority, also known as legal-rational authority, is where an individual or institution exerts power by virtue of the legal office that they hold. It is the authority that demands obedience to the office rather than the office holder; once they leave office, their rational-legal authority is lost. Weber identified *"rationally-created rules"* as the central feature of this form of authority. Modern democracies contain many examples of legal-rational regimes. There are different ways in which legal authority can develop. Many societies have developed a system of laws and regulations and there exist many different principles of legality. With the development of a legal-rational system, the political system is likely to be rationalized similarly. Constitutions, written documents, established offices and regular elections are often associated with modern legal-rational political systems. These in the past have tended to develop in opposition to earlier traditional systems such as monarchies, where the set of rules are not well developed. As these systems develop in a rational manner, authority takes on a legal-rational form. Those who govern have the legitimate legal right to do so and those subordinated accept the legality of the rulers.

Albeit rational-legal authority may be challenged by those subordinated, it is unlikely to result in a quick change in the nature of the system. Such power-struggles, according to Weber, may be based on nationalism, ethnicity and are mostly political struggles.

The Classification of Authority in the Context of History

Weber also notes that legal domination is the most advanced, and that societies evolve from having mostly traditional and charismatic authorities to mostly rational and legal ones, because the instability of charismatic authority inevitably forces it to "routinize" into a more structured form of authority. Likewise he notes that in a pure type of traditional rule, sufficient resistance to a master can lead to a "traditional revolution". Thus he alludes to an inevitable move towards a rational-legal structure of authority, utilizing a bureaucratic structure. This ties to his broader concept of rationalization by suggesting the inevitability of a move in this direction. Thus this theory can be sometimes viewed as part of the social evolutionism theory.

In traditional authority, the legitimacy of the authority comes from tradition, in charismatic authority from the personality and leadership qualities of the individual (charisma), and in legal (or rational-legal) authority from powers that are bureaucratically and legally attached to certain positions. A classic example of these three types may be found in religion:

priests (traditional), Jesus (charismatic), and the Roman Catholic Church (legal-rational). Weber also conceived of these three types within his three primary modes of conflict: traditional authority within status groups, charismatic authority within class, and legal-rational authority within party organizations.

In his view every historical relation between rulers and ruled contained elements that can be analyzed on the basis of the above distinction.

Anthropological Overview

Anthropologists have found that social stratification is not the standard among all societies. John Gowdy writes, "Assumptions about human behaviour that members of market societies believe to be universal, that humans are naturally competitive and acquisitive, and that social stratification is natural, do not apply to many hunter-gatherer peoples." Non-stratified egalitarian or acephalous ("headless") societies exist which have little or no concept of social hierarchy, political or economic status, class, or even permanent leadership.

Kinship-orientation

Anthropologists identify egalitarian cultures as "kinship-oriented," because they appear to value social harmony more than wealth or status. These cultures are contrasted with economically-oriented cultures (including states) in which status and material wealth are prized, and stratification, competition, and conflict are common. Kinship-oriented cultures actively work to prevent social hierarchies from developing because they believe that such stratification could lead to conflict and instability.

Reciprocal altruism is one process by which this is accomplished.

A good example is given by Richard Borshay Lee in his account of the Khoisan, who practice *"insulting the meat."* Whenever a hunter makes a kill, he is ceaselessly teased and ridiculed (in a friendly, joking fashion) to prevent him from becoming too proud or egotistical. The meat itself is then distributed evenly among the entire social group, rather than kept by the hunter. The level of teasing is proportional to the size of the kill. Lee found this out when he purchased an entire cow as a gift for the group he was living with, and was teased for weeks afterward about it (since obtaining that much meat could be interpreted as showing off).

Another example is the Indigenous Australians of Groote Eylandt and Bickerton Island, off the coast of Arnhem Land, who have arranged their entire society, spirituality, and economy around a kind of gift economy called *renunciation.* According to David H. Turner, in this arrangement, every person is expected to give *everything* of any resource they have to any other person who needs or lacks it at the time.

This has the benefit of largely eliminating social problems like theft and relative poverty. However, misunderstandings obviously arise when attempting to reconcile Aboriginal *renunciative economics* with the competition/scarcity-oriented economics introduced to Australia by Anglo-European colonists.

Social Impact

Social stratification has been shown to cause many social problems. A comprehensive study of major world economies revealed that homicide, infant mortality, obesity, teenage pregnancies, emotional depression and prison population all correlate with higher social inequality.

Power Distribution

- Autocracy: One individual retains complete and absolute power over others. This is also known as despotism.
- Monarchism: A king or queen has ultimate control over the power, but does share it with other individuals. Power is usually transmitted by heredity— in the primogeniture system, for example, the eldest son of a king will ascend to that position when the current king dies or resigns.
- Oligarchy: Political power is vested in a few individuals, who usually pass power by a hereditary system.
- Republic: Voting citizens elect representatives who propose, make, and enforce laws instead of citizens directly affecting the government. Also known as *representative democracy.*

- Democracy: Citizens directly vote in lawmaking. In contrast to *representative democracy*, this is sometimes known as a *direct democracy*.
- Anarchism: An absence of hierarchy in economic and political relations—a decentralized participatory system of councils, assemblies and federations.
- Ochlocracy: What some argue to be the end product of an unstable lawless system, is absolute power and a system known as "rule by organized crime". Such a system emerges when powerful gang-like organizations arrogate power and develop a semi-legitimate status.
- Plutocracy: A society in which power is distributed according to wealth or the ability to abstain from relations for exchange of cash or property.

Three Characteristics of Stratified Systems

The rankings apply to social categories of people who share a common characteristic without necessarily interacting or identifying with each other. The process of being ranked can be changed by the person being ranked.

- Example: The way we rank people differently by race, gender, and social class.

People's life experiences and opportunities depend on their social category. This characteristic can be changed by the amount of work a person can put into their interests.

- Example: The greater advantage had by the son or daughter of a king to have a successful life than the son or daughter of a minimum-wage factory worker, because the king has a greater amount of resources than the factory worker — The use of resources can influence others.

The ranks of different social categories change slowly over time. This has occurred frequently in the United States ever since the American revolution. The U.S. Constitution has been altered several times to contain rights for everyone.

- Examples:
  * The Declaration of Independence: Abolished the monarchy

* Article I, Section 9 of U.S. Constitution: "No Title of Nobility shall be granted by the United States," Abolished aristocracy
* Thirteenth Amendment: Ended slavery in the United States
* Fourteenth Amendment: Granted African-Americans citizenship in the United States
* Fifteenth Amendment: Ended the denial of suffrage based on race
* Nineteenth Amendment: The United States government's recognition of women's suffrage
* The Civil Rights Act of 1964: Ended racial segregation in public places in the United States — Also extended the right to vote.

3

Social Thought for Social Change

Social change refers to an alteration in the social structure of a social group or society, i.e. a change in the nature, social institutions, social behaviours or social relations of a society.

Social change is a very basic term and must be assigned further context. It may refer to the notion of social progress or sociocultural evolution; the philosophical idea that society moves forward by dialectical or evolutionary means. It may refer to a paradigmatic change in the socio-economic structure, for instance a shift away from feudalism and towards capitalism. Accordingly it may also refer to social revolution, such as the Communist revolution presented in Marxism, or to other social movements, such as Women's suffrage or the Civil rights movement. Social change may be driven by cultural, religious, economic, scientific or technological forces.

Prominent Theories of Social Change

- Hegelian: The classic Hegelian dialectic model of change is based on the interaction of opposing forces. Starting from a point of momentary stasis, Thesis countered by Antithesis first yields conflict, then it subsequently results in a new Synthesis.
- Marxist: Marxism presents a dialectical and materialist concept of history; Humankind's history is a fundamental struggle between social classes.
- Kuhnian: The philosopher of science, Thomas Kuhn argues in *The Structure of Scientific Revolutions* with

respect to the Copernican Revolution that people are unlikely to jettison an unworkable paradigm, despite many indications that the paradigm is not functioning properly, until a better paradigm can be presented.

- Heraclitan: The Greek philosopher Heraclitus used the metaphor of a river to speak of change thus, "On those stepping into rivers staying the same other and other waters flow" (DK22B12). What Heraclitus seems to be suggesting here, later interpretations notwithstanding, is that, in order for the river to remain the river, change must constantly be taking place. Thus one may think of the Heraclitan model as parallel to that of a living organism, which, in order to remain alive, must constantly be changing.
- Daoist: The Chinese philosophical work Dao De Jing, I.8 and II.78 uses the metaphor of water as the ideal agent of change. Water, although soft and yielding, will eventually wear away stone. Change in this model is to be natural, harmonious and steady, albeit imperceptible.

Social Darwinism

Social Darwinism is a pejorative term used for various late nineteenth century ideologies which, while often contradictory, exploited ideas of survival of the fittest. It especially refers to notions of struggle for existence being used to justify social policies which show no sympathy for those unable to support themselves. While the most prominent form of such views stressed competition between individuals in free market capitalism, it is also associated with ideas of struggle between national or racial groups. In sociology it has been defined as a theory of social evolution which asserts that "There are underlying, and largely irresistible, forces acting in societies which are like the natural forces that operate in animal and plant communities. One can therefore formulate social laws similar to natural ones. These social forces are of such a kind as to produce evolutionary progress through the natural conflicts between social groups. The best-adapted and most successful social groups survive these conflicts, raising the evolutionary level of society generally (the 'survival of the fittest')." The term has very rarely been used as a self description. The term first appeared in Europe in 1877, and around this time it was used by sociologists opposed to the concept. The term was popularized in the United States in 1944 by the American historian Richard Hofstadter who used it in the ideological war effort against fascism to denote a reactionary creed which promoted competitive strife, racism and nationalism. Before Hofstadter's work the use of the term in English academic journals was quite rare. The term "social darwinism" has rarely been used by advocates of the supposed ideologies or ideas; instead it has almost always been used (pejoratively) by its opponents.

The term draws upon the common use of the term *Darwinism*, which has been used to describe a range of evolutionary views, but in the late 19th century was applied more specifically to natural selection as first advanced by Charles Darwin to explain speciation in populations of organisms. The process includes competition between individuals for limited resources, popularly but inaccurately described by the phrase "survival of the fittest", a term coined by sociologist Herbert Spencer.

While the term has been applied to the claim that Darwin's theory of evolution by natural selection can be used to understand the social endurance of a nation or country, social Darwinism commonly refers to ideas that predate Darwin's publication of *On the Origin of Species*. Others whose ideas are given the label include the 18th century clergyman Thomas Malthus, and Darwin's cousin Francis Galton who founded eugenics towards the end of the 19th century.

Theories and Origins

The term Darwinism had been coined by Thomas Henry Huxley in his April 1860 review of *On the Origin of Species*, and by the 1870s it was used to describe a range of concepts of evolutionism or development, without any specific commitment to Charles Darwin's own theory.

The first use of the phrase "social Darwinism" was in Joseph Fisher's 1877 article on *The History of Landholding in Ireland* which was published in the *Transactions of the Royal Historical Society*. Fisher was commenting on how a system for borrowing livestock which had been called "tenure" had led to the false impression that the early Irish had already evolved or developed land tenure;

These arrangements did not in any way affect that which we understand by the word " tenure," that is, a man's farm, but they related solely to cattle, which we consider a chattel. It has appeared necessary to devote some space to this subject, inasmuch as that usually acute writer Sir Henry Maine has accepted the word " tenure " in its modern interpretation, and has built up a theory under which the Irish chief " developed " into a feudal baron. I can find nothing in the Brehon laws to warrant this theory of social Darwinism, and believe further study will show that the Cain Saerrath and the Cain Aigillue relate solely to what we now call chattels, and did not in any way affect what we now call the freehold, the possession of the land. – *Fisher 1877.*

Despite the fact that social Darwinism bears Charles Darwin's name, it is also linked today with others, notably Herbert Spencer, Thomas Malthus, and Francis Galton, the founder of eugenics. In fact, Spencer was not described as a social Darwinist until the 1930s, long after his death.

Darwin himself gave serious consideration to Galton's work, but considered the ideas of "hereditary improvement" impractical. Aware of weaknesses in his own family, Darwin was sure that families would naturally refuse such selection and wreck the scheme. He thought that even if compulsory registration was the only way to improve the human race, this illiberal idea would be unacceptable, and it would be better to publicize the "principle of inheritance" and let people decide for themselves.

In *The Descent of Man, and Selection in Relation to Sex* of 1882 Darwin described how medical advances meant that the weaker were able to survive and have families, and commented on the effects of this, while cautioning that hard reason should not override sympathy, and considering how other factors might reduce the effect:

Thus the weak members of civilized societies propagate their kind. No one who has attended to the breeding of domestic animals will doubt that this must be highly injurious to the race of man. It is surprising how soon a want of care, or care wrongly directed, leads to the degeneration of a domestic race; but excepting in the case of man himself, hardly any one is so ignorant as to allow his worst animals to breed.

The aid which we feel impelled to give to the helpless is mainly an incidental result of the instinct of sympathy, which was originally acquired as part of the social instincts, but subsequently rendered, in the manner previously indicated, more tender and more widely diffused. Nor could we check our sympathy, even at the urging of hard reason, without deterioration in the noblest part of our nature. The surgeon may harden himself whilst performing an operation, for he knows that he is acting for the good of his patient; but if we were intentionally to neglect the weak and helpless, it could only be for a contingent benefit, with an overwhelming present evil.... We must therefore bear the undoubtedly bad effects of the weak surviving and propagating their kind; but there appears to be at least one check in steady action, namely that the weaker and inferior members of society do not marry so freely as the sound; and this check might be indefinitely increased by the weak in body or mind refraining from marriage, though this is more to be hoped for than expected.

Social Darwinists

Herbert Spencer's ideas, like those of evolutionary progressivism, stemmed from his reading of Thomas Malthus, and his later theorics were influenced by those of Darwin. However, Spencer's major work, *Progress: Its Law and Cause* (1857) was released two years before the publication of Darwin's *On the Origin of Species*, and *First Principles* was printed in 1860. Although Spencer's writings were never described as 'social Darwinist' in his lifetime, some authors describe him as such. In *The Social Organism* (1860), Spencer compares society to a living organism and argues that, just as biological organisms evolve through natural selection, society evolves and increases in complexity through analogous processes.

In many ways, Spencer's theory of cosmic evolution has much more in common with the works of Lamarck and Auguste Comte's positivism than with Darwin's.

Spencer's work also served to renew interest in the work of Malthus. While Malthus's work does not itself qualify as social Darwinism, his 1798 work *An Essay on the Principle of Population*, was incredibly popular and widely read by social Darwinists. In that book, for example, the author argued that as an increasing population would normally outgrow its food supply, this would result in the starvation of the weakest and a Malthusian catastrophe.

According to Michael Ruse, Darwin read Malthus' famous *Essay on a Principle of Population* in 1838, four years after Malthus' death. Malthus himself anticipated the social Darwinists in suggesting that charity could exacerbate social problems.

Another of these social interpretations of Darwin's biological views, later known as eugenics, was put forth by Darwin's cousin, Francis Galton, in 1865 and 1869. Galton argued that just as physical traits were clearly inherited among generations of people, so could be said for mental qualities (genius and talent). Galton argued that social morals needed to change so that heredity was a conscious decision, in order to avoid over-breeding by less fit members of society and the under-breeding of the more fit ones.

In Galton's view, social institutions such as welfare and insane asylums were allowing inferior humans to survive and reproduce at levels faster than the more "superior" humans in respectable society, and if corrections were not soon taken, society would be awash with "inferiors." Darwin read his cousin's work with interest, and devoted sections of *Descent of Man* to discussion of Galton's theories. Neither Galton nor Darwin, though, advocated any eugenic policies such as those that would be undertaken in the early 20th century, as government coercion of any form was very much against their political opinions.

Friedrich Nietzsche's philosophy addressed the question of artificial selection, but it was built against Darwinian theories of natural selection. His point of view on sickness and health, in particular, opposed him to the concept of biological adaptation, forged by Spencer's "fitness". He criticized Haeckel, Spencer, and Darwin, sometimes under the same banner. Nietzsche thought that, in specific cases, sickness was necessary and even helpful. Thus, he wrote: Wherever progress is to ensue, deviating natures are of greatest importance. Every progress of the whole must be preceded by a partial weakening. The strongest natures retain the type, the weaker ones help to advance it. Something similar also happens in the individual. There is rarely a degeneration, a truncation, or even a vice or any physical or moral loss without an advantage somewhere else. In a warlike and restless clan, for example, the sicklier man may have occasion to be alone, and may therefore become quieter and wiser; the one-eyed man will have one eye the stronger; the blind man will see deeper inwardly, and certainly hear better. To this extent, the famous theory of the survival of the fittest does not seem to me to be the only viewpoint from which to explain the progress of strengthening of a man or of a race.

The publication of Ernst Haeckel's best-selling *Welträtsel* ('Riddle of the Universe') in 1899 brought social Darwinism and earlier ideas of racial hygiene to a wider audience, and its recapitulation theory (since heavily refuted on many fronts) became famous. This led to the formation of the Monist League in 1904 with many prominent citizens among its members, including the Nobel Prize winner Wilhelm Ostwald. By 1909, it had a membership of some six thousand people.

The simpler aspects of social Darwinism followed the earlier Malthusian ideas that humans, especially males, need competition in their lives in order to survive in the future, and that the poor should have to provide for themselves and not be given any aid, although most social Darwinists of the early twentieth century supported better working conditions and salaries, thus giving the poor a better chance to provide for themselves and distinguishing those who are capable of succeeding from those who are poor out of laziness, weakness, or inferiority.

Darwinism and Hypotheses of Social Change

"Social Darwinism" was first described by Oscar Schmidt of the University of Strasbourg, reporting at a scientific and medical conference held in Munich in 1877. He noted how socialists, although opponents of Darwin's theory, nonetheless used it to add force to their political arguments. Schmidt's essay first appeared in English in *Popular Science* in March

1879. There followed an anarchist tract published in Paris in 1880 entitled "Le darwinisme social" by Émile Gautier. However, the use of the term was very rare—at least in the English-speaking world (Hodgson, 2004)—until the American historian Richard Hofstadter published his influential *Social Darwinism in American Thought* (1944) during World War II.

Hypotheses of social evolution and cultural evolution are common in Europe. The Enlightenment thinkers who preceded Darwin, such as Hegel, often argued that societies progressed through stages of increasing development. Earlier thinkers also emphasized conflict as an inherent feature of social life. Thomas Hobbes's 17th century portrayal of the state of nature seems analogous to the competition for natural resources described by Darwin. Social Darwinism is distinct from other theories of social change because of the way it draws Darwin's distinctive ideas from the field of biology into social studies.

Darwin's unique discussion of evolution considered the supernatural in human development. Unlike Hobbes, he believed that this struggle for natural resources allowed individuals with certain physical and mental traits to succeed more frequently than others, and that these traits accumulated in the population over time, which under certain conditions could lead to the descendants being so different that they would be defined as a new species.

However, Darwin felt that "social instincts" such as "sympathy" and "moral sentiments" also evolved through natural selection, and that these resulted in the strengthening of societies in which they occurred, so much so that he wrote about it in *Descent of Man*:

The following proposition seems to me in a high degree probable- namely, that any animal whatever, endowed with well-marked social instincts, the parental and filial affections being here included, would inevitably acquire a moral sense or conscience, as soon as its intellectual powers had become as well, or nearly as well developed, as in man. For, firstly, the social instincts lead an animal to take pleasure in the society of its fellows, to feel a certain amount of sympathy with them, and to perform various services for them. After the 1906 election, David Lloyd George and Winston Churchill began to reform society according to the Rowntree Report. The report detailed poor people from York and explained that although they tried hard to lift themselves out of their poverty, it was nearly always impossible. This contributed to changing the prevalent social view that the poor were lazy and stupid, and new policies were made concerning the 'Deserving Poor'. These social reforms earned the Liberal Party the title 'Fathers of the Welfare State' and were largely due to the implementation of Social Darwinist philosophies.

Altruism

Altruism is selfless concern for the welfare of others. It is a traditional virtue in many cultures, and a core aspect of various religious traditions, though the concept of 'others' toward whom concern should be directed can vary among religions. Altruism is the opposite of selfishness.

Altruism can be distinguished from feelings of loyalty and duty. Altruism focuses on a motivation to help others or a want to do good without reward, while duty focuses on a moral obligation towards a specific individual (for example, God, a king), a specific organization (for example, a government), or an abstract concept (for example, patriotism etc.). Some individuals may feel both altruism and duty, while others may not. Pure altruism is giving without regard to reward or the benefits of recognition and need.

The term *altruism* may also refer to an ethical doctrine that claims that individuals are morally obliged to benefit others. Used in this sense, it is the opposite of egoism.

The Notion of Altruism

The concept has a long history in philosophical and ethical thought. The term was originally coined in the 19th century by the founding sociologist and philosopher of science, Auguste Comte, and has become a major topic for psychologists (especially evolutionary psychology researchers), evolutionary biologists, and ethologists.

While ideas about altruism from one field can have an impact on the other fields, the different methods and focuses of these fields lead to different perspectives on altruism.

Scientific Viewpoints

Anthropology

Marcel Mauss's book *The Gift* contains a passage "Note on alms". This note describes the evolution of the notion of alms (and by extension of altruism) from the notion of sacrifice.

"Alms are the fruits of a moral notion of the gift and of fortune on the one hand, and of a notion of sacrifice, on the other. Generosity is an obligation, because Nemesis avenges the poor and the gods for the superabundance of happiness and wealth of certain people who should rid themselves of it. This is the ancient morality of the gift, which has become a principle of justice.

The gods and the spirits accept that the share of wealth and happiness that has been offered to them and had been hitherto destroyed in useless sacrifices should serve the poor and children."

- Compare Altruism (ethics) - perception of altruism as self-sacrifice.
- Compare explanation of alms in various scriptures.

Evolutionary Explanations

In the science of ethology (the study of animal behaviour), and more generally in the study of social evolution, altruism refers to behaviour by an individual that increases the fitness of another individual while decreasing the fitness of the actor. Researchers on alleged altruist behaviours among animals have been ideologically opposed to the sociological social Darwinist concept of the "survival of the fittest", under the name of "survival of the nicest"—not to be confused with the biological concept of Darwin's theory of evolution.

Insistence on such cooperative behaviours between animals was first exposed by the Russian zoologist and anarchist Peter Kropotkin in his 1902 book, *Mutual Aid: A Factor of Evolution*.

Theories of apparently-altruistic behaviour were accelerated by the need to produce theories compatible with evolutionary origins. Two related strands of research on altruism have emerged out of traditional evolutionary analyses, and from game theory respectively.

Some of the proposed mechanisms are:

- Behavioural manipulation (for example, by certain parasites that can alter the behaviour of the host)
- Bounded rationality (for example, Herbert Simon)
- Conscience
- Kin selection including eusociality
- Reciprocal altruism, mutual aid
- Selective investment theory - a theoretical proposal for the evolution of long-term, high-cost altruism
- Sexual selection, in particular, the Handicap principle
- Reciprocity
  - o Direct reciprocity (repeated encounters)
  - o Indirect reciprocity (for example, reputation)
  - o Strong reciprocity
  - o Pseudo-reciprocity.

The study of altruism was the initial impetus behind George R. Price's development of the Price equation, which is a mathematical equation used to study genetic evolution. An interesting example of altruism is found in the cellular slime moulds, such as *Dictyostelium mucoroides*. These protists live as individual amoebae until starved, at which point they aggregate and form a multicellular fruiting body in which some cells sacrifice themselves to promote the survival of other cells in the fruiting body. Social behaviour and altruism share many similarities to the interactions between the many parts (cells, genes) of an organism, but are distinguished by the ability of each individual to reproduce indefinitely without an absolute requirement for its neighbours.

Neurobiology

Jorge Moll and Jordan Grafman, neuroscientists at the National Institutes of Health and LABS-D'Or Hospital Network (J.M.) provided the first evidence for the neural bases of altruistic giving in normal healthy volunteers, using functional magnetic resonance imaging. In their research, published in the Proceedings of the National Academy of Sciences USA in October, 2006, they showed that both pure monetary rewards and charitable donations activated the mesolimbic reward pathway, a primitive part of the brain that usually lights up in response to food and sex. However, when volunteers generously placed the interests of others before their own by making charitable donations, another brain circuit was selectively activated: the subgenual cortex/septal region. These structures are intimately related to social attachment and bonding in other species. Altruism, the experiment suggested, was not a superior moral faculty that suppresses basic selfish urges but rather was basic to the brain, hard-wired and pleasurable.

Another experiment funded by the National Institutes of Health and conducted in 2007 at the Duke University in Durham, North Carolina suggests a different view, "that altruistic behaviour may originate from how people view the world rather than how they act in it". In the study published in the February 2007 print issue of Nature Neuroscience, researchers have found a part of the brain that behaves differently for altruistic and selfish people.

The researchers invited 45 volunteers to play a computer game and also to watch the computer play the game. In some instances, successful completion of the game resulted in them winning money for themselves, and in other instances, it resulted in money being donated to a charity which each person had chosen. During these activities, the researchers took functional magnetic resonance imaging (fMRI) scans of the participants' brains and were "surprised by the results". Although they "were expecting to see activity in the brain's reward centres" and that "people perform altruistic acts because they feel good about it", what they found was that "another part of the brain was also involved, and it was quite sensitive to the difference between doing something for personal gain and doing it for someone else's gain". That part of the brain is called the posterior superior temporal cortex (pSTC).

In the next stage, the scientists asked the participants some questions about type and frequency of their altruistic or helping behaviours. They then analysed the responses to generate an estimate of a person's tendency to act altruistically and compared each person's level against their fMRI brain scan. The results showed that pSTC activity rose in proportion to a person's estimated level of altruism. According to the researchers, the results suggest that altruistic behaviour may originate from how people view the world rather than how they act in it. "We believe that the ability to perceive other people's actions as meaningful is critical for altruism", said lead study investigator Dharol Tankersley.

Genetics

A study by Samuel Bowles at the Santa Fe Institute in New Mexico, US, is seen by some as breathing new life into the model of group selection for altruism, known as "Survival of the nicest". Bowles conducted a genetic analysis of contemporary foraging groups, including Australian aboriginals, native Siberian Inuit populations and indigenous tribal groups in Africa. It was found that hunter-gatherer bands of up to 30 individuals were considerably more closely related than was previously thought. Under these conditions, thought to be similar to those of the middle and upper Paleolithic, altruism towards other group-members would improve the overall fitness of the group. This is however simply a form of inclusive fitness - one vehicle helping other vehicles likely to contain the same genes.

If an individual defends the group, risking death or simply reducing his reproductive fitness, genes that this individual shares with those he successfully defends (group members) would increase in frequency (thanks to his defence supporting their reproduction). If such helpful acts are rewarded with food sharing, sexual access, monogamy or other benefits, there is not average "cost" of altruistic behaviour to be repaid. Bowles assembled genetic, climactic, archaeological, ethnographic and experimental data to examine the cost-benefit relationship of human cooperation in ancient populations. In his model, altruism is selected for when members of a group bearing genes for altruistic behaviour pay a cost - limiting their reproductive opportunities - but receive a benefit from sharing food and information. If their acts increase the average fitness of group members, altruism increase so long as group members tend also to maintain or increase their inter-relatedness (in-group mating). Bands of such altruistic humans could then act together not only defensively, but aggressively, to gain resources from other groups.

Altruist theories in evolutionary biology were contested by Amotz Zahavi, the inventor of the signal theory and its correlative, the handicap principle, based mainly on his observations of the Arabian Babbler, a bird commonly known for its surprising (alleged) altruistic behaviours.

Religious Viewpoints

Most, if not all, of the world's religions promote altruism as a very important moral value. Judaism, Jainism, Hinduism, Islam, Christianity, Buddhism, and Sikhism, etc., place particular emphasis on altruistic morality.

Buddhism

Altruism figures prominently in Buddhism. Love and compassion are components of all forms of Buddhism, and both are focused on all beings equally: the wish that all beings be happy (love) and the wish that all beings be free from suffering (compassion). "Many illnesses can be cured by the one medicine of love and compassion. These qualities are the ultimate source of human happiness, and the need for them lies at the very core of our being" (Dalai Lama).

Since "all beings" includes the individual, love and compassion in Buddhism are outside the opposition between self and other. It is even said that the very distinction between self and other is part of the root cause of our suffering. In practical terms, however, because of the spontaneous self-centeredness of most of us, Buddhism encourages us to focus love and compassion on others, and thus can be characterized as "altruistic." Many would agree with the Dalai Lama that Buddhism as a religion is kindness toward others.

Still, the very notion of altruism is modified in such a world-view, since the belief is that such a practice promotes our own happiness: "The more we care for the happiness of others, the greater our own sense of well-being becomes" (Dalai Lama).

In the context of larger ethical discussions on moral action and judgment, Buddhism is characterized by the belief that negative (unhappy) consequences of our actions derive not from punishment or correction based on moral judgment, but on the law of karma, which functions like a natural law of cause and effect. One simple illustration of such cause and effect would be the case of experiencing the effects of what I myself cause: if I cause suffering, I will as a natural consequence experience suffering; if I cause happiness, I will as a natural consequence experience happiness.

In Buddhism, *karma* (Pali *kamma*) is strictly distinguished from *vipaka*, meaning "fruit" or "result". Karma is categorized within the group or groups of cause (Pali *hetu*) in the chain of cause and effect, where it comprises the elements of "volitional activities" (Pali *sankhara*) and "action" (Pali *bhava*). Any action is understood to create "seeds" in the mind that will sprout into the appropriate result (Pali *vipaka*) when they meet with the right conditions. Most types of karmas, with good or bad results, will keep one within the wheel of samsara; others will liberate one to nirvana.

Buddhism relates karma directly to motives behind an action. Motivation usually makes the difference between "good" and "bad", but included in the motivation is also the aspect of ignorance; so a well-intended action from an ignorant mind can easily be "bad" in the sense that it creates unpleasant results for the "actor".

In Buddhism, karma is not the only cause of everything that happens. The commentarial tradition classified causal mechanisms governing the universe as taught in the early texts in five categories, known as Niyama Dhammas:

- Kamma Niyama — Consequences of one's actions
- Utu Niyama — Seasonal changes and climate
- Biija Niyama — Laws of heredity
- Citta Niyama — Will of mind
- Dhamma Niyama — Nature's tendency to produce a perfect type.

Jainism

The fundamental principles of Jainism revolve around the concept of altruism, not only for humans but for all sentient beings. This religion preaches the view of Ahimsa - to live and let live, thereby not harming sentient beings, i.e. uncompromising reverence for all life. Jainism considers all living things to be equal. The first Thirthankar, Rishabh introduced the concept of altruism for all living beings, from extending knowledge and experience to others to donation, giving oneself up for others, non-violence and compassion for all living things.

Jainism prescribes a path of non-violence to progress the soul to this ultimate goal. Jains believe that to attain enlightenment and ultimately liberation, one must practice the following ethical principles (major vows) in thought, speech and action. The degree to which these principles are practiced is different for householders and monks. They are:

1. Non-violence (Ahimsa)
2. Truthfulness (Satya)
3. Non-stealing (Asteya)
4. Celibacy (Brahmacharya)
5. Non-possession or non-materialism (Aparigraha).

A major characteristic of Jain belief is the emphasis on the consequences of not only physical but also mental behaviours. One's unconquered mind with anger, pride (ego), deceit, greed and uncontrolled sense organs are the powerful enemies of humans. Anger spoils good relations, pride destroys humility, deceit destroys peace and greed destroys everything. Jainism recommends conquering anger by forgiveness, pride (ego) by humility, deceit by straight-forwardness and greed by contentment.

The principle of non-violence seeks to minimize karmas which limit the capabilities of the soul. Jainism views every soul as worthy of respect because it has the potential to become Siddha (Param-atma – "highest soul"). Because all living beings possess a soul, great care and awareness is essential in one's actions. Jainism emphasizes the equality of all life, advocating harmlessness towards all, whether the creatures are great or small. This policy extends even to microscopic organisms. Jainism acknowledges that every person has different capabilities and capacities to practice and therefore accepts different levels of compliance for ascetics and householders. The "great vows" (mahavrata) are prescribed for monks and "limited vows" (anuvrata) are prescribed for householders. In other words, the house-holders are encouraged to practice the five cardinal principles of non-violence, truthfulness, non-stealing, celibacy and non-possessiveness with their current practical limitations while the monks have to observe them very strictly. With consistent practice, it will be possible to overcome the limitations gradually, accelerating the spiritual progress.

Christianity

Altruism was central to the teachings of Jesus found in the Gospel especially in the Sermon on the Mount and the Sermon on the Plain. From biblical to medieval Christian traditions, tensions between self-affirmation and other-regard were sometimes discussed under the heading of "disinterested love," as in the Pauline phrase "love seeks not its own interests." In his book *Indoctrination and Self-deception*, Roderick Hindery tries to shed light on these tensions by contrasting them with impostors of authentic self-affirmation and altruism, by analysis of other-regard within creative individuation of the self, and by contrasting love for the few with love for the many. Love confirms others in their freedom, shuns propagandas and masks, assures others of its presence, and is ultimately confirmed not by mere declarations from others, but by each person's experience and practice from within. As in practical arts, the presence and meaning of love becomes validated and grasped not by words and reflections alone, but in the making of the connection.

Though it might seem obvious that altruism is central to the teachings of Jesus, one important and influential strand of Christianity would qualify this. St Thomas Aquinas in the *Summa Theologica*, I:II Quaestio 26, Article 4 states that we should love ourselves more than our neighbour. His interpretation of the Pauline phrase is that we should seek the common good more than the private good but this is because the common good is a more desirable good for the individual. 'You should love your neighbour as yourself' from Leviticus 19 and Matthew 22 is interpreted by St Thomas as meaning that love for ourselves is the exemplar of love for others. He does think though, that we should love God more than ourselves and our neighbour, taken as an entirety, more than our bodily life, since the ultimate purpose of love of our neighbour is to share in eternal beatitude, a more desirable thing than bodily well being. Comte was probably opposing this Thomistic doctrine, which is present in some theological schools within Catholicism, in coining the word Altruism, as stated above.

Thomas Jay Oord has argued in several books that altruism is but one possible form of love. An altruistic action is not always a loving action. Oord defines altruism as acting for the good of the other, and he agrees with feminists who note that sometimes love requires acting for one's own good when the demands of the other undermine overall well-being.

Islam and Sufism

In Sufism, the concept of i'thar (altruism) is the notion of 'preferring others to oneself'. For Sufis, this means devotion to others through complete forgetfulness of one's own concerns. The importance lies in sacrifice for the sake of the greater good; Islam considers those practicing i'thar as abiding by the highest degree of nobility. This is similar to the notion of chivalry, but unlike the European concept there is a focus on attention to everything in existence. A constant concern for Allah results in a careful attitude towards people, animals, and other things in this world. This concept was emphasized by Sufi mystics like Rabia al-Adawiyya who paid attention to the difference in dedication to Allah and dedication to people. 13th century Turkish sufi poet Yunus Emre explained this philosophy as "Yaratýlaný severiz, Yaratandan ötürü" or "We love the creature, because of The Creator"

Judaism

Judaism defines altruism as the desired goal of creation. The famous Rabbi Abraham Isaac Kook stated that love is the most important attribute in humanity. This is defined as bestowal, or giving, which is the intention of altruism. This can be altruism towards humanity that leads to altruism towards the creator or God. Kabbalah defines God as the force of giving in existence. Rabbi Moshe Chaim Luzzatto in particular focused on the 'purpose of creation' and how the will of God was to bring creation into perfection and adhesion with this upper force.

Modern Kabbalah developed by Rabbi Yehuda Ashlag, in his writings about the future generation, focuses on how society could achieve an altruistic social framework. Ashlag proposed that such a framework is the purpose of creation, and everything that happens is to raise humanity to the level of altruism, love for one another. Ashlag focused on society and its relation to divinity.

Sikhism

Altruism is essential to the Sikh religion. In the late 17th century, Guru Gobind Singh Ji (the tenth guru in Sikhism), was in war with the Moghul rulers to protect the people of different faiths, when a fellow Sikh, Bhai Kanhaiya, attended the troops of the enemy. He gave water to both friends and foes who were wounded on the battlefield. Some of the enemy began to fight again and some Sikh warriors were annoyed by Bhai Kanhaiya as he was helping their enemy. Sikh soldiers brought Bhai Kanhaiya before Guru Gobind Singh Ji, and complained of his action that they considered counterproductive to their struggle on the battlefield. "What were you doing, and why?" asked the Guru. "I was giving water to the wounded because I saw your face in all of them," replied Bhai Kanhaiya. The Guru responded, "Then you should also give them ointment to heal their wounds. You were practicing what you were coached in the house of the Guru."

It was under the tutelage of the Guru that Bhai Kanhaiya subsequently founded a volunteer corps for altruism. This volunteer corps still to date is engaged in doing good to others and trains new volunteering recruits for doing the same.

Vedanta

Vedanta differs from the view that karma is a law of cause and effect but instead additionally hold that karma is mediated by the will of a personal supreme god. This view of karma is in contradiction to Buddhism, Jain and other Hindu religions that do view karma as a law of cause and effect.

Swami Sivananda, an Advaita scholar, reiterates the same views in his commentary synthesising Vedanta views on the Brahma Sutras, a Vedantic text. Hence, karma cannot bestow the fruits of actions at a future date according to one's merit. Furthermore, one cannot argue that karma generates apurva or punya, which gives fruit. Since apurva is non-sentient, it cannot act unless moved by an intelligent being such as a god. It cannot independently bestow reward or punishment.

United States

Spencer proved to be a popular figure in the 1870s primarily because his application of evolution to all areas of human endeavor promoted an optimistic view of the future as inevitably becoming better; in the United States, writers and thinkers of the gilded age such as Edward L. Youmans, William Graham Sumner, John Fiske, John W. Burgess, and others all developed theories of social evolution as a result of their exposure to the works of Darwin and Spencer.

Sumner never fully embraced Darwinian ideas, and some contemporary historians do not believe that Sumner ever actually believed in social Darwinism. The great majority of American businessmen rejected the anti-philanthropic implications of the theory. Instead they gave millions to build schools, colleges, hospitals, art institutes, parks and many other institutions. Andrew Carnegie, who admired Spencer, was the leading philanthropist in the world (1890–1920), and a major leader against imperialism and warfare.

H. G. Wells was heavily influenced by Darwinist thoughts, and novelist Jack London wrote stories of survival that incorporated his views on social Darwinism.

Japan

Social Darwinism has influenced political, public health and social movements in Japan since the late 19th and early 20th century. Originally brought to Japan through the works of Francis Galton, Ernst Haeckel and German orthodox mendelian, United States, British and French Lamarkian eugenical written studies of the late 19th and early 20th centuries, eugenism as a science, was hotly debated at the beginning of the 20th, in *Jinsei-Der Mensch*, the first eugenics journal in the empire. As the Japanese sought to close ranks with the west, this practice was adopted wholesale along with colonialism and its justifications.

Eugenics in Japan

Eugenics in Japan has influenced political, public health and social movements in Japan since the late 19th and early 20th century. Originally brought to Japan through the United States (like Charles Davenport and John Coulter), through

Mendelian Inheritance by way of German influences, and French Lamarkian eugenic written studies of the late 19th and early 20th centuries. Eugenics as a science was hotly debated at the beginning of the 20th, in *Jinsei-Der Mensch*, the first eugenics journal in the Empire. As the Japanese sought to close ranks with the West, this practice was adopted wholesale, along with colonialism and its justifications..

The concept of pure blood as a criterion for the uniqueness of the Yamato people began circulating around 1880 in Japan, while eugenics in the sense of instrumental and selective procreation, clustered around two positions concerning blood, the pure blood and the mixed blood.

Popularity of the pure-blood eugenics theory came from a homegrown racial purity or monoculture national belief that has been part of Japanese society since ancient times. The local movement was however less focused on modern scientific ideals and more on the "outside person" vs the "native or inside person" and blood purity.

Later legal measures were supported by certain politicians and movements that sought to increase the number of healthy pure Japanese, while simultaneously decreasing the number of people suffering mental retardation, disability, genetic disease and other conditions that led to them being viewed as "inferior" contributions to the Japanese gene pool.

Opposition to the eugenics movement persisted amongst several right-wing ultra-nationalist factions, including members of the Diet of Japan and obstetricians, who perceived eugenics as suggesting that the Japanese people were only animals, not people of divine origin as believed by the Japanese national Shinto tradition. Similar resistance to these theories occurred within conservative and traditional Christian communities in the United States.

Origins of Japanese Domestic Scientific Eugenics

Yamanouchi Shige (1876-1973), a plant cytologist, was one of the early and important members of the Japanese eugenics movement, who was trained under John Coulter (1851-1928) an American eugenicist and botanist. He was a major promoter and academic of early Lamarckian theory, but later blended his ideas with Mendelian evolutionary theory.

His career is a direct link between United States and Japanese eugenics. His approach has been credited with searching for a way for the Japanese *race* to genetically "catch up" with the "dominant Western race" of the 19th and early 20th centuries. According to Jennifer Robertson of the University of Michigan, eugenism, as part of the new scientific order, was introduced in Japan "under the aegis of nationalism and empire building." She identifies "positive eugenism" and "negative eugenism." Positive eugenism, promoted by Ikeda Shigenori, refers to "the improvement of circumstances of sexual reproduction and thus incorporates advances in sanitation, nutrition and physical education into strategies to shape the reproductive choices and decisions of individual and families" Negative Eugenism, promoted by Hisomu Nagai, "involves the prevention of sexual reproduction, through induced abortion or sterilization among people deemed unfit". "Unfit" included people such as alcoholics, lepers, the mentally ill, the physically disabled, and criminals.

Eugenic Policies

Ikeda Shigenori, a journalist who had been sent to Germany, started the magazine *Eugenics movement* in 1926. In 1928, he promoted December 21 as "Blood-purity day" (*junketsu de*) and sponsored free blood-test at the Tokyo Hygiene Laboratory.

Nagai, the "Doctor of Eugenics", assumed the position of chief director of The Japanese Society of Health and Human Ecology (JSHHE), which was established in 1930.

By early 1930s' detailed "eugenic marriage" questionnaires were printed or inserted in popular magazines for public consumption. Promoters like Ikeda were convinced that these marriage surveys would not only insure the eugenic fitness of spouses but also help avoid class differences that could disrupt and even destroy marriage. The goal was to create a database of individuals and their entire households which would enable eugenicists to conduct in-depth surveys of any given family's genealogy.

Race Eugenic Protection Law

The *Race Eugenic Protection Law* was submitted from 1934 to 1938 to the Diet. After four amendments, this draft was promulgated as a National Eugenic Law in 1940 by the Konoe government.

This law limited compulsory sterilization to "inherited mental disease", promoted genetic screening and restricted birth control access. According to Matsubara Yoko, from 1940 to 1945, 454 people were sterilized in Japan under this law.

There were also campaigns to ensure reproduction amongst the "intelligent or superior elements" in the population.

Family center staff also attempted to discourage marriage between Japanese women and Korean men who had been recruited from the peninsula as labourers following its annexation by Japan in 1910. In 1942, a survey report argued that

"the Korean labourers brought to Japan, where they have established permanent residency, are of the lower classes and therefore of inferior constitution...By fathering children with Japanese women, these men could lower the caliber of the *Yamato minzoku*."

Eugenism was criticized by some Shinto ultranationalists as it seemed to treat Japanese people, considered of divine origin, as animals to be "bred". According to Nagai Hisomu, the Japanese Army's ignorance and dismissal of the science behind eugenics also stalled the spread of eugenic ideology.

After 1945

One of the last eugenic measures of the pre-war regime was taken by the Higashikuni government. On 19 August 1945, the Home Ministry ordered local government offices to establish a prostitution service for allied soldiers to preserve the "purity" of the "Japanese race". The official declaration stated that :

Through the sacrifice of thousands of "Okichis" of the Shôwa era, we shall construct a dike to hold back the mad frenzy of the occupation troops and cultivate and preserve the purity of our race long into the future...

Such clubs were soon established by cabinet councillor Yoshio Kodama and Ryoichi Sasakawa.

In postwar Japan, the Eugenic Protection Law was enacted in 1948 to replace the National Eugenic Law of 1940. The main provisions allowed for the surgical sterilization of women, when the woman, her spouse, or family member within the 4th degree of kinship had a serious genetic disorder, and where pregnancy would endanger the life of the woman. The operation required consent of the woman, her spouse and the approval of the Prefectural Eugenic Protection Council.

The law also allowed for abortion for pregnancies in the cases of rape, leprosy, hereditary-transmitted disease, or if the physician determined that the fetus would not be viable outside of the womb. Again, the consent of the woman and her spouse were necessary. Birth control guidance and implementation was restricted to doctors, nurses and professional midwives accredited by the Prefectural government. The law was also amended in May 1949 to allow abortions for economic reasons at the sole discretion of the doctor, which in effect fully legalized abortion in Japan.

Despite the unambiguous wording of the law, the law was used by local authorities as justification for measures enforcing forced sterilization and abortions upon people with certain genetic disorders, as well as leprosy, as well as an excuse for legalized discrimination against people with physical and mental handicaps.

Abolition of Eugenics Laws

Laws that decreed compulsory sterilization of the disabled were abolished with the approval of the Mother's Body Protection Law on June 18, 1996.

Leprosy Policies

The *Leprosy Prevention laws* of 1907, 1931 and 1953, the last one only repealed in 1996, permitted the segregation of patients in sanitarium where forced abortions and sterilization were common, even if the laws did not refer to it, and authorized punishment of patients "disturbing peace" as most Japanese leprologists believed that vulnerability to the disease was inheritable.

There were a few Japanese leprologists such as Noburo Ogasawara who argued against the "isolation-sterilization policy" but he was denounced as a traitor to the nation at 15th Conference of the Japanese Association of Leprology in 1941. Under the colonial Korean *Leprosy prevention ordinance*, Korean patients were also subjected to hard labour. In postwar Japan, the Eugenic Protection Law was enacted in 1948 to replace the National Eugenic Law of 1940. The indications of the Eugenic Protection Law includede leprosy. This condition discontinued when the law changed into Women's Body Protection Law.

China

Social Darwinism was formally introduced to China through the translations by Yan Fu of Huxley, in the course of an extensive series of translations of influential Western thought. By the 1920s, it found expression in the tireless promotion of eugenics by the Chinese sociologist Pan Guangdan.

Criticisms and Controversies

As Social Darwinism has many definitions, it is hard for some to be either for or against it; some of the definitions oppose the others. John Halliday & Iain McLean state that

Part of the difficulty in establishing sensible and consistent usage is that commitment to the biology of natural selection and to 'survival of the fittest' entailed nothing uniform either for sociological method or for political doctrine. A 'social Darwinist' could just as well be a defender of laissez-faire as a defender of state socialism, just as much an imperialist as a domestic eugenist.

Some pre-twentieth century doctrines subsequently described as social Darwinism appear to anticipate eugenics and the race doctrines of Nazism. Critics have frequently linked evolution, Charles Darwin and social Darwinism with racialism, nationalism, imperialism and eugenics, contending that social Darwinism became one of the pillars of Fascism and Nazi ideology, and that the consequences of the application of policies of "survival of the fittest" by Nazi Germany eventually created a very strong backlash against the theory.

As mentioned above, Social Darwinism has often been linked to nationalism and imperialism. During the age of New Imperialism, the concepts of evolution justified the exploitation of "lesser breeds without the law" by "superior races." To elitists, strong nations were composed of white people who successful at expanding their empires, and as such, these strong nations would survive in the struggle for dominance. With this attitude,

Europeans, except for Christian missionaries, seldom adopted the customs and languages of local people under their empires.

Nazi Germany's justification for its aggression was regularly promoted in Nazi propaganda films depicting scenes such as beetles fighting in a lab setting to demonstrate the principles of "survival of the fittest" as depicted in Alles Leben ist Kampf (English translation: All Life is Struggle). Hitler often refused to intervene in the promotion of officers and staff members, preferring instead to have them fight amongst themselves to force the "stronger" person to prevail - "strength" referring to those social forces void of virtue or principle.

The argument that Nazi ideology was strongly influenced by social Darwinist ideas is often found in historical and social science literature. For example, the Jewish philosopher and historian Hannah Arendt analysed the historical development from a politically indifferent scientific Darwinism via social Darwinist ethics to racist ideology. In the last years the argument has increasingly been taken up by opponents of evolutionary theory. The creationist ministry Answers in Genesis is especially known for some of these claims. Intelligent design supporters have promoted this position as well. For example, it is a theme in the work of Richard Weikart, who is a historian at California State University, Stanislaus and is a senior fellow for the Center for Science and Culture of the Discovery Institute.

It is also a main argument in the 2008 movie *Expelled: No Intelligence Allowed*. These claims are widely criticized within the academic community. The Anti-Defamation League has rejected such attempts to link Darwin's ideas with Nazi atrocities, and has stated that "Using the Holocaust in order to tarnish those who promote the theory of evolution is outrageous and trivializes the complex factors that led to the mass extermination of European Jewry."

Weickart himself writes in his book "From Darwin to Hitler": "The multivalence of Darwinism and eugenics ideology, especially when applied to ethical, political, and social thought, together with the multiple roots of Nazi ideology, should make us suspicious of monocausal arguments about the origins of the Nazi worldview".

Similar criticisms are sometimes applied (or misapplied) to other political or scientific theories that resemble social Darwinism, for example criticisms leveled at evolutionary psychology. For example, a critical reviewer of Weikart's book writes that "(h)is historicization of the moral framework of evolutionary theory poses key issues for those in sociobiology and evolutionary psychology, not to mention bioethicists, who have recycled many of the suppositions that Weikart has traced."

Another example is recent scholarship that portrays Ernst Haeckel's Monist League as a mystical progenitor of the Völkisch movement and, ultimately, of the Nazi Party of Adolf Hitler. Scholars opposed to this interpretation, however, have pointed out that the Monists were freethinkers who opposed all forms of mysticism, and that their organizations were immediately banned following the Nazi takeover in 1933 because of their association with a wide variety of progressive causes including feminism, pacifism, human rights, and early gay liberation movements.

Similarly, capitalist economics, especially laissez-faire economics, is attacked by some socialists by equating it to social Darwinism because it is premised on the idea of natural scarcity, and because it is often interpreted to involve a "sink or swim" attitude toward economic activity. However, while many industrialists supported social Darwinism during the gilded age, later notable advocates of *laissez-faire* rejected it.

Ludwig von Mises argued in his book Human Action that social Darwinism contradicts the principles of liberalism, however this conclusion was based on the definition of social Darwinism as *"that individuals or groups achieve advantage over others as the result of genetic or biological superiority"*. He addresses this definition of social Darwinism by stating *"Darwinism does not in any way invalidate the liberal creed; on the contrary, the traits conducive to social cooperation (rather than the allegedly "natural" instincts of aggression) are precisely those that maximize one's offspring in the current environment. Far from being unnatural, reason is the foremost biological mark of homo sapiens."*

Social Darwinist theory itself does not necessarily engender a political position: some social Darwinists would argue for the inevitability of progress, while others emphasize the potential for the degeneration of humanity, and some even attempt to enroll social Darwinism in a reformist politics. Rather, social Darwinism is an eclectic set of closely interrelated social theories—much in the way that existentialism is not one philosophy but a set of closely interrelated philosophical principles.

Some economic critics of social Darwinism point to David Ricardo's comparative advantage and claim that weaker members of society are valuable even if the stronger members are better at doing everything. However, social Darwinism does not necessarily assert the latter. Comparative advantage relies on the idea that trade and cooperation are more important than pure competitiveness, which might inhibit trade by erecting protective barriers.

4

Stratification and Social Distance

Social distance describes the distance between different groups of society and is opposed to *locational distance*. The notion includes all differences such as social class, race/ethnicity or sexuality, but also the fact that the different groups do not mix. The term is often applied in cities, but its use is not limited to that.

In the sociological literature, the concept of social distance is conceptualized in several different ways.

1. Affective social distance: One widespread conception of social distance focuses on affectivity. According to this approach, social distance is associated with affective distance, i.e. how much or little sympathy the members of a group feel for another group. Emory Bogardus, the creator of "Bogardus social distance scale" was typically basing his scale on this subjective-affective conception of social distance: "[i]n social distance studies the center of attention is on the feeling reactions of persons toward other persons and toward groups of people."
2. Normative social distance: A second approach views social distance as a normative category. Normative social distance refers to the widely accepted and often consciously expressed norms about who should be considered as an "insider" and who an "outsider/ foreigner." Such norms, in other words, specify the distinctions between "us" and "them." In this respect,

normative social distance is very different from affective social distance, because here social distance is conceived as a non-subjective, structural aspect of social relations. Examples of this conception can be found in some of the works of sociologists such as Georg Simmel, Emile Durkheim and to some extent Robert Park.

3. Interactive social distance: A third conceptualization of social distance focuses on the frequency and intensity of interactions between two groups. The main idea here is that the more the members of two groups interact, the closer they are socially. This conception is similar to the approaches in sociological network theory, where the frequency of interaction between two parties is used as a measure of the "strength" of the social tie between them.

It is possible to view these different conceptions as "dimensions" of social distance. However, it is important to note that these dimensions do not necessarily overlap. The members of two groups might interact with each other quite frequently, but this does not always mean that they will feel "close" to each other or that normatively they will consider each other as the members of the same group. In other words, interactive, normative and affective dimensions of social distance might not be linearly associated.

Social distancing is the public health practice of encouraging people to keep their physical distance from each other during disease outbreaks in order to slow the spread of infection.

Social periphery is a term often used in conjunction with social distance. It refers to people distant with regard to social relations. It is often implied that it is measured from the dominant *city élite*. The social periphery of a city is often located in the centre.

Locational periphery in contrast is used to describe places physically distant from the heart of the city. These places often include suburbs and are socially close to the core of the city. In some cases the locational periphery overlaps with the social periphery, such as in Paris' *banlieues*.

In 1991 Mulgan stated that "The centres of two cities are often for practical purposes closer to each other than to their own peripheries." This reference to social distance is especially true for global cities.

Bogardus Social Distance Scale

The Bogardus Social Distance Scale is a psychological testing scale created by Emory S. Bogardus to empirically measure people's willingness to participate in social contacts of varying degrees of closeness with members of diverse social groups, such as other racial and ethnic groups, sex offenders, and homosexuals.

The scale asks people the extent to which they would be accepting of each group (a score of 1.00 for a group is taken to indicate no social distance):

- As close relatives by marriage (score 1.00)
- As my close personal friends (2.00)
- As neighbours on the same street (3.00)
- As co-workers in the same occupation (4.00)
- As citizens in my country (5.00)
- As only visitors in my country (6.00)
- Would exclude from my country (7.00).

The Bogardus Social Distance Scale is a cumulative scale (a Guttman scale), because agreement with any item implies agreement with all preceding items. The scale has been criticized as too simple because the social interactions and attitudes in close familial or friendship-type relationships may be qualitatively different from social interactions with and attitudes toward relationships with far-away contacts such as citizens or visitors in one's country.

Research by Bogardus first in 1925 and then repeated in 1946, 1956, and 1966 shows that the extent of social distancing in the US is decreasing slightly and fewer distinctions are being made among groups. A Web-based questionnaire has been running since late 1993. Internet users are encouraged to submit their responses here where the maintainer of this site has posted at least two papers that update research on social distance.

For Bogardus, social distance is a function of affective distance between the members of two groups: "[i]n social distance studies the center of attention is on the feeling reactions of persons toward other persons and toward groups of people." Thus, for him, social distance is essentially a measure of how much or little sympathy the members of a group feel for another group. It might be important to note that Bogardus's conceptualization is not the only one in the sociological literature. Several sociologists have pointed out that social distance can also be conceptualized on the basis of other parameters such as the frequency of interaction between different groups or the normative distinctions in a society about who should be considered an "insider" or "outsider."

Discrimination

Discrimination is a sociological term referring to the treatment taken toward or against an individual of a certain group in consideration based solely on class or category. Discrimination is the *actual behaviour* towards another group. It involves excluding or restricting members of one group from opportunities that are available to other groups. The United Nations explains: "Discriminatory behaviours take many forms, but they all involve some form of exclusion or rejection." Discriminatory laws such as redlining have existed in many countries. In some countries, controversial attempts such as racial quotas have been used to redress negative effects of discrimination.

Race and Ethnicity Discrimination

Racial discrimination differentiates between individuals on the basis of real and perceived racial differences, and has been official government policy in several countries, such as South Africa in the apartheid era, and the USA.

In the United States, racial profiling of minorities by law enforcement officials has been called racial discrimination. As early as 1865, the Civil Rights Act provided a remedy for intentional race discrimination in employment by private employers and state and local public employers. The Civil Rights Act of 1871 applies to public employment or employment involving state action prohibiting deprivation of rights secured by the federal constitution or federal laws through action under colour of law. Title VII is the principal federal statute with regard to employment discrimination prohibiting unlawful employment discrimination by public and private employers, labor organizations, training programs and employment agencies based on race or colour, religion, gender, and national origin.

Within the criminal justice system in some Western countries, minorities are convicted and imprisoned disproportionately when compared with whites. In 1998, nearly one out of three black men between the ages of 20-29 were in prison or jail, on probation or parole on any given day in the United States. First Nations make up about 2% of Canada's population, but account for 18% of the federal prison population as of 2000. According to the Australian government's June 2006 publication of prison statistics, indigenous peoples make up 24% of the overall prison population in Australia. In 2004, Maori made up just 15% of the total population of New Zealand but 49.5% of prisoners. Maori were entering prison at 8 times the rate of non-Maori. A quarter of the people in England's prisons are from an ethnic minority. The Equality and Human Rights Commission found that five times more black people than white people per head of population in England and Wales are imprisoned. Experts and politicians said over-representation of black men was a result of decades of racial prejudice in the criminal justice system.

Racism

Racism is the belief that the genetic factors which constitute race are a primary determinant of human traits and capacities and that racial differences produce an inherent superiority of a particular race. Racism's effects are called "racial discrimination." In the case of institutional racism, certain racial groups may be denied rights or benefits, or receive preferential treatment.

Racial discrimination typically points out taxonomic differences between different groups of people, although anyone may be discriminated against on an ethnic or cultural basis, independently of their somatic differences. According to the United Nations conventions, there is no distinction between the term racial discrimination and ethnicity discrimination. There is some evidence that the meaning of the term has changed over time, and that earlier definitions of racism involved the simple belief that human populations are divided into separate races. Many biologists, anthropologists, and sociologists reject this taxonomy in favor of more specific and/or empirically verifiable criteria, such as geography, ethnicity, or a history of endogamy.

Definitions

Although the term racism usually denotes race-based prejudice, violence, dislike, discrimination, or oppression, the term can also have varying and contested definitions. *Racialism* is a related term, sometimes intended to avoid these negative meanings. According to the *Oxford English Dictionary*, racism is a belief or ideology that all members of each racial group possess characteristics or abilities specific to that race, especially to distinguish it as being either superior or inferior to another racial group or racial groups.

The *Merriam-Webster's Dictionary* defines racism as a belief that race is the primary determinant of human traits and capacities and that racial differences produce an inherent superiority or inferiority of a particular racial group, and that it is also the prejudice based on such a belief. The *Macquarie Dictionary* defines racism as: "the belief that human races have distinctive characteristics which determine their respective cultures, usually involving the idea that one's own race is superior and has the right to rule or dominate others."

Legal

The UN does not define "racism", however it does define "racial discrimination": according to the United Nations Convention on the Elimination of All Forms of Racial Discrimination, *the term "racial discrimination" shall mean any distinction, exclusion, restriction or preference based on race, colour, descent, or national or ethnic origin which has the purpose or effect of nullifying or impairing the recognition, enjoyment or exercise, on an equal footing, of human rights and fundamental freedoms in the political, economic, social, cultural or any other field of public life.*

This definition does not make any difference between discrimination based on ethnicity and race, in part because the distinction between the two remains debatable among anthropologists. Similarly, in British law the phrase *racial group* means "any group of people who are defined by reference to their race, colour, nationality (including citizenship) or ethnic or national origin".

Sociological

Some sociologists have defined racism as a system of group privilege. In *Portraits of White Racism*, David Wellman has defined racism as "culturally sanctioned beliefs, which, regardless of intentions involved, defend the advantages whites have because of the subordinated position of racial minorities". Sociologists Noël A. Cazenave and Darlene Alvarez Maddern define racism as "...a highly organized system of 'race'-based group privilege that operates at every level of society and is held together by a sophisticated ideology of colour/'race' supremacy. Sellers and Shelton (2003) found that a relationship between racial discrimination and emotional distress was moderated by racial ideology and public regard beliefs. That is, racial centrality appears to promote the degree of discrimination African American young adults perceive whereas racial ideolog, may buffer the detrimental emotional effects of that discrimination. Racist systems include, but cannot be reduced to, racial bigotry,". Sociologist and former American Sociological Association president Joe Feagin argues that the United States can be characterized as a "total racist society"

"Police harassment and brutality directed at black men, women, and children are as old as American society, dating back to the days of slavery and Jim Crow segregation. Such police actions across the nation today reveal important aspects of... the commonplace discriminatory practices of individual whites... [and] white dominated institutions that allow or encourage such practices.."

Types

Racial Discrimination

Racial discrimination is treating people differently through a process of social division into categories not necessarily related to races. Racial segregation policies may officialize it, but it is also often exerted without being legalized. Researchers, including Dean Karlan and Marianne Bertrand, at the MIT and the University of Chicago found in a 2003 study that there was widespread discrimination in the workplace against job applicants whose names were merely perceived as "sounding black". These applicants were 50% less likely than candidates perceived as having "white-sounding names" to receive callbacks for interviews. In contrast, institutions and courts have upheld discrimination against whites when it is done to promote a diverse work or educational environment, even when it was shown to be to the detriment of qualified applicants. The researchers view these results as strong evidence of unconscious biases rooted in the United States' long history of discrimination (i.e. Jim Crow laws, etc.)

Institutional

Institutional racism (also known as structural racism, state racism or systemic racism) is racial discrimination by governments, corporations, religions, or educational institutions or other large organizations with the power to influence the lives of many individuals. Stokely Carmichael is credited for coining the phrase *institutional racism* in the late 1960s. He defined the term as "the collective failure of an organization to provide an appropriate and professional service to people because of their colour, culture or ethnic origin".

Maulana Karenga argued that racism constituted the destruction of culture, language, religion and human possibility, and that the effects of racism were "the morally monstrous destruction of human possibility involved redefining African humanity to the world, poisoning past, present and future relations with others who only know us through this stereotyping and thus damaging the truly human relations among peoples."

Economic

Historical economic or social disparity is alleged to be a form of discrimination which is caused by past racism and historical reasons, affecting the present generation through deficits in the formal education and kinds of preparation in the parents' generation, and, through primarily unconscious racist attitudes and actions on members of the general population. (e.g. A member of race Y, Mary, has her opportunities adversely affected (directly and/or indirectly) by the mistreatment of her ancestors of race Y.)

A hypothesis embraced by classical economists is that competition in a capitalist economy decreases the impact of discrimination. The thinking behind the hypothesis is that discrimination imposes a cost on the employer, and thus a profit-driven employer will avoid racist hiring policies.

Although a capitalist economy would avoid discrimination in order to avoid extra cost, this can be avoided in other ways. A capitalist company for example may use racist hiring policies as it deviates towards the "cultural norm".

These "norms" albeit unquestioned are evident within society. In a predominantly white society when hiring a person of colour into a position of management this may then cause disputes, and damage communications between other employers. Thus the company would be economically put in a deficit because of the discrimination of other companies, as they invoke discrimination and isolate that company. Although this may be a radical, over exaggerated point of view, it portrays how pervasive racism is and how company will some time deviate towards racist hiring policies in order to henceforth be not isolated, thus preventing the company from going into an economic deficit. (Burton 2009:1)

For decades, African American farmers said they were unjustly being denied farm loans or subjected to longer waits for loan approval because of racism, and accused the U.S. Department of Agriculture (USDA) of not responding to their complaints.

During the Spanish colonial period, Spaniards developed a complex caste system based on race, which was used for social control and which also determined a person's importance in society. While many Latin American countries have long since rendered the system officially illegal through legislation, usually at the time of independence, prejudice based on degrees of perceived racial distance from European ancestry combined with one's socioeconomic status remain, an echo of the colonial caste system.

Almost uniformly, people who are darker-skinned and of indigenous descent make up the peasantry and working classes, while lighter-skinned, Spanish-descent Latin Americans are in the ruling elite.

Declarations against Racial Discrimination

In 1950, UNESCO suggested in *The Race Question* —a statement signed by 21 scholars such as Ashley Montagu, Claude Lévi-Strauss, Gunnar Myrdal, Julian Huxley, etc. — to "drop the term *race* altogether and instead speak of ethnic groups". The statement condemned scientific racism theories which had played a role in the Holocaust. It aimed both at debunking scientific racist theories, by popularizing modern knowledge concerning "the race question," and morally condemned racism as contrary to the philosophy of the Enlightenment and its assumption of equal rights for all. Along with Myrdal's *An American Dilemma: The Negro Problem and Modern Democracy* (1944), *The Race Question* influenced the 1954 U.S. Supreme Court desegregation decision in "Brown v. Board of Education of Topeka".

The United Nations uses the definition of racial discrimination laid out in the *International Convention on the Elimination of All Forms of Racial Discrimination*, adopted in 1966:*...any distinction, exclusion, restriction or preference based on race, colour, descent, or national or ethnic origin which has the purpose or effect of nullifying or impairing the recognition, enjoyment or exercise, on an equal footing, of human rights and fundamental freedoms in the political, economic, social, cultural or any other field of public life.*(Part 1 of Article 1 of the U.N. International Convention on the Elimination of All Forms of Racial Discrimination)

In 2001, the European Union explicitly banned racism along with many other forms of social discrimination in the Charter of Fundamental Rights of the European Union, the legal effect of which, if any, would necessarily be limited to Institutions of the European Union: "Article 21 of the charter prohibits discrimination on any ground such as race, colour, ethnic or social origin, genetic features, language, religion or belief, political or any other opinion, membership of a national minority, property, disability, age or sexual orientation and also discrimination on the grounds of nationality."

Ideology

As an ideology, racism existed during the 19th century as "scientific racism", which attempted to provide a racial classification of humanity. Although such racist ideologies have been widely discredited after World War II and the Holocaust, racism and of racial discrimination have remained widespread all over the world. Some examples of this in present day are statistics including, but not limited to, the ratio of black men in prison to free black men vs. other races, physical abilities and mental ability statistics, and other data gathered by scientific groups. While these statistics are accurate, and can show trends, it's inappropriate in most countries to assume that because a particular race has a high crime or low literacy rate, that the entire race of people automatically are criminals or unintelligent.

It was already noted by DuBois that, in making the difference between races, it is not race that we think about, but culture: "...a common history, common laws and religion, similar habits of thought and a conscious striving together for certain ideals of life" Late 19th century nationalists were the first to embrace contemporary discourses on "race", ethnicity and "survival of the fittest" to shape new nationalist doctrines. Ultimately, race came to represent not only the most important traits of the human body, but was also regarded as decisively shaping the character and personality of the nation.

According to this view, culture is the physical manifestation created by ethnic groupings, as such fully determined by racial characteristics. Culture and race became considered intertwined and dependent upon each other, sometimes even to the extent of including nationality or language to the set of definition. Pureness of race tended to be related to rather superficial characteristics that were easily addressed and advertised, such as blondness. Racial qualities tended to be related to nationality and language rather than the actual geographic distribution of racial characteristics. In the case of Nordicism, the denomination "Germanic" became virtually equivalent to superiority of race.

Bolstered by some nationalist and ethnocentric values and achievements of choice, this concept of racial superiority evolved to distinguish from other cultures, that were considered inferior or impure. This emphasis on culture corresponds to the modern mainstream definition of racism: "Racism does not originate from the existence of 'races'. It *creates* them through a process of social division into categories: anybody can be racialised, independently of their somatic, cultural, religious differences."

This definition explicitly ignores the fiery polemic on the biological concept of race, still subject to scientific debate. In the words of David C. Rowe "A racial concept, although sometimes in the guise of another name, will remain in use in biology and in other fields because scientists, as well as lay persons, are fascinated by human diversity, some of which is captured by race."

Until recent history this racist abuse of physical anthropology has been politically exploited. Apart from being unscientific, racial prejudice became subject to international legislation. For instance, the Declaration on the Elimination of all Forms of Racial Discrimination, adopted by the United Nations General Assembly on November 20, 1963, address racial prejudice explicitly next to discrimination for reasons of race, colour or ethnic origin.

Racism has been a motivating factor in social discrimination, racial segregation, hate speech and violence (such as pogroms, genocides and ethnic cleansings). Despite the persistence of racial stereotypes, humour and epithets in much everyday language, racial discrimination is illegal in many countries.

Ironically, anti-racism has also become a political instrument of abuse. Some politicians have practised *race baiting* in an attempt to win votes. In a reversal of values, anti-racism is being propagated by despots in the service of obscurantism and the suppression of women. Philosopher Pascal Bruckner claimed that *"Anti-racism in the UN has become the ideology of totalitarian regimes who use it in their own interests."*

Ethnic Nationalism

After the Napoleonic Wars, Europe was confronted with the new "nationalities question," leading to ceaseless reconfigurations of the European map, on which the frontiers between the states had been delimited during the 1648 Peace of Westphalia. Nationalism had made its first striking appearance with the invention of the *levée en masse* by the

French revolutionaries, thus inventing mass conscription in order to be able to defend the newly founded Republic against the *Ancien Régime* order represented by the European monarchies. This led to the French Revolutionary Wars (1792–1802) and then to the Napoleonic conquests, and to the subsequent European-wide debates on the concepts and realities of nations, and in particular of nation-states. The Westphalia Treaty had divided Europe into various empires and kingdoms (Ottoman Empire, Holy Roman Empire, Swedish Empire, Kingdom of France, etc.), and for centuries wars were waged between princes (*Kabinettskriege* in German).

Modern nation-states appeared in the wake of the French Revolution, with the formation of patriotic sentiments for the first time in Spain during the Peninsula War (1808–1813 – known in Spanish as the Independence War). Despite the restoration of the previous order with the 1815 Congress of Vienna, the "nationalities question" became the main problem of Europe during the Industrial Era, leading in particular to the 1848 Revolutions, the Italian unification completed during the 1871 Franco-Prussian War, which itself culminated in the proclamation of the German Empire in the Hall of Mirrors in the Palace of Versailles, thus achieving the German unification.

Meanwhile, the Ottoman Empire, the "sick man of Europe", was confronted with endless nationalist movements, which, along with the dissolving of the Austrian-Hungarian Empire, would lead to the creation after World War I of the various nation-states of the Balkans, with "national minorities" in their borders. Ethnic nationalism, which advocated the belief in a hereditary membership of the nation, made its appearance in the historical context surrounding the creation of the modern nation-states.

One of its main influences was the Romantic nationalist movement at the turn of the 19th century, represented by figures such as Johann Herder (1744–1803), Johan Fichte (1762–1814) in the *Addresses to the German Nation* (1808), Friedrich Hegel (1770–1831), or also, in France, Jules Michelet (1798–1874). It was opposed to liberal nationalism, represented by authors such as Ernest Renan (1823–1892), who conceived of the nation as a community which, instead of being based on the *Volk* ethnic group and on a specific, common language, was founded on the subjective will to live together ("the nation is a daily plebiscite", 1882) or also John Stuart Mill (1806–1873).

Ethnic nationalism quickly blended itself with scientific racist discourses, as well as with "continental imperialist" discourses, for example in the pan-Germanism discourses, which postulated the racial superiority of the German Volk. The Pan-German League (*Alldeutscher Verband*), created in 1891, promoted German imperialism, "racial hygiene" and was opposed to intermarriage with Jews. Another, popular current, the *Völkisch movement*, was also an important proponent of the German ethnic nationalist discourse, which it also combined with modern antisemitism. Members of the Völkisch movement, in particular the Thule Society, would participate in the founding of the German Workers' Party (DAP) in Munich in 1918, the predecessor of the NSDAP Nazi party. Pan-Germanism and played a decisive role in the interwar period of the 1920s–1930s.

These currents began to associate the idea of the nation with the biological concept of a "master race" (often the "Aryan race" or "Nordic race") issued from the scientific racist discourse. They conflated nationalities with ethnic groups, called "races", in a radical distinction from previous racial discourses which posited the existence of a "race struggle" inside the nation and the state itself. Furthermore, they believed that political boundaries should mirror these alleged racial and ethnic groups, thus justifying ethnic cleansing in order to achieve "racial purity" and also to achieve ethnic homogeneity in the nation-state.

Such racist discourses, combined with nationalism, were not however limited to pan-Germanism. In France, the transition from Republican, liberal nationalism, to ethnic nationalism, which made nationalism a characteristic of far-right movements in France, took place during the Dreyfus Affair at the end of the 19th century. During several years, a nation-wide crisis affected French society, concerning the alleged treason of Alfred Dreyfus, a French Jewish military officer. The country polarized itself into two opposite camps, one represented by Émile Zola, who wrote *J'accuse* in defense of Alfred Dreyfus, and the other represented by the nationalist poet Maurice Barrès (1862–1923), one of the founders of the ethnic nationalist discourse in France. At the same time, Charles Maurras (1868–1952), founder of the monarchist *Action française* movement, theorized the "anti-France," composed of the "four confederate states of Protestants, Jews, Freemasons and foreigners" (his actual word for the latter being the pejorative *métèques*)). Indeed, to him the first three were all "internal foreigners," who threatened the ethnic unity of the French people.

Ethnic Conflicts

Debates over the origins of racism often suffer from a lack of clarity over the term. Many use the term "racism" to refer to more general phenomena, such as xenophobia and ethnocentrism, although scholars attempt to clearly distinguish those phenomena from racism as an ideology or from scientific racism, which has little to do with ordinary xenophobia. Others conflate recent forms of racism with earlier forms of ethnic and national conflict. In most cases, ethno-national conflict seems to owe itself to conflict over land and strategic resources. In some cases ethnicity and nationalism were harnessed to rally combatants in wars between great religious empires (for example, the Muslim Turks and the Catholic Austro-Hungarians).

Notions of race and racism often have played central roles in such ethnic conflicts. Historically, when an adversary is identified as "other" based on notions of race or ethnicity (particularly when "other" is construed to mean "inferior"), the means employed by the self-presumed "superior" party to appropriate territory, human chattel, or material wealth often have been more ruthless, more brutal, and less constrained by moral or ethical considerations. According to historian Daniel Richter, Pontiac's Rebellion saw the emergence on both sides of the conflict of "the novel idea that all Native people were 'Indians,' that all Euro-Americans were 'Whites,' and that all on one side must unite to destroy the other." (Richter, *Facing East from Indian Country*) Basil Davidson insists in his documentary, *Africa: Different but Equal*, that racism, in fact, only just recently surfaced—as late as the 19th century, due to the need for a justification for slavery in the Americas.

The idea of slavery as an "equal-opportunity employer" was denounced with the introduction of Christian theory in the

West. Maintaining that Africans were "subhuman" was the only loophole in the then accepted law that "men are created equal" that would allow for the sustenance of the Triangular Trade. New peoples in the Americas, possible slaves, were encountered, fought, and ultimately subdued, but then due to European diseases, their populations drastically decreased. Through both influences, theories about "race" developed, and these helped many to justify the differences in position and treatment of people whom they categorized as belonging to different races.

Juan Ginés de Sepúlveda argued that, during the Valladolid controversy in the middle of the 16th century, the Native Americans were natural slaves because they had no *souls*. In Asia, the Chinese and Japanese Empires were both strong colonial powers, with the Chinese making colonies and vassal states of much of East Asia throughout history, and the Japanese doing the same in the 19th–20th centuries. In both cases, the Asian imperial powers believed they were ethnically and racially preferenced too.

Academic Variants

Owen 'Alik Shahadah comments on this racism by stating: "Historically Africans are made to sway like leaves on the wind, impervious and indifferent to any form of civilization, a people absent from scientific discovery, philosophy or the higher arts. We are left to believe that almost nothing can come out of Africa, other than raw material."

Scottish philosopher and economist David Hume said, "I am apt to suspect the Negroes to be naturally inferior to the Whites. There scarcely ever was a civilised nation of that complexion, nor even any individual, eminent either in action or in speculation. No ingenious manufacture among them, no arts, no sciences." German philosopher Immanuel Kant stated: "The yellow Indians do have a meagre talent. The Negroes are far below them, and at the lowest point are a part of the American people."

In the 19th century, the German philosopher Georg Wilhelm Friedrich Hegel declared that "Africa is no historical part of the world." Hegel further claimed that blacks had no "sense of personality; their spirit sleeps, remains sunk in itself, makes no advance, and thus parallels the compact, undifferentiated mass of the African continent".

Fewer than 30 years before Nazi Germany started World War II, the German Otto Weininger, claimed: "A genius has perhaps scarcely ever appeared amongst the negroes, and the standard of their morality is almost universally so low that it is beginning to be acknowledged in America that their emancipation was an act of imprudence".

The German conservative Oswald Spengler remarked on what he perceived as the culturally degrading influence of Africans in modern Western culture: in *The Hour of Decision* Spengler denounced "the 'happy ending' of an empty existence, the boredom of which has brought to jazz music and Negro dancing to perform the Death March for a great Culture". During the Nazi era, German scientists rearranged academia to support claims of a grand "Aryan" agent behind the splendors of all human civilizations, including India and Ancient Egypt.

Scientific Variants

The modern biological definition of race developed in the 19th century with scientific racist theories. The term *scientific racism* refers to the use of science to justify and support racist beliefs, which goes back to at least the early 18th century, though it gained most of its influence in the mid-19th century, during the New Imperialism period. Also known as academic racism, such theories first needed to overcome the Church's resistance to positivist accounts of history, and its support of monogenism, that is that all human beings were originated from the same ancestors, in accordance with creationist accounts of history.

These racist theories put forth on scientific hypothesis were combined with unilineal theories of social progress which postulated the superiority of the European civilization over the rest of the world. Furthermore, they frequently made use of the idea of "survival of the fittest", a term coined by Herbert Spencer in 1864, associated with ideas of competition which were named social Darwinism in the 1940s. Charles Darwin himself opposed the idea of rigid racial differences in *The Descent of Man* (1871) in which he argued that humans were all of one species, sharing common descent. He recognised racial differences as varieties of humanity, and emphasised the close similarities between people of all races in mental faculties, tastes, dispositions and habits, while still contrasting the culture of the "lowest savages" with European civilization.

At the end of the 19th century, proponents of scientific racism intertwined themselves with eugenics discourses of "degeneration of the race" and "blood heredity." Henceforth, scientific racist discourses could be defined as the combination of polygenism, unilinealism, social darwinism and eugenism. They found their scientific legitimacy on physical anthropology, anthropometry, craniometry, phrenology, physiognomy and others now discredited disciplines in order to formulate racist prejudices.

Before being disqualified in the 20th century by the American school of cultural anthropology (Franz Boas, etc.), the British school of social anthropology (Bronishaw Malinowski, Alfred Radcliffe-Brown, etc.), the French school of ethnology (Claude Lévi-Strauss, etc.), as well as the discovery of the neo-Darwinian synthesis, such sciences, in particular anthropometry, were used to deduce behaviours and psychological characteristics from outward, physical appearances.

The neo-Darwinian synthesis, first developed in the 1930s, eventually led to a gene-centred view of evolution in the 1960s. According to the Human Genome Project, the most complete mapping of human DNA to date indicates that there is no clear genetic basis to racial groups. While some genes are more common in certain populations, there are no genes which exist in all members of one population and no members of any other.

Heredity and Eugenics

The first theory of eugenics was developed in 1869 by Francis Galton (1822–1911), who used the then popular concept of *degeneration*. He applied statistics to study human differences and the alleged "inheritance of intelligence", foreshadowing future uses of "intelligence testing" by the anthropometry school. Such theories were vividly described by the writer Émile Zola (1840–1902), who started publishing in 1871 a twenty-novel cycle, *Les Rougon-Macquart*, where he linked heredity to behaviour. Thus, Zola described the high-born Rougons as those involved in politics (*Son Excellence Eugène Rougon*) and medicine (*Le Docteur Pascal*) and the low-born Macquarts as those fatally falling into alcoholism (*L'Assommoir*), prostitution (*Nana*), and homicide (*La Bête humaine*).

During the rise of Nazism in Germany, some scientists in Western nations worked to debunk the regime's racial theories. A few argued against racist ideologies and discrimination, even if they believed in the alleged existence of biological races. However, in the fields of anthropology and biology, these were minority positions until the mid-20th century. According to the 1950 UNESCO statement, *The Race Question*, an international project to debunk racist theories had been attempted in the mid-1930s. However, this project had been abandoned. Thus, in 1950, UNESCO declared that it had resumed:

Up again, after a lapse of fifteen years, a project which the International Institute for Intellectual Cooperation has wished to carry through but which it had to abandon in deference to the appeasement policy of the pre-war period. The race question had become one of the pivots of Nazi ideology and policy. Masaryk and Beneš took the initiative of calling for a conference to re-establish in the minds and consciences of men everywhere the truth about race... Nazi propaganda was able to continue its baleful work unopposed by the authority of an international organisation.

The Third Reich's racial policies, its eugenics programs and the extermination of Jews in the Holocaust, as well as Romani people in the Porrajmos (the Romani Holocaust) and others minorities led to a change in opinions about scientific research into race after the war. Changes within scientific disciplines, such as the rise of the Boasian school of anthropology in the United States contributed to this shift. These theories were strongly denounced in the 1950 UNESCO statement, signed by internationally renowned scholars, and titled *The Race Question*.

Eugenics

Eugenics is the "applied science or the biosocial movement which advocates the use of practices aimed at improving the genetic composition of a population," usually referring to human populations. Eugenics was widely popular in the early decades of the 20th century, but has fallen into disfavor after having become associated with Nazi Germany and with the discovery of molecular evolution. Since the postwar period, both the public and the scientific communities have associated eugenics with Nazi abuses, such as enforced racial hygiene, human experimentation, and the extermination of "undesired" population groups. However, developments in genetic, genomic, and reproductive technologies at the end of the 20th century have raised many new questions and concerns about the meaning of *eugenics* and its ethical and moral status in the modern era.

Overview

As a social movement, eugenics reached its height of popularity in the early decades of the 20th century. By the end of World War II eugenics had been largely abandoned. Although current trends in genetics have raised questions amongst critical academics concerning parallels between pre-war attitudes about eugenics and current "utilitarian" and social theories allegedly related to Darwinism, they are, in fact, only superficially related and somewhat contradictory to one another. At its pre-war height, the movement often pursued pseudoscientific notions of racial supremacy and purity.

Eugenics was practiced around the world and was promoted by governments, and influential individuals and institutions. Its advocates regarded it as a social philosophy for the improvement of human hereditary traits through the promotion of higher reproduction of certain people and traits, and the reduction of reproduction of other people and traits.

Today it is widely regarded as a brutal movement which inflicted massive human rights violations on millions of people. The "interventions" advocated and practiced by eugenicists involved prominently the identification and classification of individuals and their families, including the poor, mentally ill, blind, promiscuous women, homosexuals and entire racial groups — such as the Roma and Jews — as "degenerate" or "unfit"; the segregation or institutionalisation of such individuals and groups, their sterilization, euthanasia, and in the extreme case of Nazi Germany, their mass extermination.

The practices engaged in by eugenicists involving violations of privacy, attacks on reputation, violations of the right to life, to found a family, to freedom from discrimination are all today classified as violations of human rights. The practice of negative racial aspects of eugenics, after World War II, fell within the definition of the new international crime of genocide, set out in the Convention on the Prevention and Punishment of the Crime of Genocide.

The modern field and term were first formulated by Sir Francis Galton in 1883, drawing on the recent work of his half-cousin Charles Darwin. At its peak of popularity eugenics was supported by prominent people, including Margaret Sanger, Marie Stopes, H. G. Wells, Theodore Roosevelt, George Bernard Shaw, John Maynard Keynes, John Harvey Kellogg, Linus Pauling and Sidney Webb. Its most infamous proponent and practitioner was, however, Adolf Hitler who praised and incorporated eugenic ideas in Mein Kampf and emulated Eugenic legislation for the sterilization of "defectives" that had been pioneered in the United States.

G. K. Chesterton was an early critic of the philosophy of eugenics, expressing this opinion in his book, *Eugenics and Other Evils*. Eugenics became an academic discipline at many colleges and universities, and received funding from many sources. Three International Eugenics Conferences presented a global venue for eugenicists with meetings in 1912 in London, and in 1921 and 1932 in New York. Eugenic policies were first implemented in the early 1900s in the United States. Later, in the 1920s and 30s, the eugenic policy of sterilizing certain mental patients was implemented in a variety of other countries, including Belgium, Brazil, Canada, and Sweden, among others. The scientific reputation of eugenics started to decline in the 1930s, a time when Ernst Rüdin used eugenics as a justification for the racial policies of Nazi Germany, and when proponents of eugenics among scientists and thinkers prompted a backlash in the public. Nevertheless, the second largest known eugenics program, created by social democrats in Sweden, continued until 1975.

Since the postwar period, both the public and the scientific communities have associated eugenics with Nazi abuses, such as enforced racial hygiene, human experimentation, and the extermination of "undesired" population groups. However, developments in genetic, genomic, and reproductive technologies at the end of the 20th century have raised many new questions and concerns about what exactly constitutes the meaning of *eugenics* and what its ethical and moral status is in the modern era.

Meanings and Types

The word *eugenics* derives from the Greek word *eu* (*good* or *well*) and the suffix *-gençs* (*born*), and was coined by Sir Francis Galton in 1883, who defined it as "the study of all agencies under human control which can improve or impair the racial quality of future generations". Eugenics has, from the very beginning, meant many different things to many different people. Historically, the term has referred to everything from prenatal care for mothers to forced sterilization and euthanasia. Much debate has taken place in the past, as it does today, as to what exactly counts as eugenics. Some types of eugenics deal only with perceived beneficial and/or detrimental genetic traits. These are sometimes called "pseudo-eugenics' by proponents of strict eugenics.

The term *eugenics* is often used to refer to movements and social policies influential during the early twentieth century. In a historical and broader sense, eugenics can also be a study of "improving human genetic qualities." It is sometimes broadly applied to describe any human action whose goal is to improve the gene pool. Some forms of infanticide in ancient societies, present-day reprogenetics, preemptive abortions and designer babies have been (sometimes controversially) referred to as eugenic. Because of its normative goals and historical association with scientific racism, as well as the development of the science of genetics, the western scientific community has mostly disassociated itself from the term "eugenics", although one can find advocates of what is now known as *liberal eugenics*. Despite its ongoing criticism in the United States, several regions globally practice different forms of eugenics.

Eugenicists advocate specific policies that (if successful) they believe will lead to a perceived improvement of the human gene pool. Since defining what improvements are desired or beneficial is perceived by many as a cultural choice rather than a matter that can be determined objectively (e.g., by empirical, scientific inquiry), eugenics has often been deemed a pseudoscience. The most disputed aspect of eugenics has been the definition of "improvement" of the human gene pool, such as what is a beneficial characteristic and what is a defect. This aspect of eugenics has historically been tainted with scientific racism.

Early eugenicists were mostly concerned with perceived intelligence factors that often correlated strongly with social class. Many eugenicists took inspiration from the selective breeding of animals (where purebreds are often strived for) as their analogy for improving human society. The mixing of races (or miscegenation) was usually considered as something to be avoided in the name of racial purity. At the time this concept appeared to have some scientific support, and it remained a contentious issue until the advanced development of genetics led to a scientific consensus that the division of the human species into unequal races is unjustifiable.

Eugenics has also been concerned with the elimination of hereditary diseases such as hemophilia and Huntington's disease. However, there are several problems with labeling certain factors as genetic defects. In many cases there is no scientific consensus on what a genetic defect is. It is often argued that this is more a matter of social or individual choice. What appears to be a genetic defect in one context or environment may not be so in another. This can be the case for genes with a heterozygote advantage, such as sickle-cell disease or Tay-Sachs disease, which in their heterozygote form may offer an advantage against, respectively, malaria and tuberculosis. Although some birth defects are uniformly lethal, disabled persons can succeed in life. Many of the conditions early eugenicists identified as inheritable (pellagra is one such example) are currently considered to be at least partially, if not wholly, attributed to environmental conditions. Similar concerns have been raised when a prenatal diagnosis of a congenital disorder leads to abortion.

Eugenic policies have been conceptually divided into two categories. Positive eugenics is aimed at encouraging reproduction among the genetically advantaged. Possible approaches include financial and political stimuli, targeted demographic analyses, in vitro fertilization, egg transplants, and cloning. Negative eugenics is aimed at lowering fertility among the genetically disadvantaged. This includes abortions, sterilization, and other methods of family planning. Both positive and negative eugenics can be coercive. Abortion by biologically fit women was illegal in Nazi Germany and in the Soviet Union during Stalin's reign.

During the 20th century, many countries enacted various eugenics policies and programs, including: genetic screening, birth control, promoting differential birth rates, marriage restrictions, segregation (both racial segregation as well as segregation of the mentally ill from the rest of the population), compulsory sterilization, forced abortions or forced pregnancies and genocide. Most of these policies were later regarded as coercive and/or restrictive, and now few jurisdictions implement policies that are explicitly labelled as eugenic or unequivocally eugenic in substance. However, some private organizations assist people in genetic counseling, and reprogenetics may be considered as a form of non-state-enforced liberal eugenics.

Implementation Methods

There are three main ways by which the methods of eugenics can be applied. One is mandatory eugenics or authoritarian eugenics, in which the government mandates a eugenics program. Policies and/or legislation are often seen as being coercive and restrictive. Another is promotional voluntary eugenics, in which eugenics is voluntarily practiced and promoted to the general population, but not officially mandated. This is a form of non-state enforced eugenics, using a liberal or democratic approach, which can mostly be seen in the 1900s. The third is private eugenics, which is practiced voluntarily by individuals and groups, but not promoted to the general population.

Notable Proponents

Charles Davenport, a scientist from the United States, stands out as history's leading eugenicist. He took eugenics from a scientific idea to a worldwide movement implemented in many countries. Davenport obtained funding to establish the Biological Experiment Station at Cold Spring Harbor in 1904 and the Eugenics Records Office in 1910, which provided the scientific basis for later Eugenic policies. He became the first

President of the International Federation of Eugenics Organizations (IFEO) in 1925, an organization he was instrumental in building. However, Davenport's racist views were not supported by all geneticists at Cold Spring Harbor.

In 1932 Davenport welcomed Ernst Rüdin, a prominent Swiss eugenicist and race scientist, as his successor in the position of President of the IFEO. Rüdin worked closely with Alfred Ploetz, his brother-in-law and co-founder with him of the German Society for the Racial Hygiene. Other prominent figures in the Eugenics included Harry Laughlin (United States), Havelock Ellis (United Kingdom), Irving Fischer (United States), Eugen Fischer (Germany), Madison Grant (United States), Lucien Howe (United States), and Margaret Sanger (United States, founder of Planned Parenthood).

History

Pre-Galtonian Philosophies

Tribes such as the Fans, aboriginal tribes and ancient Prussian tribes all carried out policies reminiscent of eugenics. A form of eugenics is even advocated in the Tanakh and Catholic Bible. Taking a wife from outside one's kinsmen was considered tantamount to sin. Despite all the prohibitions concerning sex in Leviticus, marriage with one's first cousin is still permitted.

The philosophy was most famously expounded by Plato, who believed human reproduction should be monitored and controlled by the state. However, Plato understood this form of government control would not be readily accepted, and proposed the truth be concealed from the public via a fixed lottery. Mates, in Plato's Republic, would be chosen by a "marriage number" in which the quality of the individual would be quantitatively analyzed, and persons of high numbers would be allowed to procreate with other persons of high numbers. In theory, this would lead to predictable results and the improvement of the human race. However, Plato acknowledged the failure of the "marriage number" since "gold soul" persons could still produce "bronze soul" children.

Plato's ideas may have been one of the earliest attempts to mathematically analyze genetic inheritance, which was not perfected until the development of Mendelian genetics and the mapping of the human genome. Other ancient civilizations, such as Rome, Athens and Sparta, practiced infanticide through exposure as a form of phenotypic selection. In Sparta, newborns were inspected by the city's elders, who decided the fate of the infant. If the child was deemed incapable of living, it was usually exposed in the *Apothetae* near the Taygetus mountain. It was more common for boys than girls to be killed this way in Sparta. Trials for babies included bathing them in wine and exposing them to the elements. To Sparta, this would ensure only the strongest survived and procreated. Adolf Hitler considered Sparta to be the first "Völkisch State," and much like Ernst Haeckel before him, praised Sparta due to its primitive form of eugenics practice of selective infanticide policy which was applied on deformed children though the Nazis believed the children were killed outright and not exposed.

In addition, patriarchs in Roman society were given the right to "discard" infants at their discretion. This was often done by drowning undesired newborns in the Tiber River. The practice of open infanticide in the Roman Empire did not subside until its Christianization.

Galton's Theory

Sir Francis Galton systematized these ideas and practices according to new knowledge about the evolution of man and animals provided by the theory of his cousin Charles Darwin during the 1860s and 1870s. After reading Darwin's *Origin of Species*, Galton built upon Darwin's ideas, whereby the mechanisms of natural selection were potentially thwarted by human civilization. He reasoned that, since many human societies sought to protect the underprivileged and weak, those societies were at odds with the natural selection responsible for extinction of the weakest; and only by changing these social policies could society be saved from a "reversion towards mediocrity," a phrase he first coined in statistics and which later changed to the now common "regression towards the mean".

Galton first sketched out his theory in the 1865 article "Hereditary Talent and Character," then elaborated further in his 1869 book *Hereditary Genius*. He began by studying the way in which human intellectual, moral, and personality traits tended to run in families. Galton's basic argument was "genius" and "talent" were hereditary traits in humans (although neither he nor Darwin yet had a working model of this type of heredity). He concluded since one could use artificial selection to exaggerate traits in other animals, one could expect similar results when applying such models to humans. As he wrote in the introduction to *Hereditary Genius*:

> I propose to show in this book that a man's natural abilities are derived by inheritance, under exactly the same limitations as are the form and physical features of the whole organic world. Consequently, as it is easy, notwithstanding those limitations, to obtain by careful selection a permanent breed of dogs or horses gifted with peculiar powers of running, or of doing anything else, so it would be quite practicable to produce a highly-gifted race of men by judicious marriages during several consecutive generations.

Galton claimed that the less intelligent were more fertile than the more intelligent of his time. Galton did not propose any selection methods; rather, he hoped a solution would be found if social mores changed in a way that encouraged people to see the importance of breeding. He first used the word *eugenic* in his 1883 *Inquiries into Human Faculty and Its Development*, a book in which he meant "to touch on various topics more or less connected with that of the cultivation of race, or, as we might call it, with 'eugenic' questions." He included a footnote to the word "eugenic" which read:

> That is, with questions bearing on what is termed in Greek, *eugenes* namely, good in stock, hereditary endowed with noble qualities. This, and the allied words, *eugeneia*, etc., are equally applicable to men, brutes, and plants. We greatly want a brief word to express the science of improving stock, which is by no means confined to questions of judicious mating, but which, especially in the case of man, takes cognizance of all influences that tend in however remote a degree to give to the more suitable races or strains of blood a better chance of prevailing speedily over the less suitable than they otherwise would have had. The word *eugenics* would sufficiently express the idea; it is at least a neater word and a more generalized one than *viticulture* which I once ventured to use. In 1904 he clarified his definition of eugenics as "the science which deals with all

influences that improve the inborn qualities of a race; also with those that develop them to the utmost advantage."

Galton's formulation of eugenics was based on a strong statistical approach, influenced heavily by Adolphe Quetelet's "social physics". Unlike Quetelet, however, Galton did not exalt the "average man" but decried him as mediocre. Galton and his statistical heir Karl Pearson developed what was called the biometrical approach to eugenics, which developed new and complex statistical models (later exported to wholly different fields) to describe the heredity of traits. However, with the rediscovery of Gregor Mendel's hereditary laws, two separate camps of eugenics advocates emerged. One was made up of statisticians, the other of biologists. Statisticians thought the biologists had exceptionally crude mathematical models, while biologists thought the statisticians knew little about biology.

Eugenics eventually referred to human selective reproduction with an intent to create children with desirable traits, generally through the approach of influencing differential birth rates. These policies were mostly divided into two categories: *positive eugenics*, the increased reproduction of those seen to have advantageous hereditary traits; and *negative eugenics*, the discouragement of reproduction by those with hereditary traits perceived as poor. Negative eugenic policies in the past have ranged from attempts at segregation to sterilization and even genocide. Positive eugenic policies have typically taken the form of awards or bonuses for "fit" parents who have another child. Relatively innocuous practices like marriage counseling had early links with eugenic ideology. Eugenics is superficially related to what would later be known as Social Darwinism. While both claimed intelligence was hereditary, eugenics asserted new policies were needed to actively change the status quo towards a more "eugenic" state, while the Social Darwinists argued society itself would naturally "check" the problem of "dysgenics" if no welfare policies were in place (for example, the poor might reproduce more but would have higher mortality rates).

Britain

In Britain, eugenics never received significant state funding, but it was supported by many prominent figures of different political persuasions before World War I, including: Liberal economists William Beveridge and John Maynard Keynes; Fabian socialists such as Irish author George Bernard Shaw, H. G. Wells and Sidney Webb; the future Prime Minister Winston Churchill; and Conservatives such as Arthur Balfour.

Furthermore, its emphasis was more upon social class, rather than race. Indeed, Galton expressed these views during a lecture in 1901 in which he placed the British society into groups. These groupings are shown in the figure and indicate the proportion of society falling into each group and their perceived genetic worth. Galton suggested that negative eugenics (i.e. an attempt to prevent them from bearing offspring) should be applied only to those in the lowest social group (the "Undesirables"), while positive eugenics applied to the higher classes. However, he appreciated the worth of the higher working classes to society and industry.

Sterilisation programmes were never legalised, although some were carried out in private upon the mentally ill by clinicians who were in favour of a more widespread eugenics plan. Indeed, those in support of eugenics shifted their lobbying of Parliament from enforced to voluntary sterilization, in the hope of achieving more legal recognition. But leave for the Labour Party Member of Parliament Major A. C. Church, to propose a Private Member's Bill in 1931, which would legalise the operation for voluntary sterilization, was rejected by 167 votes to 89. The limited popularity of eugenics in Britain was reflected by the fact that only two universities established courses in this field (University College London and Liverpool University). The Galton Institute, affiliated to UCL, was headed by Galton's protégé, Karl Pearson.

United States

One of the earliest modern advocates of eugenics (before it was labelled as such) was Alexander Graham Bell. In 1881 Bell investigated the rate of deafness on Martha's Vineyard, Massachusetts. From this he concluded that deafness was hereditary in nature and, through noting that congenitally deaf parents were more likely to produce deaf children, tentatively suggested that couples where both were deaf should not marry, in his lecture *Memoir upon the formation of a deaf variety of the human race* presented to the National Academy of Sciences on 13 November 1883. However, it was his hobby of livestock breeding which led to his appointment to biologist David Starr Jordan's Committee on Eugenics, under the auspices of the American Breeders Association. The committee unequivocally extended the principle to man.

During the 20th century, researchers interested in familial mental disorders conducted a number of studies to document the heritability of such illnesses as schizophrenia, bipolar disorder, and depression. Their findings were used by the eugenics movement as proof for its cause. State laws were written in the late 19th and early 20th centuries to prohibit marriage and force sterilization of the mentally ill in order to prevent the "passing on" of mental illness to the next generation. These laws were upheld by the U.S. Supreme Court in 1927 and were not abolished until the mid-20th century. All in all, 60,000 Americans were sterilized.

In 1907 Indiana became the first of more than thirty states to adopt legislation aimed at compulsory sterilization of certain individuals. Although the law was overturned by the Indiana Supreme Court in 1921, the U.S. Supreme Court upheld the constitutionality of a Virginia law allowing for the compulsory sterilization of patients of state mental institutions in 1927.

Beginning with Connecticut in 1896, many states enacted marriage laws with eugenic criteria, prohibiting anyone who was "epileptic, imbecile or feeble-minded" from marrying. In 1898 Charles B. Davenport, a prominent American biologist, began as director of a biological research station based in Cold Spring Harbor where he experimented with evolution in plants and animals. In 1904 Davenport received funds from the Carnegie Institution to found the Station for Experimental Evolution. The Eugenics Record Office (ERO) opened in 1910 while Davenport and Harry H. Laughlin began to promote eugenics.

The Immigration Restriction League (founded in 1894) was the first American entity associated officially with eugenics. The League sought to bar what it considered dysgenic members of certain races from entering America and diluting what it saw as the superior American racial stock through procreation.

They lobbied for a literacy test for immigrants, based on the belief that literacy rates were low among "inferior races". Literacy test bills were vetoed by Presidents in 1897, 1913 and 1915; eventually, President Wilson's second veto was overruled by Congress in 1917. Membership in the League included: A. Lawrence Lowell, president of Harvard, William DeWitt Hyde, president of Bowdoin College, James T. Young, director of Wharton School and David Starr Jordan, president of Stanford University. The League allied themselves with the American Breeder's Association to gain influence and further its goals and in 1909 established a eugenics committee chaired by David Starr Jordan with members Charles Davenport, Alexander Graham Bell, Vernon Kellogg, Luther Burbank, William Earnest Castle, Adolf Meyer, H. J. Webber and Friedrich Woods. The ABA's immigration legislation committee, formed in 1911 and headed by League's founder Prescott F. Hall, formalized the committee's already strong relationship with the Immigration Restriction League.

In years to come, the ERO collected a mass of family pedigrees and concluded that those who were unfit came from economically and socially poor backgrounds. Eugenicists such as Davenport, the psychologist Henry H. Goddard and the conservationist Madison Grant (all well respected in their time) began to lobby for various solutions to the problem of the "unfit". (Davenport favored immigration restriction and sterilization as primary methods; Goddard favored segregation in his *The Kallikak Family*; Grant favored all of the above and more, even entertaining the idea of extermination.) Though their methodology and research methods are now understood as highly flawed, at the time this was seen as legitimate scientific research. It did, however, have scientific detractors (notably, Thomas Hunt Morgan, one of the few Mendelians to explicitly criticize eugenics), though most of these focused more on what they considered the crude methodology of eugenicists, and the characterization of almost every human characteristic as being hereditary, rather than the idea of eugenics itself.

Some states sterilized "imbeciles" for much of the 20th century. The U.S. Supreme Court ruled in the 1927 *Buck v. Bell* case that the state of Virginia could sterilize those it thought unfit. The most significant era of eugenic sterilization was between 1907 and 1963, when over 64,000 individuals were forcibly sterilized under eugenic legislation in the United States. A favorable report on the results of sterilization in California, the state with the most sterilizations by far, was published in book form by the biologist Paul Popenoe and was widely cited by the Nazi government as evidence that wide-reaching sterilization programs were feasible and humane.

Public acceptance in the U.S. was the reason eugenic legislation was passed. Over 19 million people attended the Panama-Pacific International Exposition in San Francisco, open for 10 months from February 20 to December 4, 1915. The PPIE was a fair devoted to extolling the virtues of a rapidly progressing nation, featuring new developments in science, agriculture, manufacturing and technology. A subject that received a large amount of time and space was that of the developments concerning health and disease, particularly the areas of tropical medicine and race betterment (tropical medicine being the combined study of bacteriology, parasitology and entomology while racial betterment being the promotion of eugenic studies). Having these areas so closely intertwined, it seemed that they were both categorized in the main theme of the fair, the advancement of civilization. Thus in the public eye, the seemingly contradictory areas of study were both represented under progressive banners of improvement and were made to seem like plausible courses of action to better American society.

The state of California was at the vanguard of the American eugenics movement, performing about 20,000 sterilizations or one third of the 60,000 nationwide from 1909 up until the 1960s. By 1910, there was a large and dynamic network of scientists, reformers and professionals engaged in national eugenics projects and actively promoting eugenic legislation. The American Breeder's Association was the first eugenic body in the U.S., established in 1906 under the direction of biologist Charles B. Davenport. The ABA was formed specifically to "investigate and report on heredity in the human race, and emphasize the value of superior blood and the menace to society of inferior blood." Membership included Alexander Graham Bell, Stanford president David Starr Jordan and Luther Burbank.

When Nazi administrators went on trial for war crimes in Nuremberg after World War II, they justified the mass sterilizations (over 450,000 in less than a decade) by citing the United States as their inspiration. The Nazis had claimed American eugenicists inspired and supported Hitler's racial purification laws, and failed to understand the connection between those policies and the eventual genocide of the Holocaust.

The idea of "genius" and "talent" is also considered by William Graham Sumner, a founder of the American Sociological Society (now called the American Sociological Association). He maintained that if the government did not meddle with the social policy of *laissez-faire*, a class of genius would rise to the top of the system of social stratification, followed by a class of talent. Most of the rest of society would fit into the class of mediocrity. Those who were considered to be defective (mentally retarded, handicapped, etc.) had a negative effect on social progress by draining off necessary resources. They should be left on their own to sink or swim. But those in the class of delinquent (criminals, deviants, etc.) should be eliminated from society ("Folkways", 1907). (Compare to ideals in Plato's *Republic*.)

However, methods of eugenics were applied to reformulate more restrictive definitions of white racial purity in existing state laws banning interracial marriage: the so-called anti-miscegenation laws. The most famous example of the influence of eugenics and its emphasis on strict racial segregation on such "anti-miscegenation" legislation was Virginia's Racial Integrity Act of 1924. The U.S. Supreme Court overturned this law in 1967 in Loving v. Virginia, and declared anti-miscegenation laws unconstitutional.

With the passage of the Immigration Act of 1924, eugenicists for the first time played an important role in the Congressional debate as expert advisers on the threat of "inferior stock" from eastern and southern Europe. This reduced the number of immigrants from abroad to 15 percent from previous years, to control the number of "unfit" individuals entering the country. While eugenicists did support the act, the most important backers were union leaders like Samuel Gompers The new act, inspired by the eugenic belief in the racial superiority of "old stock" white Americans as members of the "Nordic race" (a form of white supremacy), strengthened the position of existing laws prohibiting race-mixing. Eugenic considerations also lay behind the adoption of incest laws in much of the U.S. and were used to justify many anti-miscegenation laws.

Stephen Jay Gould asserted that restrictions on immigration passed in the United States during the 1920s (and overhauled in 1965 with the Immigration and Nationality Act) were motivated by the goals of eugenics. During the early 20th century, the United States and Canada began to receive far higher numbers of Southern and Eastern European immigrants. Influential eugenicists like Lothrop Stoddard and Harry Laughlin (who was appointed as an expert witness for the House Committee on Immigration and Naturalization in 1920) presented arguments they would pollute the national gene pool if their numbers went unrestricted.

It has been argued that this stirred both Canada and the United States into passing laws creating a hierarchy of nationalities, rating them from the most desirable Anglo-Saxon and Nordic peoples to the Chinese and Japanese immigrants, who were almost completely banned from entering the country.

However, several people, in particular Franz Samelson, Mark Snyderman and Richard Herrnstein, have argued, based on their examination of the records of the congressional debates over immigration policy, Congress gave virtually no consideration to these factors. According to these authors, the restrictions were motivated primarily by a desire to maintain the country's cultural integrity against the heavy influx of foreigners.

In the USA, eugenic supporters included Theodore Roosevelt, the National Academy of Sciences, and the National Research Council. Research was funded by distinguished philanthropies and carried out at prestigious universities. It was taught in college and high school classrooms. Margaret Sanger founded Planned Parenthood of America to urge the legalization of contraception for poor, immigrant women. In its time eugenics was touted by some as scientific and progressive, the natural application of knowledge about breeding to the arena of human life. Before the realization of death camps in World War II, the idea that eugenics would lead to genocide was not taken seriously by the average American.

The Negro Project was a Eugenics program originated by Margaret Sanger. Her ideas of racial hygiene to reduce or eliminate what she considered undesirable people groups included the hereditary poor and indigent (indicators to Eugenicists of low intelligence), the infirm, the daft, and criminals (petty and otherwise); and these undesirable characteristics ran uncommonly high among minority groups, the largest of which was the black population. Clinics were set up primarily in black neighbourhoods under the auspices of providing health care and education services for women about sexuality and contraception in order to give those women and the children they would choose to raise a better chance at a middle-class future.

The Negro Project is considered controversial and thought by many to be a conspiracy theory, but Sanger's own words (from a sympathetic source on the subject) demonstrate her not-uncommon-for-the-age race-based ideals and involvement in the origins of The Negro Project. The referenced paper suggests Sanger "lost control" of The Negro Project just after it received initial funding (yet it then goes on to cite repeated instances of her continued influence on it), that she later spoke generously toward blacks, and that she actually said she was opposed to abortion in an attempt to exonerate her. Sanger may have intended the clinics to be health care and education centres, but in fact they became primarily abortion providers. The placement of the clinics in black neighbourhoods and their renowned provision mainly of abortion services without so much as a peep of opposition from the otherwise outspoken woman's rights advocate, Sanger; suggest if not active complicity then her tacit approval of the abortions. And those continue to be abortions of disproportionate numbers of children of African heritage, under the guise of Planned Parenthood - which is what has become of the Eugenicist Sanger's Negro Project.

Although the U.S. state of Oregon did not repeal its forced sterilization law until 1983, the last known forced sterilization there was performed in 1978.

Australia

The policy of removing mixed race Aboriginal children from their parents emerged from an opinion based on Eugenics theory in late nineteenth and early twentieth-century Australia that the 'full-blood' tribal Aborigine would be unable to sustain itself, and was doomed to inevitable extinction, as at the time huge numbers of aborigines were in fact dying out, from diseases caught from European settlers. An ideology at the time held that mankind could be divided into a civilizational hierarchy. This notion supposed that Northern Europeans were superior in civilization and that Aborigines were inferior. According to this view, the increasing numbers of mixed-descent children in Australia, labelled as 'half-castes' (or alternatively 'crossbreeds', 'quadroons' and 'octoroons') should develop within their respective communities, white or aboriginal, according to their dominant parentage.

In the first half of the twentieth century, this led to policies and legislation that resulted in the removal of children from their tribe. The stated aim was to culturally assimilate mixed-descent people into contemporary Australian society. In all states and territories legislation was passed in the early years of the twentieth century which gave Aboriginal protectors guardianship rights over Aborigines up to the age of sixteen or twenty-one. Policemen or other agents of the state (such as Aboriginal Protection Officers), were given the power to locate and transfer babies and children of mixed descent, from their communities into institutions. In these Australian states and territories, half-caste institutions (both government or missionary) were established in the early decades of the twentieth-century for the reception of these separated children. The 2002 movie Rabbit-Proof Fence portrays this system and the harrowing consequences of attempting to overcome it.

In 1922 A.O. Neville was appointed the second Western Australia State *Chief Protector of Aborigines*. During the next quarter-century, he presided over the now notorious 'Assimilation' policy of removing mixed-race Aboriginal children from their parents. This policy in turn created the Stolen Generations and set in motion a grieving process that has become known as the concept of trans-generational grief, and would affect many generations to come. Albert Namatjira, Ernie

Dingo, Lionel Rose, Cathy Freeman, Nova Peris-Kneebone, Michael Long, Gavin Wanganeen, and many other successful Australian Aboriginals, were all products of the "Stolen Generation". In 1936 Neville became the *Commissioner for Native Affairs*, a post he held until his retirement in 1940.

Neville believed that biological absorption was the key to 'uplifting the Native race.' Speaking before the Moseley Royal Commission, which investigated the administration of Aboriginals in 1934, he defended the policies of forced settlement, removing children from parents, surveillance, discipline and punishment, arguing that "they have to be protected against themselves whether they like it or not. They cannot remain as they are. The sore spot requires the application of the surgeon's knife for the good of the patient, and probably against the patients will." In his twilight years Neville continued to actively promote his policy. Towards the end of his career, Neville published *Australia's Coloured Minority*, a text outlining his plan for the biological absorption of aboriginal people into white Australia.

Canada

In Canada, the eugenics movement gained support early in the 20th century as prominent physicians drew a direct link between heredity and public health. Eugenics was enforced by law in two Canadian provinces. In Alberta, the Sexual Sterilization Act was enacted in 1928, focusing the movement on the sterilization of mentally deficient individuals, as determined by the Alberta Eugenics Board. The campaign to enforce this action was backed by groups such as the United Farm Women's Group, including key member Emily Murphy.

Individuals were assessed using IQ tests like the Stanford-Binet. This posed a problem to new immigrants arriving in Canada, as many had not mastered the English language, and often their scores denoted them as having impaired intellectual functioning. As a result, many of those sterilized under the Sexual Sterilization Act were immigrants who were unfairly categorized. The province of British Columbia enacted its own Sexual Sterilization Act in 1933. As in Alberta, the British Columbia Eugenics Board could recommend the sterilization of those it considered to be suffering from "mental disease or mental deficiency." The popularity of the eugenics movement peaked during the Depression when sterilization was widely seen as a way of relieving society of the financial burdens imposed by defective individuals. Although the eugenics excesses of Nazi Germany diminished the popularity of the eugenics movement, the Sexual Sterilization Acts of Alberta and British Columbia were not repealed until 1972.

Germany

Nazi Germany under Adolf Hitler was well known for eugenics programs which attempted to maintain a "pure" German race through a series of programs that ran under the banner of racial hygiene. Among other activities, the Nazis performed extensive experimentation on live human beings to test their genetic theories, ranging from simple measurement of physical characteristics to the experiments carried out by Josef Mengele for Otmar von Verschuer on twins in the concentration camps. During the 1930s and 1940s, the Nazi regime forcibly sterilized hundreds of thousands of people whom they viewed as mentally and physically unfit, an estimated 400,000 between 1934 and 1937. The scale of the Nazi program prompted one American eugenics advocate to seek an expansion of their program, with one complaining that "the Germans are beating us at our own game".

The Nazis went further, however, killing tens of thousands of the institutionalized disabled through compulsory "euthanasia" programs such as Aktion T4. The methods of murder developed in the euthanasia policy led directly to their widespread use in concentration camps and extermination camps, especially the use of carbon monoxide followed by hydrogen cyanide in Zyklon B.

They also implemented a number of positive eugenics policies, giving awards to Aryan women who had large numbers of children and encouraged a service in which "racially pure" single women could deliver illegitimate children. Allegations that such women were also impregnated by SS officers in the *Lebensborn* were not proven at the Nuremberg trials, but new evidence (and the testimony of Lebensborn children) has established more details about Lebensborn practices. Also, "racially valuable" children from occupied countries were forcibly removed from their parents and adopted by German people. Many of their concerns for eugenics and racial hygiene were also explicitly present in their systematic killing of millions of "undesirable" people, especially Jews and Gypsies, in the Holocaust. The scope and coercion involved in the German eugenics programs along with a strong use of the rhetoric of eugenics and so-called "racial science" throughout the regime created an indelible cultural association between eugenics and the Third Reich in the post-war years.

Two scholars, John Glad and Seymour W. Itzkoff of Smith College, have questioned the relation between eugenics and the Holocaust. They argue that, contrary to popular beliefs Hitler did not regard the Jews as intellectually inferior and did not send them to the concentration camps on these grounds. They argue that Hitler had different reasons for his genocidal policies toward the Jews. Seymour W. Itzkoff writes that the Holocaust was "a vast dysgenic program to rid Europe of highly intelligent challengers to the existing Christian domination by a numerically and politically minuscule minority". Therefore, according to Itzkoff, "the Holocaust was the very antithesis of eugenic practice."

China

Eugenics was one of many ideas and programs debated in the 1920s and 1930s in Republican China, as a means of improving society and raising China's stature in the world. The principal Chinese proponent of eugenics was the prominent sociologist Pan Guangdan, and a significant number of intellectuals entered into the debate, including Gao Xisheng, biologist Zhou Jianren, sociologist Chen Da, and Chen Jianshan, and many others. Chen Da is notable for the link he provides to the family planning policy and One Child Policy enacted in China after the establishment of the People's Republic of China.

Sweden

In Sweden, the Sterilization Act of 1934 provided for the voluntary sterilization of some mental patients. The law was passed while the Swedish Social Democratic Party was in power, though it was also supported by all other political parties in Parliament at the time, as well as the Lutheran Church and much of the medical profession. From about 1934 to until 1975, Sweden sterilized more than 62,000 people, with Herman Lundborg in the lead of the project. Sweden sterilized more people than any other European state except Nazi Germany. However, it is more reasonable to compare numbers per caipita. If so, Finland has sterilised the most and the Nordic countries and the state of California sterilised about the same percentage. More people were sterilized in 1948 than any other year.

Sweden's large-scale eugenics program targeted the deviant and the mentally ill. Most sterilizations were vóluntary (though voluntary does not necessarily mean free from persuasion or exhortation). The Swedish government inquiry found that about 30.000 of the 62.000 were sterilised under some form of pressure or coercion.

As was the case in other programs, ethnicity and race were believed to be connected to mental and physical health. The Swedish government inquiry denied that the Swedish sterilisation program targeted ethnic minorities but did not provide any evidence for this and the government´s claims are contradicted by the experiences recounted by Swedish gypsies and travellers.

There is proof that the program targeted women. The goal of the program was to decrease deviant offspring. If one member of a family was considered deviant the whole family became the target of an investigation. It was perceived to be easier to persuade a woman to be sterilized than it was to persuade a man. For this reason women were more often sterilized than men, despite the fact that the medical procedure involved in the sterilization was simpler to carry out on a man.

Even as far as 1996, social democrats rejected paying compensation to those who had been sterilized. No one in Sweden raised the issue of compensation to the victims until there was international attention to Swedish eugenics following a 1997 series of articles in by the Polish-born journalist Maciej Zaremba, in Sweden´s largest daily, Dagens Nyheter. In 1999 the Swedish government began paying compensation to the sterilized and their families an equivalent to 21,000 USD to those who had "not consented" and who applied for the compensation.

Other Countries

Other countries that adopted some form of eugenics program include Norway, France, Finland, Denmark, Estonia, Iceland, and Switzerland with programs to sterilize people the government declared to be mentally deficient. Singapore practiced a limited form of eugenics that involved discouraging marriage between university graduates and the rest through segregation in matchmaking agencies, in the hope that the former would produce better children, although this point is contestable. Most notably its government introduced the "Graduate Mother Scheme" in the early 1980s to entice graduate women with incentives to get married, which was eventually scrapped due to public criticism and the implications it had on meritocracy.

Marginalization after World War II

After the experience of Nazi Germany, many ideas about "racial hygiene" and "unfit" members of society were publicly renounced by politicians and members of the scientific community. The Nuremberg Trials against former Nazi leaders revealed to the world many of the regime's genocidal practices and resulted in formalized policies of medical ethics and the 1950 UNESCO statement on race. Many scientific societies released their own similar "race statements" over the years, and the Universal Declaration of Human Rights, developed in response to abuses during the Second World War, was adopted by the United Nations in 1948 and affirmed, "Men and women of full age, without any limitation due to race, nationality or religion, have the right to marry and to found a family." In continuation, the 1978 UNESCO declaration on race and racial prejudice states that the fundamental equality of all human beings is the ideal toward which ethics and science should converge.

In reaction to Nazi abuses, eugenics became almost universally reviled in many of the nations where it had once been popular (however, some eugenics programs, including sterilization, continued quietly for decades). Many pre-war eugenicists engaged in what they later labelled "crypto-eugenics", purposefully taking their eugenic beliefs "underground" and becoming respected anthropologists, biologists and geneticists in the postwar world (including Robert Yerkes in the U.S. and Otmar von Verschuer in Germany). Californian eugenicist Paul Popenoe founded marriage counseling during the 1950s, a career change which grew from his eugenic interests in promoting "healthy marriages" between "fit" couples.

The American Life League, an opponent of abortion, charges that eugenics was merely "re-packaged" after the war, and promoted anew in the guise of the population-control and environmentalism movements. They claim, for example, that Planned Parenthood was funded and cultivated by the Eugenics Society for these reasons. Julian Huxley, the first Director-General of UNESCO and a founder of the World Wildlife Fund was also a Eugenics Society president and a strong supporter of eugenics

[E]ven though it is quite true that any radical eugenic policy will be for many years politically and psychologically impossible, it will be important for UNESCO to see that the eugenic problem is examined with the greatest care, and that the public mind is informed of the issues at stake so that much that now is unthinkable may at least become thinkable. — Julian Huxley

High school and college textbooks from the 1920s through the '40s often had chapters touting the scientific progress to be had from applying eugenic principles to the population. Many early scientific journals devoted to heredity in general were run by eugenicists and featured eugenics articles alongside studies of heredity in nonhuman organisms. After eugenics fell out of scientific favor, most references to eugenics were removed from textbooks and subsequent editions of relevant journals. Even the names of some journals changed to reflect new attitudes.

For example, *Eugenics Quarterly* became *Social Biology* in 1969 (the journal still exists today, though it looks little like its predecessor). Notable members of the American Eugenics Society (1922–94) during the second half of the 20th century included Joseph Fletcher, originator of Situational ethics; Dr. Clarence Gamble of the Procter & Gamble fortune; and Garrett Hardin, a population control advocate and author of the essay *The Tragedy of the Commons*. In the United States, the eugenics movement had largely lost most popular and political support by the end of the 1930s while forced sterilizations mostly ended in the 1960s with the last performed in 1981. Many US states continued to prohibit biracial marriages with "anti-miscegenation laws" such as Virginia's The Racial Integrity Act of 1924, until they were over-ruled by the Supreme Court in 1967 in Loving v. Virginia. The Immigration Restriction Act of 1924, which was designed to limit the immigration of "dysgenic" Italians, and eastern European Jews, was repealed and replaced by the Immigration and Nationality Act in 1965.

However, some prominent academics continued to support eugenics after the war. In 1963 the Ciba Foundation convened a conference in London under the title "Man and His Future," at which three distinguished biologists and Nobel laureates (Hermann Muller, Joshua Lederberg, and Francis Crick) all spoke strongly in favor of eugenics. A few nations, notably Sweden and the Canadian province of Alberta, maintained large-scale eugenics programs, including forced sterilization of mentally handicapped individuals, as well as other practices, until the 1970s.

Modern Eugenics, Genetic Engineering, and Ethical Re-evaluation

Beginning in the 1980s, the history and concept of eugenics were widely discussed as knowledge about genetics advanced significantly, making practical genetic engineering, which has been widely used to produce genetically modified organisms, with genetically modified foods being most visible to the general public. Endeavors such as the Human Genome Project made the effective modification of the human species seem possible again (as did Darwin's initial theory of evolution in the 1860s, along with the rediscovery of Mendel's laws in the early 20th century). The difference at the beginning of the 21st century was the guarded attitude towards eugenics, which had become a watchword to be feared rather than embraced.

A few scientific researchers such as psychologist Richard Lynn, psychologist Raymond Cattell, and scientist Gregory Stock have openly called for eugenic policies using modern technology, but they represent a minority opinion in current scientific and cultural circles. One attempted implementation of a form of eugenics was a "genius sperm bank" (1980–99) created by Robert Klark Graham, from which nearly 230 children were conceived (the best-known donors were Nobel Prize winners William Shockley and J.D.Watson). In the U.S. and Europe, though, these attempts have frequently been criticized as in the same spirit of classist and racist forms of eugenics of the 1930s. Because of its association with compulsory sterilization and the racial ideals of the Nazi Party, the word *eugenics* is rarely used by the advocates of such programs.

Eugenicists have argued that immigration from countries with low national IQ is undesirable. According to Raymond Cattell "when a country is opening its doors to immigration from diverse countries, it is like a farmer who buys his seeds from different sources by the sack, with sacks of different average quality of contents."

Polygenism and Racial Typologies

Works such as Arthur de Gobineau's *An Essay on the Inequality of the Human Races* (1853–1855) may be considered as one of the first theorizations of this new racism, founded on an essentialist notion of race, which opposed the former racial discourse, of Boulainvilliers for example, which saw in races a fundamentally historical reality which changed over time. Gobineau thus attempted to frame racism within the terms of biological differences among humans, giving it the legitimacy of biology. He was one of the first theorists to postulate polygenism, stating that there were, at the origins of the world, various discrete "races."

Gobineau's theories would be expanded, in France, by Georges Vacher de Lapouge (1854–1936)'s typology of races, who published in 1899 *The Aryan and his Social Role*, in which he claimed that the white, "Aryan race", "dolichocephalic", was opposed to the "brachycephalic" race, of whom the "Jew" was the archetype. Vacher de Lapoug thus created a hierarchical classification of races, in which he identified the "*Homo europaeus* (Teutonic, Protestant, etc.), the "*Homo alpinus*" (Auvergnat, Turkish, etc.), and finally the "*Homo mediterraneus*" (Neapolitan, Andalus, etc.) He assimilated races and social classes, considering that the French upper class was a representation of the *Homo europaeus*, while the lower class represented the *Homo alpinus*. Applying Galton's eugenics to his theory of races, Vacher de Lapouge's "selectionism" aimed first at achieving the annihilation of trade unionists, considered to be a "degenerate"; second, creating types of man each destined to one end, in order to prevent any contestation of labour conditions. His "anthroposociology" thus aimed at blocking social conflict by establishing a fixed, hierarchical social order

The same year than Vacher de Lapouge, William Z. Ripley used identical racial classification in *The Races of Europe* (1899), which would have a great influence in the United States. Others famous scientific authors include H.S. Chamberlain at the end of the 19th century (a British citizen who naturalized himself as German because of his admiration for the "Aryan race") or Madison Grant, a eugenicist and author of *The Passing of the Great Race* (1916).

Human Zoos

Human zoos (called "People Shows"), were an important means of bolstering *popular racism* by connecting it to scientific racism: they were both objects of public curiosity and of anthropology and anthropometry. Joice Heth, an African American slave, was displayed by P.T. Barnum in 1836, a few years after the exhibition of Saartjie Baartman, the "Hottentot Venus", in England. Such exhibitions became common in the New Imperialism period, and remained so until World War II. Carl Hagenbeck, inventor of the modern zoos, exhibited animals beside humans who were considered as "savages".

Congolese pygmy Ota Benga was displayed in 1906 by eugenicist Madison Grant, head of the Bronx Zoo, as an attempt to illustrate the "missing link" between humans and orangutans: thus, racism was tied to Darwinism, creating a social Darwinism ideology which tried to ground itself in Darwin's scientific discoveries. The 1931 Paris Colonial Exhibition displayed Kanaks from New Caledonia. A "Congolese village" was on display as late as 1958 at the Brussels' World Fair.

Evolutionary Theories about the Origins of Racism

Biologists John Tooby and Leda Cosmides were puzzled by the fact that race is one of the three characteristics most often used in brief descriptions of individuals (the others are age and sex). They reasoned that natural selection would not have favoured the evolution of an instinct for using race as a classification, because for most of human history, humans almost never encountered members of other races. Tooby and Cosmides hypothesized that modern people use race as a proxy (rough-and-ready indicator) for coalition membership, since a better-than-random guess about "which side" another person is on will be helpful if one does not actually know in advance.

Their colleague Robert Kurzban designed an experiment whose results appeared to support this hypothesis. Using the Memory confusion protocol, they presented subjects with pictures of individuals and sentences, allegedly spoken by these individuals, which presented two sides of a debate. The errors which the subjects made in recalling who said what indicated that they sometimes misattributed a statement to a speaker of the same race as the "correct" speaker, although they also sometimes misattributed a statement to a speaker "on the same side" as the "correct" speaker. In a second run of the experiment, the team also distinguished the "sides" in the debate by clothing of similar colors; and in this case the effect of racial similarity in causing mistakes almost vanished, being replaced by the colour of their clothing. In other words, the first group of subjects, with no clues from clothing, used race as a visual guide to guessing who was on which side of the debate; the second group of subjects used the clothing colour as their main visual clue, and the effect of race became very small.

Some research suggests that ethnocentric thinking may have actually contributed to the development of cooperation. Political scientists Ross Hammond and Robert Axelrod created a computer simulation wherein virtual individuals were randomly assigned one of a variety of skin colors, and then one of a variety of trading strategies: be colour-blind, favor those of your own colour, or favor those of other colors. They found that the ethnocentric individuals clustered together, then grew until all the non-ethnocentric individuals were wiped out.

As State-sponsored Activity

State racism – that is, institutions and practices of a nation-state that are grounded in racist ideology – has played a major role in all instances of settler colonialism, from the United States to Australia to Israel. It also played a prominent role in the Nazi Germany regime and fascist regimes in Europe, and in the first part of Japan's Shôwa period. The politics of Zimbabwe promote discrimination against whites, in an effort of ethnically cleansing the country.

State racism contributed as well to the formation of the Dominican Republic's identity and violent actions encouraged by Dominican governmental xenophobia against Haitians and "Haitian looking" people. Currently the Dominican Republic employs a de facto system of separatism for children and grandchildren of Haitians and black Dominicans, denying them birth certificates, education and access to health care. These governments advocated and implemented policies that were racist, xenophobic and, in case of Nazism, genocidal.

In History

In Antiquity

According to the Indo-Aryan migrations theory, Indo-Aryans migrated from Central Asia to India sometime after the collapse of the Indus Valley Civilization. They are believed to have been related to Indo-European-speaking peoples from the Near East, Anatolia, the Caucasus, and Europe. Following the discovery of the Indo-European languages in the 19th century, British historians put forth the Aryan invasion theory which argued that it was "Aryans" who established the caste system, an elitist form of social organization that (according to the British) separated the "light-skinned" Indo-Aryan conquerors from the "conquered dark-skinned" indigenous Dravidian tribes through enforcement of "racial endogamy". This claim was used by the British, defining themselves as "purely Aryan", to justify British Rule in India. Much of this was simply conjecture, fueled by British imperialism. Since the independence of South Asia from British rule, the Aryan invasion theory and subjugation of the dark skinned Dravidians in India" has become a staple polemic in South Asian geopolitics, including the propaganda of Indophobia in Pakistan.

Chouki El Hamel has cited the Babylonian Talmud, which divides mankind between the three sons of Noah, stating that "the descendants of Ham are cursed by being black, and [it] depicts Ham as a sinful man and his progeny as degenerates." Bernard Lewis has cited the Greek philosopher Aristotle who, in his discussion of slavery, stated that while Greeks are free by nature, 'barbarians' (non-Greeks) are slaves by nature, in that it is in their nature to be more willing to submit to despotic government. Though Aristotle does not specify any particular races, he argues that people from outside Greece are more prone to the burden of slavery than those from Ancient Greece.

Middle Ages and Renaissance

In the Middle East and North Africa region, racist opinions were expressed within the works of some of its historians and geographers including Al-Muqaddasi, Al-Jahiz, Al-Masudi, Abu Rayhan Biruni, Nasir al-Din al-Tusi, and Ibn Qutaybah. In the 14th century CE, the Tunisian Ibn Khaldun wrote:

"beyond [known peoples of black West Africa] to the south there is no civilization in the proper sense. There are only humans who are closer to dumb animals than to rational beings. They live in thickets and caves, and eat herbs and unprepared grain. They frequently eat each other. They cannot be considered human beings." "Therefore, the Negro nations are, as a rule, submissive to slavery, because (Negroes) have little that is (essentially) human and possess attributes that are quite similar to those of dumb animals, as we have stated."

Though the Qur'an expresses no racial prejudice, such prejudices later developed among Arabs due to several reasons: their extensive conquests and slave trade; the influence of Aristotelian ideas regarding slavery, which some Muslim philosophers directed towards Zanj (East African) and Turkic peoples; and the influence of Judeo-Christian ideas regarding divisions among humankind. In response to such views, the Afro-Arab author Al-Jahiz, himself of East African descent, wrote a book entitled *Superiority Of The Blacks To The Whites*, and explained why the Zanj were black in terms of environmental determinism in the "On the Zanj" chapter of *The Essays*. By the 14th century, a significant number of slaves came from sub-Saharan Africa, leading to the likes of Egyptian historian Al-Abshibi (1388–1446) writing: "It is said that when the [black] slave is sated, he fornicates, when he is hungry, he steals." According to J. Philippe Rushton, Arab relations with blacks whom the Muslims had dealt as slave traders for over 1,000 years could be summed up as follows:

> *"Although the Qur'an stated that there were no superior and inferior races and therefore no bar to racial intermarriage, in practice this pious doctrine was disregarded. Arabs did not want their daughters to marry even hybridized blacks. The Ethiopians were the most respected, the "Zanj" (Bantu and other Negroid tribes from East and West Africa south of the Sahara) the least respected, with Nubians occupying an intermediate position."*

It should be noted that ethnic prejudice among some elite Arabs was not limited to darker-skinned black people, but was also directed towards fairer-skinned "ruddy people" (including Persians, Turks, Caucasians and Europeans), while Arabs referred to themselves as "swarthy people". According to Arnold J. Toynbee: "The extinction of race consciousness as between Muslims is one of the outstanding achievements of Islam and in the contemporary world there is, as it happens, a crying need for the propagation of this Islamic virtue."

Richard E. Nisbett has said that the question of racial superiority may go back at least a thousand years, to the time when the Umayyad Caliphate invaded Hispania, occupying most of the Iberian Peninsula for six centuries, where they founded the advanced civilization of Al-Andalus (711–1492). Al-Andalus coincided with *La Convivencia*, an era of religious tolerance, and with the Golden age of Jewish culture in Iberia (912, the rule of Abd-ar-Rahman III – 1066, Granada massacre). It was followed by a violent *Reconquista* under the *Reyes Catolicos* (Catholic Kings), Ferdinand V and Isabella I. The Catholic Spaniards then formulated the *Cleanliness of blood* doctrine. It was during this time in history that the Western concept of aristocratic "blue blood" emerged in a highly racialized and implicitly white supremacist context, as author Robert Lacey explains:

It was the Spaniards who gave the world the notion that an aristocrat's blood is not red but blue. The Spanish nobility started taking shape around the ninth century in classic military fashion, occupying land as warriors on horseback. They were to continue the process for more than five hundred years, clawing back sections of the peninsula from its Moorish occupiers, and a nobleman demonstrated his pedigree by holding up his sword arm to display the filigree of blue-blooded veins beneath his pale skin—proof that his birth had not been contaminated by the dark-skinned enemy. Sangre azul, blue blood, was thus a euphemism for being a white man—Spain's own particular reminder that the refined footsteps of the aristocracy through history carry the rather less refined spoor of racism.

Following the expulsion of most Sephardic Jews from the Iberian peninsula, the remaining Jews and Muslims were forced to convert to Roman Catholicism, becoming "New Christians" which were despised and discriminated by the "Old Christians". An Inquisition was carried out by members of the Dominican Order in order to weed out converts that still practiced Judaism and Islam in secret. The system and ideology of the *limpieza de sangre* ostracized Christian converts from society, regardless of their actual degree of sincerity in their faith.

In Portugal, the legal distinction between New and Old Christian was only ended through a legal decree issued by the Marquis of Pombal in 1772, almost three centuries after the implementation of the racist discrimination. The *limpieza de sangre* doctrine was also very common in the colonization of the Americas, where it led to the racial separation of the various peoples in the colonies and created a very intricate list of nomenclature to describe one's precise race and, by consequence, one's place in society. This precise classification was described by Eduardo Galeano in the *Open Veins of Latin America* (1971). It included, among others terms, *mestizo* (50% Spaniard and 50% Native American), *castizo* (75% European and 25% Native American), *Spaniard* (87.5% European and 12.5% Native American), *Mulatto* (50% European and 50% African), *Albarazado* (43.75% Native American, 29.6875% European, and 26.5625% African), etc.

At the end of the Renaissance, the Valladolid debate (1550–1551) concerning the treatment of natives of the "New World" opposed the Dominican friar and Bishop of Chiapas Bartolomé de Las Casas to another Dominican philosopher Juan Ginés de

Sepúlveda. The latter argued that "Indians" were natural slaves because they had no souls, and were therefore beneath humanity. Thus, reducing them to slavery or serfdom was in accordance with Catholic theology and natural law. To the contrary, Bartolomé de Las Casas argued that the Amerindians were free men in the natural order and deserved the same treatment as others, according to Catholic theology. It was one of the many controversy concerning racism, slavery and Eurocentrism that would arise in the following centuries.

Although anti-Semitism has a long European history, related to Christianism (anti-Judaism), racism itself is frequently described as a *modern* phenomenon. In the view of the French intellectual Michel Foucault, the first formulation of racism emerged in the Early Modern period as the "discourse of race struggle", a historical and political discourse which Foucault opposed to the philosophical and juridical discourse of sovereignty. Philosopher and historian Michel Foucault argued that the first appearance of racism as a social discourse (as opposed to simple xenophobia, which some might argue has existed in all places and times) may be found during the 1688 Glorious Revolution in Great Britain, in Edward Coke or John Lilburne's work.

However, this "discourse of race struggle", as interpreted by Foucault, must be distinguished from the 19th century biological racism, also known as "race science" or "scientific racism". Indeed, this early modern discourse has many points of difference with modern racism. First of all, in this "discourse of race struggle", "race" is not considered a biological notion — which would divide humanity into distinct biological groups — but as a *historical notion*. Moreover, this discourse is opposed to the sovereign's discourse: it is used by the bourgeoisie, the people and the aristocracy as a mean of struggle against the monarchy. This discourse, which first appeared in Great Britain, was then carried on in France by people such as Boulainvilliers, Nicolas Fréret, and then, during the 1789 French Revolution, Sieyès, and afterward Augustin Thierry and Cournot. Boulainvilliers, which created the matrix of such racist discourse in medieval France, conceived the "race" as something closer to the sense of "nation", that is, in his times, the "people". He conceived France as divided between various nations — the unified nation-state is, of course, here an anachronism — which themselves formed different "races". Boulainvilliers opposed the absolute monarchy, who tried to bypass the aristocracy by establishing a direct relationship to the Third Estate. Thus, he created this theory of the French aristocrats as being the descendants of foreign invaders, whom he called the "Franks", while the Third Estate constituted according to him the autochthonous, vanquished Gallo-Romans, who were dominated by the Frankish aristocracy as a consequence of the right of conquest. Early modern racism was opposed to nationalism and the nation-state: the Comte de Montlosier, in exile during the French Revolution, who borrowed Boulainvilliers' discourse on the "Nordic race" as being the French aristocracy that invaded the plebeian "Gauls", thus showed his despise for the Third Estate calling it "this new people born of slaves... mixture of all races and of all times".

While 19th century racism became closely intertwined with nationalism, leading to the ethnic nationalist discourse which identified the "race" to the "folk", leading to such movements as pan-Germanism, Zionism, pan-Turkism, pan-Arabism, pan-Farism (related to Persian racism), and pan-Slavism, medieval racism precisely divided the nation into various non-biological "races", which were thought as the consequences of historical conquests and social conflicts. Michel Foucault traced the genealogy of modern racism to this medieval "historical and political discourse of race struggle". According to him, it divided itself in the 19th century according to two rival lines: on one hand, it was incorporated by racists, biologists and eugenicists, who gave it the modern sense of "race" and, even more, transformed this popular discourse into a "state racism" (e.g. Nazism). On the other hand, Marxists also seized this discourse founded on the assumption of a political struggle which provided the real engine of history and continued to act underneath the apparent peace. Thus, Marxists transformed the essentialist notion of "race" into the historical notion of "class struggle", defined by socially structured position: capitalist or proletarian. In *The Will to Knowledge* (1976), Foucault analyzed another opponent of the "race struggle" discourse: Sigmund Freud's psychoanalysis, which opposed the concepts of "blood heredity", prevalent in the 19th century racist discourse.

19th Century

Authors such as Hannah Arendt, in her 1951 book *The Origins of Totalitarianism*, have said that the racist ideology (*popular racism*) which developed at the end of the 19th century helped legitimize the imperialist conquests of foreign territories and the acts that accompanied them (such as the Herero and Namaqua Genocide of 1904–1907 or the Armenian Genocide of 1915–1917). Rudyard Kipling's poem *The White Man's Burden* (1899) is one of the more famous illustrations of the belief in the inherent superiority of the European culture over the rest of the world, though also thought to be a satirical appraisal of such imperialism. Racist ideology thus helped legitimize subjugation and the dismantling of the traditional societies of indigenous peoples, which were thus conceived as humanitarian obligations as a result of these racist beliefs.

However, during the 19th century, West European colonial powers were involved in the suppression of the Arab slave trade in Africa, as well as in suppression of the slave trade in West Africa. Other colonialists recognized the depravity of their actions but persisted for personal gain and there are some Europeans during the time period who objected to the injustices caused by colonialism and lobbied on behalf of aboriginal peoples. Thus, when the Hottentot Venus was displayed in England in the beginning of the 19th century, the African Association publicly opposed itself to the exhibition. The same year that Kipling published his poem, Joseph Conrad published *Heart of Darkness* (1899), a clear criticism of the Congo Free State owned by Leopold II of Belgium.

Examples of racial theories used include the creation of the Hamitic ethno-linguistic group during the European exploration of Africa. It was then restricted by Karl Friedrich Lepsius (1810–1877) to non-Semitic Afro-Asiatic languages.

The term *Hamite* then became quite popular and was applied to different populations within Africa mainly comprising Ethiopians, Eritreans, Somalis, Berbers, and Nubians. Hamites were regarded as Caucasoid peoples who probably originated in either Arabia or Asia on the basis of their cultural, physical and linguistic similarities with the peoples of those areas. Europeans considered Hamites to be more civilized than Black

Africans, and more akin to themselves and Semitic peoples. In the first two-thirds of the 20th century, the Hamitic race was, in fact, considered one of the branches of the Caucasian race, along with the Indo-Europeans, Dravidians, Semites, and the Mediterranean race.

However, the Hamitic peoples themselves were often deemed to have failed as rulers, a failing that was usually ascribed to interbreeding with Negroes. In the mid-20th century, the German scholar Carl Meinhof (1857–1944) claimed that the Bantu race was formed by a merger of Hamitic and Negro races. The Hottentots (Nama or Khoi) were formed by the merger of Hamitic and Bushmen (San) races — both being termed nowadays as Khoisan peoples).

In the United States in the early 19th century, the American Colonization Society was established as the primary vehicle for proposals to return black Americans to greater freedom and equality in Africa. The colonization effort resulted from a mixture of motives with its founder Henry Clay stating; "unconquerable prejudice resulting from their colour, they never could amalgamate with the free whites of this country. It was desirable, therefore, as it respected them, and the residue of the population of the country, to drain them off". Racism spread throughout the "New World" in the late 19th century and early 20th century. Whitecapping which started in Indiana in the late 19th century soon spread throughout all of North America, causing many African labourers to flee from the land they worked on. In the US during the 1860s, racist posters were used during election campaigns. In one of these racist posters, a black man is depicted lounging idly in the foreground as one white man ploughs his field and another chops wood. Accompanying labels are: "In the sweat of thy face shalt thou eat thy bread," and "The white man must work to keep his children and pay his taxes." The black man wonders, "Whar is de use for me to work as long as dey make dese appropriations." Above in a cloud is an image of the "Freedman's Bureau! Negro Estimate of Freedom!" The bureau is pictured as a large domed building resembling the U.S. Capitol and is inscribed "Freedom and No Work." Its columns and walls are labelled, "Candy," "Rum, Gin, Whiskey," "Sugar Plums," "Indolence," "White Women," "Apathy," "White Sugar,"

"Idleness," and so on. On June 5, 1873, Sir Francis Galton, distinguished English explorer and cousin of Charles Darwin, wrote in a letter to The Times:

"My proposal is to make the encouragement of Chinese settlements of Africa a part of our national policy, in the belief that the Chinese immigrants would not only maintain their position, but that they would multiply and their descendants supplant the inferior Negro race" "I should expect that the African seaboard, now sparsely occupied by lazy, palavering savages, might in a few years be tenanted by industrious, order-loving Chinese, living either as a semidetached dependency of China, or else in perfect freedom under their own law."

In the Age of Enlightenment

While modern racism has an essentialist and biological conception of race, racist or xenophobic opinions have been shared by some authors, from the Antiquity to the Age of Enlightenment. However, this early form of racism did not conceive of "race" as a biological concept — as biology itself did not exist as such —, but as the accidental effect of climate on physical traits. With the Age of Discovery, the diversity of mankind became an important topic of research, leading to debates concerning monogenism and polygenism, respectively endorsing the unique origin of mankind (coherent with the Genesis Biblical account) and the multiple origins of mankind.

Pierre de Maupertuis (1698–1759), for example, reconciled the Biblical account with the present diversity of "races" in his *Essai de philosophie morale* (1749, Essay on Moral Philosophy), explaining "racial" differences by climatic factors. He thus explained the colour of black people through the inheritance of acquired characteristics, claiming white was the original colour of mankind. He also highlighted the spiritual strength of Africans seized as slaves, pointing out how, like the Ancient Stoic philosophers, they prefer to die rather than to survive to capture.

Arguments on the influence of climate found additional weight with Buffon's *Histoire naturelle* in the middle of the 18th century, and his thesis on the unity of mankind was taken back by Diderot and d'Alembert's *Encyclopédie* in the article *Humaine, espèce* (Human, Specie). According to Ann Thomson, although Buffon did establish a "clear hierarchy [...] between the beautiful white civilised races of the temperate zone and those savages who have degenerated in more extreme climates, his emphasis on the unity of the human race and his distinction between humans and other animals were extremely influential. " The abolitionists thus used his arguments to show that Africans were not naturally inferior, and could be improved by different treatment and different climate.

The abbé Demanet (1767) claimed that a Portuguese colony in Africa had become black after several generations, due to the effect of climate, a story which was given wide credence by abolitionists, quoted for example by Cabanis (1757–1808) and Thomas Clarkson (1760–1846) The abolitionist Physiocrat abbé Pierre-Joseph-André Roubaud alleged that black Africans would change skin colour if they lived in different climatic conditions. According to Ann Thomson,

What emerges from these examples is the overwhelming desire to insist on the unity of the human race by emphasizing the effect of the climate and other environmental causes, but not necessarily to claim the equality of all humans; for the existence of a hierarchy is not systematically denied but, on the contrary, frequently accepted [exceptions quoted by Thomson includes James Dunbar and the abbé Grégoire.]. This of course was to have long-lasting effects in the Nineteenth Century, when the arguments about climate were countered and the hierarchy was seen to be permanent, as the differences between humans were innate.

Moral factors were also considered to influence physical and psychical traits. The American abolitionist Anthony Benezet stated, in the *Historical Account of Guinea* (1772), that Africans in Africa were a sociable, virtuous and intelligent people; but that their servile condition in America explained their "degeneration" and adoption of the vices of Europeans. Furthermore, the theory of the Great Chain of Being, which asserted a continuity between animals and humans, thus contradicting Christian religion (and henceforth supported by materialists such as Diderot) was used by some, such as Edward Long, spokesman for the West India Lobby, or Charles White's *Account of the Regular Gradation in Man* (1799 — White denied the effect of climate) to assert the animal nature of some humans. In 1919, racial equality was proposed at the Paris Peace Conference, the proposal got a large majority of votes; however, the proposal was declined by few countries with strong oppositions. During the WW2, Asian Axis allied with Germans, however they saved tens of thousands Jews from German genocide.]]. Burma, China, Free India, Japan, Philippine and Thailand held the Greater East Asia Conference in 1943, at which the countries declared their intention to work for the abolition of racial discrimination. After the war, U.N. Charter incorporated into the racial equality.

The Nazis considered Jews, Gypsies, Poles along with other Slavic people like the Russians, Ukrainians, Czechs and anyone else who was not an "Aryan" according to the contemporary Nazi race terminology to be subhuman (*Untermensch*). The Nazis rationalized that the Germans, being a super human (*Übermenschlich*) race, had a biological right to displace, eliminate and enslave inferiors. Some 6 million Jews were killed by the Nazis during the *Holocaust*. In the longer term, the Nazis wanted to exterminate some 30–45 million Slavs.

After the war, under the "Big Plan", *Generalplan Ost* foresaw the eventual expulsion of more than 50 million non-Germanized Slavs of Eastern Europe through forced migration, as well as some of the Balts, beyond the Ural Mountains and into Siberia. In their place, Germans would be settled in an extended "living space" (*Lebensraum*) of the 1000-Year Empire (*Tausendjähriges Reich*). Herbert Backe was one of the orchestrators of the Hunger Plan – the plan to starve tens of millions of Slavs in order to ensure steady food supplies for the German people and troops.

Heinrich Himmler speech to about 100 SS Group Leaders in Posen, occupied Poland, 1943:

> *"What happens to the Russians, what happens to the Czechs, is a matter of utter indifference to me... Whether the other peoples live in comfort or perish of hunger interests me only in so far as we need them as slaves for our culture; apart from that it does not interest me. Whether or not 10,000 Russian women collapse from exhaustion while digging a tank ditch interests me only in so far as the tank ditch is completed for Germany...*

We Germans, who are the only people in the world who have a decent attitude to animals, will also adopt a decent attitude to these human animals, but it is a crime against our own blood to worry about them and to bring them ideals... I shall speak to you here with all frankness of a very serious subject. We shall now discuss it absolutely openly among ourselves, nevertheless we shall never speak of it in public. I mean the evacuation of the Jews, the extermination of the Jewish race."

Inter-minority Variants

Prejudiced thinking among and between minority groups does occur, for example conflicts between blacks and Korean Americans (notably in the Los Angeles riots of 1992), by blacks towards Jews (such as the riots in Crown Heights in 1991), between new immigrant groups (such as Latinos), or towards whites. One particularly pernicious form of racism in the United States is racial segregation, which arguably continues to exist today.

There has been a long-running racial tension between African Americans and Mexican Americans. There have been several significant riots in California prisons where Mexican American inmates and African Americans have specifically targeted each other based on racial reasons. There have been reports of racially motivated attacks against African Americans who have moved into neighbourhoods occupied mostly by Mexican Americans, and vice versa. In the late 1920s in California, there was animosity between the Filipinos and the Mexicans and between whites and Filipinos since they competed for the same jobs. Recently, there has also been an increase in racial violence between African immigrants and Blacks who have already lived in the country for generations.

The Aztlan movement has been described as racist. The movement's goal involves the pursuit of repossessing the American southwest. It has also been called the Mexican "reconquista" (re-conquest) whose name was inspired by the Spanish *reconquista*, which led to the expulsion of the Moors from Spain. According to gang experts and law enforcement agents, a longstanding race war between the Mexican Mafia and the Black Guerilla family, a rival African American prison gang, has generated such intense racial hatred among Mexican Mafia leaders or shot callers, that they have issued a "green light" on all blacks. A sort of gang-life fatwa, this amounts to a standing authorization for Latino gang members to prove their mettle by terrorizing or even murdering any blacks sighted in a neighborhood claimed by a gang loyal to the Mexican Mafia.

In Britain, tensions between minority groups can be just as strong as any minority group suffers with the majority population. In Birmingham, there have been long-term divisions between the Black and South Asian communities, which were illustrated in the Handsworth riots and in the smaller 2005 Birmingham riots. In Dewsbury, a Yorkshire town with a relatively high Muslim population, there have been tensions and minor civil disturbances between Kurds and South Asians.

During the Congo Civil War (1998–2003), Pygmies were hunted down like game animals and eaten. Both sides of the war regarded them as "subhuman" and some say their flesh can confer magical powers. UN human rights activists reported in 2003 that rebels had carried out acts of cannibalism. Sinafasi Makelo, a representative of Mbuti pygmies, has asked the UN Security Council to recognise cannibalism as a crime against humanity and an act of genocide. A report released by the United Nations Committee on the Elimination of Racial Discrimination condemns Botswana's treatment of the 'Bushmen' as racist.

Some 70,000 black African Mauritanians were expelled from Mauritania in the late 1980s. In the Sudan, black African captives in the civil war were often enslaved, and female prisoners were often used sexually. The Darfur conflict has been described by some as a racial matter. In October 2006, Niger announced that it would deport the Arabs living in the Diffa region of eastern Niger to Chad. This population numbered about 150,000. While the Government was rounding Arabs in preparation for the deportation, two girls died, reportedly after fleeing Government forces, and three women suffered miscarriages. The Ethiopian Jewish community's integration to Israeli society has been complicated by racist attitudes on the part of some elements of Israeli society and the official establishment. The Israeli media reported that residents of

Pisgat Ze'ev, a large Jewish settlement in East Jerusalem, had formed a vigilante-style patrol to stop interracial dating between Arab men and local Jewish girls. In the 2007 poll, more than half of Israeli Jews said that intermarriage should be equated with "national treason".

The mass demonstrations and riots against African students in Nanjing, China, lasted from December 1988 to January 1989. Bar owners in central Beijing had been forced "not to serve black people or Mongolians" during the 2008 Summer Olympics. Some neighborhood committees in Guangzhou bar Africans from living in residential complexes. In November 2009, British newspaper *The Guardian* reported that Lou Jing, of mixed Chinese and African parentage, had emerged as the most famous talent show contestant in China and has become the subject of intense debate because of her skin colour. Her attention in the media opened serious debates about racism in China and racial prejudice. In Asia and Latin America, light skin is seen as more attractive. Thus, skin whitening cosmetic products are popular in East Asia and India.

In France, home to Europe's largest population of Muslims — about 6 million — as well as the continent's largest community of Jews, about 600,000, anti-Jewish violence, property destruction, and racist language has been wildly increasing over the last several years and French-Jews are worried more every month that it will spiral even higher. Jewish leaders perceive as intensifying anti-Semitism in France, mainly among Muslims of Arab or African heritage, but also growing among Caribbean islanders from former colonies.

Serious race riots in Durban between Indians and Zulus erupted in 1949. Ne Win's rise to power in Burma in 1962 and his relentless persecution of "resident aliens" led to an exodus of some 300,000 Burmese Indians. They migrated to escape racial discrimination and wholesale nationalisation of private enterprise a few years later in 1964. The Zanzibar Revolution of January 12, 1964 put an end to the local Arab dynasty. Thousands of Arabs and Indians in Zanzibar were massacred in riots, and thousands more were detained or fled the island. On 4 August 1972, Idi Amin, President of Uganda, ethnically cleansed Uganda's Asians giving them 90 days to leave the country. The Jakarta riots of May 1998 targeted many Chinese

Indonesians. The anti-Chinese legislation was in the Indonesian constitution until 1998. Xenophobia against Chinese migrants is currently on the rise in Africa and Oceania. Anti-Chinese rioting, involving tens of thousands of people, broke out in Papua New Guinea in May 2009. The Fiji coup of 2000 has provoked a violent backlash against the Indo-Fijians. Fiji citizens of Indian, European, mixed race or other island heritage have become second-class citizens. Racial divisions also exist in Guyana and Malaysia.

Age Discrimination

Age discrimination is discrimination on the grounds of age. Although theoretically the word can refer to the discrimination against any age group, age discrimination usually comes in one of three forms: discrimination against youth (also called adultism), discrimination against those 40 years old or older, and discrimination against elderly people.

On an institutional level, there are policies and regulations in place that limit opportunities to people of certain ages and deny them to all others. The law, for instance, requires that all young persons must be at least 16 years old in order to obtain a driver's license in the United States. There are also government regulations that determine when a worker may retire. Currently, in the US, a worker must be 66 years and 2 months old before becoming eligible for normal retirement.

A 2006/2007 survey done by the Children's Rights Alliance for England and the National Children's Bureau asked 4,060 children and young people whether they have ever been treated unfairly based on various criteria (race, age, sex, sexual orientation, etc). A total of 43% of British youth surveyed reported experiencing discrimination based on their age, far eclipsing other categories of discrimination like sex (27%), race (11%), or sexual orientation (6%).

Ageism has significant effects in two particular sectors: employment and health care.

Employment

The concept of ageism was originally developed to refer to prejudice and discrimination against older people. Over time, this association between discrimination and old age has been expanded by evidence that suggests prejudice and discrimination in employment can occur to a worker of any age.

Like racial and gender discrimination, age discrimination, at least when it affects younger workers, can result in unequal pay for equal work. Unlike racial and gender discrimination, however, age discrimination in wages is often enshrined in law. For example, in both the United States and the United Kingdom minimum wage laws allow for employers to pay lower wages to young workers. Many state and local minimum wage laws mirror such an age-based, tiered minimum wage. Outside of the law, older workers, on average, make more than younger workers do. Firms may be afraid to offer older workers lower wages than they offer to younger workers.

Therefore, younger workers may face more statistical discrimination from employers than older workers. Statistical discrimination refers to limiting the employment opportunities of an individual based on stereotypes of a group to which the person belongs. Limited employment opportunities could come in the form of lower pay for equal work or jobs with little social mobility. Younger female workers may be more statistically discriminated against than older female workers, for example, because it is socially expected that, as young women of childbearing years, they will need to leave the work force periodically to have children.

Labor regulations also limit the age at which people are allowed to work and how many hours and under what conditions they may work. In the United States, a person must generally be at least 14 years old to seek a job, and workers face additional restrictions on their work activities until they reach age 16. Many companies refuse to hire workers younger than 18.

Young workers over 18 may also have a hard time finding a white-collar job because the maximum age for some professional occupations is set as low as 30 by employers. After these workers finish obtaining the necessary professional degrees, they may have only a few years, at most, to get into a position without being too old. The upward mobility in these same jobs starts to diminish once the workers reach the age of 40. A worker who gets a job at age 30 may only work about ten years before his chances of promotion begin to dwindle.

While older workers benefit more often from higher wages than do younger workers, they face barriers in promotions and hiring. Employers may also encourage early retirement or layoffs disproportionately more for older or more experienced workers. Age discrimination in hiring has been shown to exist in the United States. Joanna Lahey, economics professor at Texas A&M University, found that firms are more than 40% more likely to interview a younger job applicant than an older job applicant.

In a survey for the University of Kent, England, 29% of respondents stated that they had suffered from age discrimination. This is a higher proportion than for gender or racial discrimination. Dominic Abrams, social psychology professor at the university, concluded that ageism is the most pervasive form of prejudice experienced in the UK population.

According to Dr. Robert M. McCann, an associate professor of management communication at the University of Southern California's Marshall School of Business, denigrating older workers, even if only subtly, can have an outsized negative impact on employee productivity and corporate profits. For American corporations, age discrimination can lead to significant expenses. In Fiscal Year 2006, the U.S. Equal Employment Opportunity Commission received nearly 17,000 charges of age discrimination, resolving more than 14,000 and recovering $51.5 million in monetary benefits. Costs from lawsuit settlements and judgments can run into the millions, most notably with the $250 million paid by the California Public Employees' Retirement System (CalPERS) under a settlement agreement in 2003.

In the UK, age discrimination has been prohibited in employment since 2006. Since then, the number of age discrimination cases has risen dramatically. The laws protect the young as well as the old, and there were over 5,200 claims submitted to the Employment Tribunal in 2009/2010 compared to just 900 in 2006/2007 (immediately after the Regulations came in force).

Healthcare

There is considerable evidence of discrimination against the elderly in health care. This is particularly true for aspects of the physician-patient interaction, such as screening procedures, information exchanges, and treatment decisions. In the patient-physician interaction, physicians and other health care providers may hold attitudes, beliefs, and behaviours that are associated with ageism against older patients. Studies have found that physicians often do not seem to show any care or concern toward treating the medical problems of older people. Then, when actually interacting with these older patients on the job, the doctors sometimes view them with disgust and describe them in negative ways, such as "depressing" or "crazy." For screening procedures, elderly people are less likely than younger people to be screened for cancers and, due to the lack of this preventative measure, less likely to be diagnosed at early stages of their conditions.

After being diagnosed with a disease that may be potentially curable, older people are further discriminated against. Though there may be surgeries or operations with high survival rates that might cure their condition, older patients are less likely than younger patients to receive all the necessary treatments. It has been posited that this is because doctors fear their older patients are not physically strong enough to tolerate the curative treatments and are more likely to have complications during surgery that may end in death. However, other studies have been done with patients with heart disease, and, in these cases, the older patients were still less likely to receive further tests or treatments, independent of the severity of their health problems. Thus, the approach to the treatment of older people is concentrated on managing the disease rather than preventing or curing it. This is based on the stereotype that it is the natural process of aging for the quality of health to decrease, and, therefore, there is no point in attempting to prevent the inevitable decline of old age.

In the United States, the Age Discrimination in Employment Act prohibits employment discrimination nationwide based on age with respect to employees 40 years of age or older. The Age Discrimination in Employment Act also addresses the difficulty older workers face in obtaining new employment after being displaced from their jobs, arbitrary age limits.

In many countries, companies more or less openly refuse to hire people above a certain age despite the increasing lifespans and average age of the population. The reasons for this range from vague feelings younger people are more "dynamic" and create a positive image for the company, to more concrete concerns about regulations granting older employees higher salaries or other benefits without these expenses being fully justified by an older employees' greater experience. Unions cite age as the most common form of discrimination in the workplace. Workers ages 45 and over form a disproportionate share of the long-term unemployed – those who have been out of work for six months or longer, according to the U.S. Bureau of Labor Statistics. Some people consider that teenagers and youth (around 15–25 years old) are victims of adultism, age discrimination framed as a paternalistic form of protection. In seeking social justice, they feel that it is necessary to remove the use of a false moral agenda in order to achieve agency and empowerment.This perspective is based on the grounds that youth should be treated more respectfully by adults and not as second-class citizens. Some suggest that social stratification in age groups causes outsiders to incorrectly stereotype and generalize the group, for instance that all adolescents are equally immature, violent or rebellious, listen to rock tunes, and do drugs. Some have organized groups against age discrimination.

Ageism is the causal effect of a continuum of fears related to age. This continuum includes:

- Ephebiphobia: the fear of youth.
- Gerontophobia: the fear of elderly people.
- Pediaphobia: the fear of infants or small children.

Related terms include:

- Adultism: Also called adultarchy, adult privilege, and adultcentrism/adultocentrism, this is the wielding of authority over young people and the preference of adults before children and youth.
- Jeunism: Also called "youthism" is the holding of beliefs or actions taken that preference 'younger' people before adults.

Sex and Gender Discrimination

Though gender discrimination and sexism refers to beliefs and attitudes in relation to the gender of a person, such beliefs and attitudes are of a social nature and do not, normally, carry any legal consequences. Sex discrimination, on the other hand, may have legal consequences.

Though what constitutes sex discrimination varies between countries, the essence is that it is an adverse action taken by one person against another person that would not have occurred had the person been of another sex. Discrimination of that nature in certain enumerated circumstances is illegal in many countries. Currently, discrimination based on sex is defined as adverse action against another person, that would not have occurred had the person been of another sex. This is considered a form of prejudice and is illegal in certain enumerated circumstances in most countries.

Sexual discrimination can arise in different contexts. For instance an employee may be discriminated against by being asked discriminatory questions during a job interview, or because an employer did not hire, promote or wrongfully terminated an employee based on his or her gender, or employers pay unequally based on gender. In an educational setting there could be claims that a student was excluded from an educational institution, program, opportunity, loan, student group, or scholarship due to his or her gender. In the housing setting there could be claims that a person was refused negotiations on seeking a house, contracting/leasing a house or getting a loan based on his or her gender. Another setting where there have been claims of gender discrimination is banking; for example if one is refused credit or is offered unequal loan terms based on one's gender.

Another setting where there is usually gender discrimination is when one is refused to extend his or her credit, refused approval of credit/loan process, and if there is a burden of unequal loan terms based on one's gender.

Socially, sexual differences have been used to justify different roles for men and women, in some cases giving rise to claims of primary and secondary roles.

While there are alleged non-physical differences between men and women, major reviews of the academic literature on gender difference find only a tiny minority of characteristics where there are consistent psychological differences between men and women, and these relate directly to experiences grounded in biological difference. However, there are also some psychological differences in regard to how problems are dealt with and emotional perceptions and reactions which may relate to hormones and the successful characteristics of each gender during longstanding roles in past primitive lifestyles.

Unfair discrimination usually follows the gender stereotyping held by a society. The United Nations had concluded that women often experience a "glass ceiling" and that there are no societies in which women enjoy the same opportunities as men. The term "glass ceiling" is used to describe a perceived barrier to advancement in employment based on discrimination, especially sex discrimination.

In the United States in 1995, the Glass Ceiling Commission, a government-funded group, stated: "Over half of all Master's degrees are now awarded to women, yet 95% of senior-level managers, of the top Fortune 1000 industrial and 500 service companies are men. Of them, 97% are white." In its report, it recommended affirmative action, which is the consideration of an employee's gender and race in hiring and promotion decisions, as a means to end this form of discrimination. In 2008, women accounted for 51% of all workers in the high-paying management, professional, and related occupations. They outnumbered men in such occupations as public relations managers; financial managers; and human resource managers.

The China's leading headhunter, Chinahr.com, reported in 2007 that the average salary for white-collar men was 44,000 yuan ($6,441), compared with 28,700 yuan ($4,201) for women.

The PwC research found that among FTSE 350 companies in the United Kingdom in 2002 almost 40% of senior management posts were occupied by women. When that research was repeated in 2007, the number of senior management posts held by women had fallen to 22%.

Transgender individuals, both male to female and female to male, often experience problems which often lead to dismissals, underachievement, difficulty in finding a job, social isolation, and, occasionally, violent attacks against them. Nevertheless, the problem of gender discrimination does not stop at trandgender individuals nor with women. Men are often the victim in certain areas of employment as men begin to seek work in office and childcare settings traditionally perceived as "women's jobs". One such situation seems to be evident in a recent case concerning alleged YMCA discrimination and a Federal Court Case in Texas. The case actually involves alleged discrimination against both men and blacks in childcare, even when they pass the same strict background tests and other standards of employment. It is currently being contended in federal court, as of fall 2009, and sheds light on how a workplace dominated by a majority (- women in this case) sometimes will seemingly "justify" whatever they wish to do, regardless of the law. This may be done as an effort at self-protection, to uphold traditional societal roles, or some other faulty, unethical or illegal prejudicial reasoning.

Affirmative action also leads to white men being discriminated against for entry level and blue collar positions. An employer cannot hire a white man with the same "on paper" qualifications over a woman or minority worker or the employer will face prosecution.

Caste Discrimination

According to UNICEF and Human Rights Watch, caste discrimination affects an estimated 250 million people worldwide. Discrimination based on caste, as perceived by UNICEF, is prevalent mainly in parts of Asia (India, Sri Lanka, Bangladesh, Nepal, Japan) and Africa

Currently, there are an estimated 160 million Dalits or Scheduled Castes (formerly known as "untouchables") in India.. Dalit people face severe problems, such as segregation and violence against them An estimated 40 million people in India, most of them Dalits, are bonded workers, many working to pay off debts that were incurred generations ago.

There have been substantial improvements in the position of Dalits in post-independence India, consequent to the strict implementation of the rights and privileges enshrined in the Constitution of India, as implemented by the Protection of Civil rights Act, 1955. India has had a Dalit president, K.R. Narayanan, and the practise had disappeared in urban public life, though persist very strongly in rural areas, where modern ideas have not penetrated, and ancient ethnic divisions and hostilities against Dalits often dominate the discourse of inter-community relations, resulting in underrepresented Dalits facing discrimination and violence.

In modern times, Dalits, as well as tribal people and members of the lowest castes in India benefit from broad affirmative action programmes and are enjoying greater political power." The Constitution of India places special emphasis on outlawing caste discrimination, especially the practice of untouchability. In addition, the Indian penal code inflicts severe punishments on those who discriminate on the basis of caste. Anti-Dalit prejudice and discrimination exists primarily in rural areas, where small societies can track the caste lineage of individuals and discriminate accordingly.

Employment Discrimination

Employment discrimination refers to disabling certain people to apply and receive jobs based on their race, age, gender, religion, sexual orientation and disability. In relationship to sociology, employment discrimination usually relates to what events are happening in society at the time. For example, it would seem ludicrous to hire an African American male and absolutely unheard of to hire an African American woman over 50 years ago. However, in our society today, it is the absolute norm to hire any qualified person.

Employment discrimination has decreased tremendously from previous years. This is due to laws that prohibit employment discrimination. In our society today, everyone is ordered to treat all different types of people equally and grant them the same opportunities. If a person hiring another breaks these rules, they can be sued for hate crimes.

The American federal laws that protect against:

- Race, colour and national origin discrimination include the Civil Rights Act of 1964, Executive Order Number 11478 among other numerous laws that protect people from race, colour and national origin discrimination.
- Sex and gender discrimination include the Civil Rights Act of 1964 and Equal Pay Act of 1963.
- age Discrimination include the Age Discrimination in Employment Act of 1967.

- Physical and mental disability discrimination include the Americans with Disabilities Act of 1990
- Religious discrimination include the Civil Rights Act of 1964.
- Military status discrimination include the Vietnam Era Veterans Readjustment Assistance Act of 1974

Most other western nations have similar laws protecting these groups.

Sexual Orientation Discrimination

In 2009, ILGA published a report based on research carried out by Daniel Ottosson at Södertörn University College, Stockholm, Sweden. This research found that of the 80 countries around the world that continue to consider homosexuality illegal, five carry the death penalty for homosexual activity, and two do in some regions of the country. In the report, this is described as "State sponsored homophobia". This happens in Islamic states, or in two cases regions under Islamic authority.

On February 5, 2005 the IRIN issued a reported titled "Iraq: Male homosexuality still a taboo." The article stated, among other things that honour killings by Iraqis against a gay family member are common and given some legal protection. In August 2009 Human Rights Watch published an extensive report detailing torture of men accused of being gay in Iraq, including the blocking of men's anuses with glue and then giving the men laxatives.

South Africa has one of the world's most progressive constitutions, but same-sex unions are often decried as "un-African." Research shows 86% of black lesbians from the Western Cape live in fear of sexual assault.

Language Discrimination

Diversity of language is protected and respected by most nations who value cultural diversity. However, people are sometimes subjected to different treatment because their preferred language is associated with a particular group, class or category. Commonly, the preferred language is just another attribute of separate ethnic groups. Discrimination exists if there is prejudicial treatment against a person or a group of people who speak a particular language or dialect. Language discrimination is suggested to be labelled linguicism or logocism. Anti-discriminatory and inclusive efforts to accommodate persons who speak different languages or cannot have fluency in the country's predominant or "official" language, is bilingualism such as official documents in two languages, and multiculturalism in more than two languages.

Reverse Discrimination

Some attempts at antidiscrimination have been criticized as reverse discrimination. In particular, minority quotas (e.g. affirmative action) discriminate against members of a dominant or majority group. In its opposition to race preferences, the American Civil Rights Institute's Ward Connerly stated, "There is nothing positive, affirmative, or equal about 'affirmative action' programs that give preference to some groups based on race." There are cases, however, such as the Noack v. YMCA case in U.S. Fifth Circuit Court, which include outright anti-male gender bias in a traditionally female work environment like childcare. That former employee claims to have suffered even physical assaults, and was allegedly also told to not hire too many blacks or men.

Disability Discrimination

Discrimination against people with disabilities in favor of people who are not is called ableism or disablism. Disability discrimination, which treats non-disabled individuals as the standard of 'normal living', results in public and private places and services, education, and social work that are built to serve 'standard' people, thereby excluding those with various disabilities.

In the United States, the Americans with Disabilities Act provides guidelines for providing wheelchair access for public institutions.

Religious Discrimination

Religious discrimination is valuing or treating a person or group differently because of what they do or do not believe. A concept like that of 'religious discrimination' is necessary to take into account ambiguities of the term *religious persecution*. The infamous cases in which people have been executed for beliefs perceived to be heretic are generally recognisable as persecution. Other cases in which adherents of different religions (or denominations) are treated unequally before the law are sometimes difficult to assess. If behind laws, regulations or acts of authority perceived to be discriminating against a certain religion, there is the intention 'encourage' people to abandon their beliefs, the laws are religious persuction. Laws which only carry light punishments are described as *mild forms of religious persecution* or as *religious discrimination*.

Furthermore, even in societies where Freedom of Religion is a constitutional right, sometimes adherents of religious minorities voice concerns about religious discrimination against them. Insofar as legal policies are concerned, cases that are perceived as religious discrimination might be the result of an interference of the religious sphere with other spheres of the public that are regulated by law (and not aimed specifically against a religious minority.) Generally people are free to have these issues clarified through the juridical system.

In a 1979 consultation on the issue, the United States commission on civil rights defined religious discrimination in relation to the civil rights guaranteed by the Fourteenth Amendment to the United States Constitution. Whereas religious civil liberties, such as the right to hold or not to hold a religious belief, are essential for Freedom of Religion (in the United States secured by the First Amendment), religious discrimination occurs when someone is denied " the equal protection of the laws, equality of status under the law, equal treatment in the administration of justice, and equality of opportunity and access to employment, education, housing, public services and facilities, and public accommodation because of their exercise of their right to religious freedom."

Situation in Western Countries

However, cases of religious discrimination might also be the result of an interference of the religious sphere with other spheres of the public that are regulated by law. Although e.g. in the United States the Free Exercise Clause of the First Amendment states that *"Congress shall make no law respecting an establishment of religion, or prohibiting the free exercise thereof"*, in *Reynolds v. United States* the U.S. supreme court decided that religious duty was not a suitable defense to a criminal indictment. In this specific case a law against bigamy was not considered to be discriminating against Mormons, who, at that time sometimes practiced Polygyny.

Similar current issues in the United States are about the policy towards drugs or environmental policy. Practitioners of one branch of the native American religion perceive the regulations regarding the use of Peyote and the eagle feather law in the United States as discriminating. Similar cases can be found in many other western countries.

Theories

Discrimination

Social theories such as Egalitarianism claim that social equality should prevail. In some societies, including most developed countries, each individual's civil rights include the right to be free from government sponsored social discrimination. Due to a belief in the capacity to perceive pain and/or suffering shared by all animals, 'abolitionist' or 'vegan' egalitarianism maintains that the interests of every individual (regardless its species), warrant equal consideration with the interests of humans, and that not doing so is "speciesist".

Conservative and Anarcho-Capitalist

In contrast, conservative writer and law professor Matthias Storme has claimed that the freedom of discrimination in human societies is a fundamental human right, or more precisely, the basis of all fundamental freedoms and therefore the most fundamental freedom. Author Hans-Hermann Hoppe, in an essay about his book Democracy: The God That Failed, asserts that a natural social order is characterized by increased discrimination.

Labeling Theory

Discrimination, in labeling theory, takes form as mental categorisation of minorities and the use of stereotype. This theory describes difference as deviance from the norm, which results in internal devaluation and social stigma that may be seen as discrimination. It is started by describing a 'natural' social order. It is distinguished between the fundamental principle of fascism and social democracy. The Nazis in 1930's-era Germany, the pre-1990 Apartheid government of South Africa used racial discriminatory agendas for their political ends. This practice continues with some present day governments.

Stereotypes and Scapegoats

Stereotyping is a type of discrimination. When a person is stereotyping they are thinking in terms of inflexible categories, and is linked to the psychological mechanism called displacement. Displacement is when one feels feelings of hostility or anger toward objects that are not the origin of those feelings. Many people blame scapegoats for problems that are not their fault. This is common when two deprived ethnic groups compete with one another for economic rewards. This is normally directed against groups that are relatively powerless, because they make an easy target. It frequently involves projection, which is the unconscious attribution to the others of ones own desires or characteristics.

5

A Woman's Place in Social Hieranchy

For centuries, women have moaned and often rightfully struggled for rights. But what exactly do we mean by rights? What is equality? I am a woman and I don't believe women have rights regardless of many claiming them to be making their own choices in education, work and relationships.

Nevertheless, I believe rights have been given but they have also been taken away. Let's start with the constant media exploitation of women today. Women think they are doing certain things such as modelling, getting cosmetic surgery, the latest fashion, the career etc etc and making the decisions themselves. However, little do we know that these are not our choices but are the choices made by money and power hungry men who are behind all this subliminal messages sent out to us all, dressed up as something it most certainly is not. 'Choice for women'? Yeah right! Exploitation of women has moved from direct and obvious stereotyping and labelling to the more damaging yet subtle exploitation through the clever use of newspapers, magazines television and radio.

So why do so many women think they are doing what they want? Are they? Really? Take a look at your life now, what is it that is making you happy and what isn't? You will find that following the constant whispers of society's norm is dictating your life without you even realising it. Women are the prime targets for exploitation due to their fragile nature and their never-ending quest to conform to the ever-changing demands of society losing sight of reality and what is really important to them. Women are going from caring individuals to superficial beings, from humans to robots, from women to puppets controlled by the individuals we are so desperate to get respect from...MEN. However, this respect will never be gained if we as women do not empower ourselves and respect ourselves.

"When you grow up, you can be whatever you want to be." Little girls in the United States hear this all the time, from their mothers to teachers to "Sesame Street" characters. Almost everywhere they go, they are encouraged to believe that girls can be just as smart, athletic, and successful as boys. Even the pictures of spunky women on magazine covers at the checkout stand tell them that when you're a girl, anything is possible.

But for little girls in developing countries, the message is just the opposite. From the day they are born, they are constantly reminded of the things they are not allowed to do.

Girls: Household Servants

When a boy is born in most developing countries, friends and relatives exclaim congratulations. A son means insurance. He will inherit his father's property and get a job to help support the family. When a girl is born, the reaction is very different. Some women weep when they find out their baby is a girl because, to them, a daughter is just another expense. Her place is in the home, not in the world of men. In some parts of India, it's traditional to greet a family with a newborn girl by saying, "The servant of your household has been born."

A girl can't help but feel inferior when everything around her tells her that she is worth less than a boy. Her identity is forged as soon as her family and society limit her opportunities and declare her to be second-rate. A combination of extreme poverty and deep biases against women creates a remorseless cycle of discrimination that keeps girls in developing countries from living up to their full potential. It also leaves them vulnerable to severe physical and emotional abuse. These "servants of the household" come to accept that life will never be any different.

Greatest Obstacles Affecting Girls

Discrimination against girls and women in the developing world is a devastating reality. It results in millions of individual tragedies, which add up to lost potential for entire countries. Studies show there is a direct link between a country's attitude toward women and its progress socially and economically. The status of women is central to the health of a society. If one part suffers, so does the whole.

Tragically, female children are most defenseless against the trauma of gender discrimination. The following obstacles are stark examples of what girls worldwide face. But the good news is that new generations of girls represent the most promising source of change for women—and men—in the developing world today.

Dowry

In developing countries, the birth of a girl causes great upheaval for poor families. When there is barely enough food to survive, any child puts a strain on a family's resources. But the monetary drain of a daughter feels even more severe, especially in regions where dowry is practiced.

Dowry is goods and money a bride's family pays to the husband's family. Originally intended to help with marriage expenses, dowry came to be seen as payment to the groom's family for taking on the burden of another woman. In some countries, dowries are extravagant, costing years' worth of wages, and often throwing a woman's family into debt. The dowry practice makes the prospect of having a girl even more distasteful to poor families. It also puts young women in danger: A new bride is at the mercy of her in-laws should they decide her dowry is too small. UNICEF estimates that around 5,000 Indian women are killed in dowry-related incidents each year.

Neglect

The developing world is full of poverty-stricken families who see their daughters as an economic predicament. That attitude has resulted in the widespread neglect of baby girls in Africa, Asia, and South America. In many communities, it's a regular practice to breastfeed girls for a shorter time than boys so that women can try to get pregnant again with a boy as soon as possible. As a result, girls miss out on life-giving nutrition during a crucial window of their development, which stunts their growth and weakens their resistance to disease.

Statistics show that the neglect continues as they grow up. Young girls receive less food, healthcare and fewer vaccinations overall than boys. Not much changes as they become women. Tradition calls for women to eat last, often reduced to picking over the leftovers from the men and boys.

Infanticide and Sex-Selective Abortion

In extreme cases, parents make the horrific choice to end their baby girl's life. One woman named Lakshmi from Tamil Nadu, an impoverished region of India, fed her baby sap from an oleander bush mixed with castor oil until the girl bled from the nose and died. "A daughter is always liabilities. How can I bring up a second?" said Lakshmi to explain why she chose to end her baby's life. "Instead of her suffering the way I do, I thought it was better to get rid of her."

Sex-selective abortions are even more common than infanticides in India. They are growing ever more frequent as technology makes it simple and cheap to determine a fetus' gender. In Jaipur, a Western Indian city of 2 million people, 3,500 sex-determined abortions are carried out every year. The gender ratio across India has dropped to an unnatural low of 927 females to 1,000 males due to infanticide and sex-based abortions.

China has its own long legacy of female infanticide. In the last two decades, the government's infamous one-child policy has weakened the country's track record even more. By restricting household size to limit the population, the policy gives parents just one chance to produce a coveted son before being forced to pay heavy fines for additional children. In 1997, the World Health Organization declared, "...more than 50 million women were estimated to be 'missing' in China because of the institutionalized killing and neglect of girls due to Beijing's population control program." The Chinese government says that sex-selective abortion is one major explanation for the staggering number of Chinese girls who have simply vanished from the population in the last 20 years.

Abuse

Even after infancy, the threat of physical harm follows girls throughout their lives. Women in every society are vulnerable to abuse. But the threat is more severe for girls and women who live in societies where women's rights mean practically nothing. Mothers who lack their own rights have little protection to offer their daughters, much less themselves, from male relatives and other authority figures. The frequency of rape and violent attacks against women in the developing world is alarming. Forty-five percent of Ethiopian women say that they have been assaulted in their lifetimes. In 1998, 48 percent of Palestinian women admitted to being abused by an intimate partner within the past year.

In some cultures, the physical and psychological trauma of rape is compounded by an additional stigma. In cultures that maintain strict sexual codes for women, if a woman steps out of bounds—by choosing her own husband, flirting in public, or seeking divorce from an abusive partner—she has brought dishonor to her family and must be disciplined. Often, discipline means execution. Families commit "honour killings" to salvage their reputation tainted by disobedient women.

Appallingly, this "disobedience" includes rape. In 1999, a 16-year-old mentally handicapped girl in Pakistan who had been raped was brought before her tribe's judicial counsel. Although she was the victim and her attacker had been arrested, the counsel decided she had brought shame to the tribe and ordered her public execution. This case, which received a lot of publicity at the time, is not unusual. Three women fall victim to honour killings in Pakistan every day—including victims of rape. In areas of Asia, the Middle East, and even Europe, all responsibility for sexual misconduct falls, by default, to women.

Labour

For the young girls who escape these pitfalls and grow up relatively safely, daily life is still incredibly hard. School might be an option for a few years, but most girls are pulled out at age 9 or 10 when they're useful enough to work all day at home. Nine million more girls than boys miss out on school every year, according to UNICEF. While their brothers continue to go to classes or pursue their hobbies and play, they join the women to do the bulk of the housework.

Housework in developing countries consists of continuous, difficult physical labor. A girl is likely to work from before daybreak until the light drains away. She walks barefoot long distances several times a day carrying heavy buckets of water, most likely polluted, just to keep her family alive. She cleans, grinds corn, gathers fuel, tends to the fields, bathes her younger siblings, and prepares meals until she sits down to her own after all the men in the family have eaten. Most families can't afford modern appliances, so her tasks must be done by hand—crushing corn into meal with heavy rocks, scrubbing laundry against rough stones, kneading bread and cooking gruel over a blistering open fire. There is no time left in the day to learn to read and write or to play with friends. She collapses exhausted each night, ready to wake up the next morning to start another long workday.

Most of this labor is performed without recognition or reward. UN statistics show that although women produce half the world's food, they own only 1 percent of its farmland. In most African and Asian countries, women's work isn't even considered real labor. Should a woman take a job, she is expected to keep up all her responsibilities at home in addition to her new ones, with no extra help. Women's labor goes overlooked, even though it is crucial to the survival of each family.

Sex Trafficking

Some families decide it's more lucrative to send their daughters to a nearby town or city to get jobs that usually involve hard labor and little pay. That desperate need for income leaves girls easy prey to sex traffickers, particularly in Southeast Asia, where international tourism gorges the illegal industry. In Thailand, the sex trade has swelled without check into a main sector of the national economy. Families in small villages along the Chinese border are regularly approached by recruiters called "aunties" who ask for their daughters in exchange for six years' wages. Most Thai farmers earn only $150 a year. The offer can be too tempting to refuse.

The girls who are forced into prostitution to support their families often feel their burden deeply. "When I was at work, 50 percent of me hated what I was doing," said one 14-year-old girl, who felt conflicted about being taken out of a brothel in Chiang Mai, Thailand. "But the other 50 percent wanted to stay so that I could earn money for my parents. My father cannot work. He is very old and I must support the family. It is my job."

It's estimated that 1 million children around the world are involved in the sex trade; a third of all sex workers in Southeast Asia are between the ages of 12 and 17.

Girls' Education: Breaking the Pattern of Gender Discrimination

Education is the tool that can help break the pattern of gender discrimination and bring lasting change for women in developing countries.

Educated women are essential to ending gender bias, starting by reducing the poverty that makes discrimination even worse in the developing world. The most basic skills in literacy and arithmetic open up opportunities for better-paying jobs for women. Uneducated women in rural areas of Zambia, for instance, are twice as likely to live in poverty as those who have had eight or more years of education. The longer a girl is able to stay in school, the greater her chances to pursue worthwhile employment, higher education, and a life without the hazards of extreme poverty.

Women who have had some schooling are more likely to get married later, survive childbirth, have fewer and healthier children, and make sure their own children complete school. They also understand hygiene and nutrition better and are more likely to prevent disease by visiting health care facilities. The UN estimates that for every year a woman spends in primary school, the risk of her child dying prematurely is reduced by 8 percent. Girls' education also means comprehensive change for a society. As women get the opportunity to go to school and obtain higher-level jobs, they gain status in their communities. Status translates into the power to influence their families and societies.

Even bigger changes become possible as girls' education becomes the cultural norm. Women can't defend themselves against physical and sexual abuse until they have the authority to speak against it without fear. Knowledge gives that authority. Women who have been educated are half as likely to undergo harmful cultural practices such as female genital mutilation

(FGM) and four times as likely to protect their daughters from it. The Global Campaign for Education also states that a primary education defends women against HIV/AIDS infection—disproportionately high for women in developing countries—by giving "the most marginalized groups in society—notably young women—the status and confidence needed to act on information and refuse unsafe sex."

Women in India

The status of women in India has been subject to many great changes over the past few millennia. From equal status with men in ancient times through the low points of the medieval period, to the promotion of equal rights by many reformers, the history of women in India has been eventful. In modern India, women have adorned high offices in India including that of the President, Prime minister, Speaker of the Lok Sabha, Leader of Opposition, etc. The incumbent President of India is a woman.

History

There are very few texts specifically dealing with the role of women; an important exception is the *strIdharmapaddhati* of Tryambakayajvan, an official at Thanjavur around c.1730. The text compiles strictures on womenly behaviour dating back to the Apastamba sutra (c. 4th c. BCE). The opening verse goes:

mukhyo dharmaH smrtishu vihito bhartr shushrushanam hi :

The primary duty of women is enjoined to be service to one's husband.

Where the term *shushrusha* (lit. "desire to hear") covers a range of meanings from the devotee's homage to god, or the obsequious service of a slave.

Ancient India

Scholars believe that in ancient India, the women enjoyed equal status with men in all fields of life. However, some others hold contrasting views. Works by ancient Indian grammarians such as Patanjali and Katyayana suggest that women were educated in the early Vedic period Rigvedic verses suggest that the women married at a mature age and were probably free to select their husband. Scriptures such as Rig Veda and

Upanishads mention several women sages and seers, notably Gargi and Maitreyi.

Some kingdoms in the ancient India had traditions such as *nagarvadhu* ("bride of the city"). Women competed to win the coveted title of the *nagarvadhu*. Amrapali is the most famous example of a nagarvadhu.

According to studies, women enjoyed equal status and rights during the early Vedic period. However, later (approximately 500 B.C.), the status of women began to decline with the Smritis (esp. Manusmriti) and with the Islamic invasion of Babur and the Mughal empire and later Christianity curtailing women's freedom and rights. Although reformatory movements such as Jainism allowed women to be admitted to the religious order, by and large, the women in India faced confinement and restrictions. The practice of child marriages is believed to have started from around sixth century.

Medieval Period

The Indian woman's position in the society further deteriorated during the medieval period when Sati among some communities, child marriages and a ban on widow remarriages became part of social life among some communities in India. The Muslim conquest in the Indian subcontinent brought the purdah practice in the Indian society. Among the Rajputs of Rajasthan, the Jauhar was practised. In some parts of India, the Devadasis or the temple women were sexually exploited. Polygamy was widely practised especially among Hindu Kshatriya rulers. In many Muslim families, women were restricted to Zenana areas.

In spite of these conditions, some women excelled in the fields of politics, literature, education and religion. Razia Sultana became the only woman monarch to have ever ruled Delhi. The Gond queen Durgavati ruled for fifteen years, before she lost her life in a battle with Mughal emperor Akbar's general Asaf Khan in 1564. Chand Bibi defended Ahmednagar against the mighty Mughal forces of Akbar in 1590s. Jehangir's wife Nur Jehan effectively wielded imperial power and was recognized as the real force behind the Mughal throne. The Mughal princesses Jahanara and Zebunnissa were well-known poets, and also influenced the ruling administration Shivaji's mother,

Jijabai was deputed as queen regent, because of her ability as a warrior and an administrator. In South India, many women administered villages, towns, divisions and heralded social and religious institutions.

The Bhakti movements tried to restore women's status and questioned some of the forms of oppression. Mirabai, a female saint-poet, was one of the most important Bhakti movement figures. Some other female saint-poets from this period include Akka Mahadevi, Rami Janabai and Lal Ded. Bhakti sects within Hinduism such as the Mahanubhav, Varkari and many others were principle movements within the Hindu fold to openly advocate social justice and equality between men and women.

Shortly after the Bhakti movement, Guru Nanak, the first Guru of Sikhs also preached the message of equality between men and women. He advocated that women be allowed to lead religious assemblies; to perform and lead congregational hymn singing called Kirtan or Bhajan; become members of religious management committees; to lead armies on the battlefield; have equality in marriage, and equality in Amrit (Baptism). Other Sikh Gurus also preached against the discrimination against women.

Historical Practices

Traditions among some communities such as sati, jauhar, and devadasi have been banned and are largely defunct in modern India. However, some cases of these practices are still found in remote parts of India. The purdah is still practised by Indian women among some communities, and child marriage remains prevalent despite it being an illegal practice, especially under current Indian laws.

Sati

Sati is an old, largely defunct custom, among some communities in which the widow was immolated alive on her husband's funeral pyre. Although the act was supposed to be a voluntary on the widow's part, it is believed to have been sometimes forced on the widow. It was abolished by the British in 1829. There have been around forty reported cases of sati since independence. In 1987, the Roop Kanwar case of Rajasthan led to The Commission of Sati (Prevention) Act.

Jauhar

Jauhar refers to the practice of the voluntary immolation of all the wives and daughters of defeated warriors, in order to avoid capture and consequent molestation by the enemy. The practice was followed by the wives of defeated Rajput rulers, who are known to place a high premium on honour.

Purdah

Purdah is the practice among some communities of requiring women to cover their bodies so as to cover their skin and conceal their form. It imposes restrictions on the mobility of women, it curtails their right to interact freely and it is a symbol of the subordination of women. It does not reflect the religious teachings of either Hinduism or Islam, contrary to common belief, although misconception has occurred due to the ignorance and prejudices of religious leaders of both faiths.

Devadasis

Devadasi is a religious practice in some parts of southern India, in which women are "married" to a deity or temple. The ritual was well established by the 10th century A.D. In the later period, the illegitimate sexual exploitation of the devadasi's became a norm in some parts of India.

India, with a population of over one billion, is the world's second most populous country. Of that number, 120 million are women who live in poverty. India has 16 percent of the world's population, but only 2.4 percent of its land, resulting in great pressures on its natural resources.

Over 70 percent of India's population currently derive their livelihood from land resources, which includes 84 percent of the economically-active women.

India is one of the few countries where males significantly outnumber females, and this imbalance has increased over time. India's maternal mortality rates in rural areas are among the world's highest. From a global perspective, Indian accounts for 19 percent of all lives births and 27 percent of all maternal deaths.

"There seems to be a consensus that higher female mortality between ages one and five and high maternal mortality rates result in a deficit of females in the population. Chatterjee (1990) estimates that deaths of young girls in India exceed those of young boys by over 300,000 each year, and every sixth infant death is specifically due to gender discrimination." Of the 15 million baby girls born in India each year, nearly 25 percent will not live to see their 15th birthday.

"Although India was the first country to announce an official family planning program in 1952, its population grew from 361 million in 1951 to 844 million in 1991. India's total fertility rate of 3.8 births per woman can be considered moderate by world standards, but the sheer magnitude of population increase has resulted in such a feeling of urgency that containment of population growth is listed as one of the six most important objectives in the Eighth Five-Year Plan."

Since 1970, the use of modern contraceptive methods has risen from 10 percent to 40 percent, with great variance between northern and southern India. The most striking aspect of contraceptive use in India is the predominance of sterilization, which accounts for more than 85 percent of total modern contraception use, with female sterilization accounting for 90 percent of all sterilizations.

The Indian constitution grants women equal rights with men, but strong patriarchal traditions persist, with women's lives shaped by customs that are centuries old. In most Indian families, a daughter is viewed as a liability, and she is conditioned to believe that she is inferior and subordinate to men. Sons are idolized and celebrated. May you be the mother of a hundred sons is a common Hindu wedding blessing.

The origin of the Indian idea of appropriate female behaviour can be traced to the rules laid down by Manu in 200 B.C.: "by a young girl, by a young woman, or even by an aged one, nothing must be done independently, even in her own house". "In childhood a female must be subject to her father, in youth to her husband, when her lord is dead to her sons; a woman must never be independent." A study of women in the Swayam Shikshan Prayog (SSP), based in 20 villages in four districts in Maharashtra state was introduced in this way:

The primary issue all women in the SSP were struggling with was that of everyday survival. Insufficient incomes and the lack of employment were reported to be their most pressing concerns. Survival is a constant preoccupation and at its most basic, survival means food (Chambers 1983). The most common problems were the lack of basic amenities such as food, water, fuel, fodder and health facilities. In addition, the deterioration of the natural environment and the fact that many of their traditional occupations were no longer viable were conditions that were making it increasingly hard for women to continue sustaining their families, as they had done in the past.

SSP is a loose, informal network of women's collectives, voluntary organizations, action groups and unions.

Women are Malnourished

The exceptionally high rates of malnutrition in South Asia are rooted deeply in the soil of inequality between men and women. "...the poor care that is afforded to girls and women by their husbands and by elders is the first major reason for levels of child malnutrition that are markedly higher in South Asia than anywhere else in the world."

This point is made in the article, The Asian Enigma, published by Unicef in the 1996 Progress of Nations, in which the rates of childhood malnutrition in South Asia are compared with those in Africa. We learn that malnutrition is far worse in South Asia, directly due to the fact that women in South Asia have less voice and freedom of movement than in Africa. "Judgement and self-expression and independence largely denied, millions of women in South Asia have neither the knowledge nor the means nor the freedom to act in their own and their children's best interests."

"Gender disparities in nutrition are evident from infancy to adulthood. In fact, gender has been the most statistically significant determinant of malnutrition among young children and malnutrition is a frequent direct or underlying cause of death among girls below age 5. Girls are breast-fed less frequently and for shorter durations in infancy; in childhood and adulthood, males are fed first and better. Adult women consume approximately 1,000 fewer calories per day than men according to one estimate from Punjab. Comparison of household dietary intake studies in different parts of the country shows that nutritional equity between males and females is lower in northern than in southern states." Nutritional deprivation has two major consequences for women: they never reach their full growth potential and anaemia. Both are risk factors in pregnancy, with anaemia ranging from 40-50 percent in urban areas to 50-70 percent in rural areas. This condition complicates childbearing and result in maternal and infant deaths, and low birth weight infants.

One study found anaemia in over 95 percent of girls ages 6-14 in Calcutta, around 67 percent in the Hyderabad area, 73 percent in the New Delhi area, and about 18 percent in the Madras area. This study states, "The prevalence of anaemia among women ages 15-24 and 25-44 years follows similar patterns and levels. Besides posing risks during pregnancy, anaemia increases women's susceptibility to diseases such as tuberculosis and reduces the energy women have available for daily activities such as household chores, child care, and agricultural labor. Any severely anaemic individual is taxed by most physical activities, including walking at an ordinary pace.

Women are in Poor Health

Surviving through a normal life cycle is a resource-poor woman's greatest challenge.

"The practice of breast-feeding female children for shorter periods of time reflects the strong desire for sons. If women are particularly anxious to have a male child, they may deliberately try to become pregnant again as soon as possible after a female is born. Conversely, women may consciously seek to avoid another pregnancy after the birth of a male child in order to give maximum attention to the new son."

A primary way that parents discriminate against their girl children is through neglect during illness. When sick, little girls are not taken to the doctor as frequently as are their brothers. A study in Punjab shows that medical expenditures for boys are 2.3 times higher than for girls.

As adults, women get less health care than men. They tend to be less likely to admit that they are sick and they'll wait until their sickness has progressed before they seek help or help is sought for them. Studies on attendance at rural primary health centres reveal that more males than females are treated in almost all parts of the country, with differences greater in northern hospitals than southern ones, pointing to regional differences in the value placed on women. Women's socialization to tolerate suffering and their reluctance to be examined by male personnel are additional constraints in their getting adequate health care.

Maternal Mortality

India's maternal mortality rates in rural areas are among the highest in the world.

A factor that contributes to India's high maternal mortality rate is the reluctance to seek medical care for pregnancy - it is viewed as a temporary condition that will disappear. The estimates nationwide are that only 40-50 percent of women receive any antenatal care. Evidence from the states of Bihar, Rajasthan, Orissa, Uttar Pradesh, Maharashtra and Gujarat find registration for maternal and child health services to be as low as 5-22 percent in rural areas and 21-51 percent in urban areas.

Even a woman who has had difficulties with previous pregnancies is usually treated with home remedies only for three reasons: the decision that a pregnant woman seek help rests with the mother-in-law and husband; financial considerations; and fear that the treatment may be more harmful than the malady.

It is estimated that pregnancy-related deaths account for one-quarter of all fatalities among women aged 15 to 29, with well over two-thirds of them considered preventable. For every maternal death in India, an estimated 20 more women suffer from impaired health. One village-level study of rural women in Maharashtra determined on the basis of physical examinations that some 92 percent suffered from one or more gynecological disorder.

Contraception Use

Women's health is harmed by lack of access to and the poor quality of reproductive services.

"About 24.6 million couples, representing roughly 18 percent of all married women, want no more children but are not using contraception. The causes of this unmet need remain poorly understood, but a qualitative study in Tamil Nadu suggests that women's lack of decision-making power in the family, opportunity costs involved in seeking contraception, fear of child death, and poor quality of contraceptive service all play an important role."

Some estimates suggest that some 5 million abortions are performed annually in India, with the large majority being illegal. As a result, abortion-related mortality is high. Although abortion has been legal since 1972 in India, "studies suggest that although official policy seeks to make pregnancy-termination services widely available, in practice guidelines on abortion limit access to services, particularly in rural areas. In 1981, of the 6,200 physicians trained to perform abortions, only 1,600 were working in rural areas."

Job Impact on Maternal Health

Working conditions result in premature and stillbirths.

The tasks performed by women are usually those that require them to be in one position for long periods of time, which can adversely affect their reproductive health. A study in a rice-growing belt of coastal Maharashtra found that 40 percent of all infant deaths occurred in the months of July to October. The study also found that a majority of births were either premature or stillbirths. The study attributed this to the squatting position that had to be assumed during July and August, the rice transplanting months.

Impact of Pollution on Women

Women's health is further harmed by air and water pollution and lack of sanitation.

The impact of pollution and industrial wastes on health is considerable. In Environment, Development and the Gender Gap, Sandhya Venkateswaran asserts that "the high incidence of malnutrition present amongst women and their low metabolism and other health problems affect their capacity to deal with chemical stress. The smoke from household biomass (made up of wood, dung and crop residues) stoves within a three-hour period is equivalent to smoking 20 packs of cigarettes. For women who spend at least three hours per day cooking, often in a poorly ventilated area, the impact includes eye problems, respiratory problems, chronic bronchitis and lung cancer. One study quoted by WHO in 1991 found that pregnant women cooking over open biomass stoves had almost a 50 percent higher chance of stillbirth.

Anaemia makes a person more susceptible to carbon monoxide toxicity, which is one of the main pollutants in the biomass smoke. Given the number of Indian women who are anaemic - 25 to 30 percent in the reproductive age group and almost 50 percent in the third trimester - this adds to their vulnerability to carbon monoxide toxicity.

Additionally, with an increasing population, diseases caused by waste disposal, such as hookworm, are rampant. People who work barefooted are particularly susceptible, and it has been found that hookworm is directly responsible for the high percentage of anaemia among rural women.

Women are Uneducated

Women and girls receive far less education than men, due both to social norms and fears of violence. India has the largest population of non-school-going working girls.

India's constitution guarantees free primary school education for both boys and girls up to age 14. This goal has been repeatedly reconfirmed, but primary education in India is not universal. Overall, the literacy rate for women is 39 percent versus 64 percent for men. The rate for women in the four large northern states - Bihar, Uttar Pradesh, Rajasthan and Madhya Pradesh - is lower than the national average: it was 25 percent in 1991. Attendance rates from the 1981 census suggest that no more than 1/3 of all girls (and a lower proportion of rural girls) aged 5-14 are attending school.

Although substantial progress has been achieved since India won its independence in 1947, when less than 8 percent of females were literate, the gains have not been rapid enough to keep pace with population growth: there were 16 million more illiterate females in 1991 than in 1981.

Sonalde Desai in Gender Inequalities and Demographic Behaviour asserts that "parents' reluctance to educate daughters has its roots in the situation of women. Parents have several incentives for not educating their daughters. Foremost is the view that education of girls brings no returns to parents and that their future roles, being mainly reproductive and perhaps including agricultural labor, require no formal education. As more and more boys are engaged in education, there is a growing reliance on the labor of girls. Girls are increasingly replacing their brothers on the farm while carrying on their usual responsibilities in housework. A large proportion of the roughly 40 million "nonworking" girls who are not in school are kept at home because of responsibilities in housework."

The role of parents is to deliver a chaste daughter to her husband's family. Sonalde Desai goes on to point out that "another disincentive for sending daughters to school is a concern for the protection of their virginity. When schools are located at a distance, when teachers are male, and when girls are expected to study along with boys, parents are often unwilling to expose their daughters to the potential assault on their virginity." There is little response to counter these obstacles: school hours remain inflexible to the labor demands of girls; many villages do not have a school; and fewer than 1/3 of India's primary and middle-school teachers are women.

According to Mapping Progress, "educational funds were cut by 801.3 million rupees in the 1991-92 budget. Funds for the mass literacy movement, in which women participate enthusiastically, have been reduced by 5 percent from the previous year. Budgetary provisions for non-formal education have been cut by 17 percent, leading to closure of many night schools and adult education programs in which working-class women participate. Reduction in government expenditures on higher education and encouragement to private colleges will reduce women's opportunities for higher education since privatization in education promotes only male-dominated professional and technical courses, as they are lucrative."

Women are Overworked

Women work longer hours and their work is more arduous than men's. Still, men report that "women, like children, eat and do nothing."

Hours Worked

Women work roughly twice as many as many hours as men. Women's contribution to agriculture - whether it be subsistence farming or commercial agriculture - when measured in terms of the number of tasks performed and time spent, is greater than men. "The extent of women's contribution is aptly highlighted by a micro study conducted in the Indian Himalayas which found that on a one-hectare farm, a pair of bullocks works 1,064 hours, a man 1,212 hours and a woman 3,485 hours in a year."

In Andhra Pradesh, (Mies 1986) found that the work day of an woman agricultural labourer during the agricultural season lasts for 15 hours, from 4 am to 8 pm, with an hour's rest in between. Her male counterpart works for seven to eight hours, from 5 am to 10 am or 11 am and from 3 pm to 5 pm.

Another study on time and energy spent by men and women on agricultural work (Batliwala 1982) found that 53 percent of the total human hours per household are contributed by women as compared to 31 percent by men. The remaining contribution comes from children.

The linking of agricultural activities to male dominance is described by Roy Burman (in Menon 1991):

The anxiety of man to monopolize his skill in plough culture is reflected in the taboo that is observed almost all over India, against the women's handling the plough. In many societies, she is not even allowed to touch it.

Mies further observed that "whereas operations performed by men were those that entailed the use of machinery and draught animals, thereby using animal, hydraulic, mechanical or electrical energy, women almost always relied on manual labour, using only their own energy." Rice transplantations, the most arduous and labour intensive task in rice cultivation, is carried out entirely by women without the help of any tools.

"Girls learn to assist their mothers in almost all tasks, and from the age of 10 years participate fully in the agricultural work done by women. Mies cites the case of Laxmi, a three-year-old infant who, along with her mother, pulled seedlings for transplanting. Boys on the other hand were seldom seen transplanting or weeding though they did help out in ploughing or watering the fields."

"Not only do women perform more tasks, their work is also more arduous than that undertaken by men. Both transplantation and weeding require women to spend the whole day and work in muddy soil with their hands. Moreover, they work the entire day under the intensely hot sun while men's work, such as ploughing and watering the fields, is invariably carried out early in the morning before the sun gets too hot. Mies argues that because women's work, unlike men's, does not involve implements and is based largely on human energy, it is considered unskilled and hence less productive. On this basis, women are invariably paid lower wages, despite the fact that they work harder and for longer hours than do men."

In contrast, a study in Uttar Pradesh reports that men "only reluctantly conceded that their womenfolk really work. The researchers in this area were repeatedly told that women, like children, simply eat food and do nothing."

The Invisibility of Women's Work

Women's work is rarely recognized.

Many maintain that women's economic dependence on men impacts their power within the family. With increased participation in income-earning activities, not only will there be more income for the family, but gender inequality should be reduced. This issue is particularly salient in India because studies show a very low level of female participation in the labor force. This under-reporting is attributed to the frequently held view that women's work is not economically productive.

In a report of the National Commission on Self-Employed Women and Women in the Informal Sector, the director of social welfare in one state said, "There are no women in any unorganized sector in our state." When the Commission probed and asked, "Are there any women who go to the forest to collect firewood? Do any of the women in rural areas have cattle?" the director responded with, "Of course, there are many women doing that type of work." Working women are invisible to most of the population.

If all activities - including maintenance of kitchen gardens and poultry, grinding food grains, collecting water and firewood, etc. - are taken into account, then 88 percent of rural housewives and 66 percent of urban housewives can be considered as economically productive. Women's employment in family farms or businesses is rarely recognized as economically productive, either by men or women. And, any income generated from this work is generally controlled by the men. Such work is unlikely to increase women's participation in allocating family finances. In a 1992 study of family-based texile workers, male children who helped in a home-based handloom mill were given pocket money, but the adult women and girls were not.

The Impact of Technology on Women

The shift from subsistence to a market economy has a dramatic negative impact on women.

According to Sandhya Venkateswaran, citing Shiva, the Green Revolution, which focused on increasing yields of rice and wheat, entailed a shift in inputs from human to technical. Women's participation, knowledge and inputs were marginalized, and their role shift from being "primary producers to subsidiary workers."

Where technology has been introduced in areas where women worked, women labourers have often been displaced by men. Threshing of grain was almost exclusively a female task, and with the introduction of automatic grain threshers - which are only operated by men - women have lost an important source of income.

Combine harvesters leave virtually no residue. This means that this source of fodder is no longer available to women, which has a dramatic impact on women's workload. So too, as cattle dung is being used as fertilizer, there is less available for fuel for cooking.

"Commercialization and the consequent focus on cash crops has led to a situation where food is lifted straight from the farm to the market. The income accrued is controlled by men. Earlier, most of the produce was brought home and stored, and the women exchanged it for other commodities. Such a system vested more control with the women."

Women are Unskilled

Women have unequal access to resources.

Extension services tend to reach only men, which perpetuates the existing division of labour in the agricultural sector, with women continuing to perform unskilled tasks. A

World Bank study in 1991 reveals that the assumption made by extension workers is that information within a family will be transmitted to the women by the men, which in actual practice seldom happens. "The male dominated extension system tends to overlook women's role in agriculture and proves ineffective in providing technical information to women farmers."

Mapping Progress, states, "in the farm sector, the process of mechanization of agricultural activities has brought in tendencies for gender discrimination by replacing men for a number of activities performed by women and also by displacing the labor of women from subsistence and marginal households. Women are employed only when there is absolute shortage of labor and for specific operations like cotton-picking.

"To supply food-processing industries being set up with foreign collaboration, there has already been a major shift from subsistence farming method of rice, millet, corn and wheat to cash-crop production of fruit, mushrooms, flowers and vegetables. This shift has led to women being the first to lose jobs."

A number of factors perpetuate women's limited job skills: if training women for economic activities requires them to leave their village, this is usually a problem for them. Unequal access to education restricts women's abilities to learn skills that require even functional levels of literacy. In terms of skill development, women are impeded by their lack of mobility, low literacy levels and prejudiced attitudes toward women. When women negotiate with banks and government officials, they are often ostracized by other men and women in their community for being 'too forward.' Government and bank officials have preconceived ideas of what women are capable of, and stereotypes of what is considered women's work.

Women are Mistreated

Violence against women and girls is the most pervasive human rights violation in the world today.

Opening the door on the subject of violence against the world's females is like standing at the threshold of an immense dark chamber vibrating with collective anguish, but with the sounds of protest throttled back to a murmur. Where there should be outrage aimed at an intolerable status quo there is instead denial, and the largely passive acceptance of 'the way things are.'

Male violence against women is a worldwide phenomenon. Although not every woman has experienced it, and many expect not to, fear of violence is an important factor in the lives of most women. It determines what they do, when they do it, where they do it, and with whom. Fear of violence is a cause of women's lack of participation in activities beyond the home, as well as inside it. Within the home, women and girls may be subjected to physical and sexual abuse as punishment or as culturally justified assaults. These acts shape their attitude to life, and their expectations of themselves.

The insecurity outside the household is today the greatest obstacle in the path of women. Conscious that, compared to the atrocities outside the house, atrocities within the house are endurable, women not only continued to accept their inferiority in the house and society, but even called it sweet.

In recent years, there has been an alarming rise in atrocities against women in India. Every 26 minutes a woman is molested. Every 34 minutes a rape takes place. Every 42 minutes a sexual harassment incident occurs. Every 43 minutes a woman is kidnapped. And every 93 minutes a woman is burnt to death over dowry.

One-quarter of the reported rapes involve girls under the age of 16 but the vast majority are never reported. Although the penalty is severe, convictions are rare.

Selective Abortions

The most extreme expression of the preference for sons is female infanticide and sex-selective abortion.

A study of amniocentesis in a Bombay hospital found that 96 percent of female fetuses were aborted, compared with only a small percentage of male fetuses.

"Government officials event suspect that the disproportionate abortion of female fetuses may be a major underlying cause of the recent decline in the nation's sex ratio. In 1971 there were 930 females for every 1,000 males. A decade later this figure had increased to 934, but by 1991, instead of continuing to rise, the ratio dropped to 927, lower than the

1971 figure. This sex ratio is one of the lowest in the world." Sonalda Desai reports that there are posters in Bombay advertising sex-determination tests that read, "It is better to pay 500 Rs. now than 50,000 Rs. (in dowry) later."

Government has passed legislation to curb the misuse of amniocentesis for sex selection and abortion of female fetuses. Women activists have been critical of this act because of its provision that calls for punishing the women who seek the procedure. These women may be under pressure to bear a male child.

Women are Powerless

Legal protection of women's rights have little effect in the face of prevailing patriarchal traditions.

Marriage: Women are subordinate in most marriages.

Exposure to and interactions with the outside world are instrumental in determining the possibilities available to women in their daily lives. The situation of women is affected by the degree of their autonomy or capacity to make decisions both inside and outside their own household.

"The position of women in northern India is notably poor. Traditional Hindu society in northern rural areas is hierarchical and dominated by men, as evidenced by marriage customs. North Indian Hindus are expected to marry within prescribed boundaries: the bride and groom must not be related, they have no say in the matter, and the man must live outside the woman's natal village.

"Wife givers" are socially and ritually inferior to "wife takers", thus necessitating the provision of a dowry. After marriage, the bride moves in with her husband's family. Such a bride is "a stranger in a strange place." They are controlled by the older females in the household, and their behaviour reflects on the honour of their husbands. Because emotional ties between spouses are considered a potential threat to the solidarity of the patrilineal group, the northern system tends to segregate the sexes and limit communication between spouses - a circumstance that has direct consequences for family planning and similar "modern" behaviours that affect health. A young Indian bride is brought up to believe that her own wishes and interests are subordinate to those of her husband and his family. The primary duty of a newly married young woman, and virtually her only means of improving her position in the hierarchy of her husband's household, is to bear sons."

Sonalde Desai points out that the perception that sons are the major source of economic security in old age is so strong in the north that "many parents, while visiting their married daughters, do not accept food or other hospitality from them. However, given women's low independent incomes and lack of control over their earnings, few can provide economic support to their parents even if parents were willing to accept it."

In the south, in contrast, a daughter traditionally marries her mother's brother or her mother's brother's son (her first cousin). Such an arrangement has a dramatic impact on women. "In southern India, men are likely to marry women to whom they are related, so that the strict distinction found in the north between patrilineal and marital relatives is absent. Women are likely to be married into family households near their natal homes, and are more likely to retain close relationships with their natal kin."

"Over the past several decades, however, marriage patterns have changed markedly. Social, economic, and demographic developments have made marriages between close relatives less common, and the bride price has given way to a dowry system akin to that in the north. Nevertheless, as long as the underlying ethic of marriage in the south remains the reinforcement of existing kinship ties, the relatively favorable situation of southern Indian women is unlikely to be threatened."

Child Marriages

Child marriages keep women subjugated.

A 1976 amendment to the Child Marriage Restraint Act raised the minimum legal age for marriage from 15 to 18 for young women and from 18 to 21 for young men. However, in many rural communities, illegal child marriages are still common. In some rural areas, nearly half the girls between 10 and 14 are married. Because there is pressure on women to prove their fertility by conceiving as soon as possible after marriage, adolescent marriage is synonymous with adolescent childbearing: roughly 10-15 percent of all births take place to women in their teens.

A May 1998 article in the New York Times states: Child marriages contribute to virtually every social malaise that keeps India behind in women's rights. The problems include soaring birth rates, grinding poverty and malnutrition, high illiteracy and infant mortality and low life expectancy, especially among rural women. The article cites a 1993 survey of more than 5,000 women in Rajasthan, which showed that 56 percent of them had married before they were 15. Barely 18 percent of them were literate and only 3 percent used any form of birth control other than sterilization. Sixty-three percent of the children under age 4 of these women were severely undernourished.

"Each year, formal warnings are posted outside state government offices stating that child marriages are illegal, but they have little impact." One man interviewed for the article has seven daughters. He borrowed some 60,000 rupees to pay for the dowries for six of his daughters, ranging in age from 4-14. He reported that "the weddings mean that he can now look forward to growing old without being trapped in the penury by the need to support his daughters." (NYT)

Dowries

Women are kept subordinate, and are even murdered, by the practice of dowry.

In India, 6,000 dowry murders are committed each year. This reality exists even though the Dowry Prohibition Act has been in existence for 33 years, and there are virtually no arrests under the Act. Since those giving as well as those accepting dowry are punishable under the existing law, no one is willing to complain. It is only after a "dowry death" that the complaints become public. It is estimated that the average dowry today is equivalent to five times the family's annual income and that the high cost of weddings and dowries is a major cause of indebtedness among India's poor.

A December 1997 article in India Today, entitled, Victims of Sudden Affluence states, "A woman on fire has made dowry deaths the most vicious of social crimes; it is an evil endemic to the subcontinent but despite every attempt at justice the numbers have continued to climb. With get-rich-quick becoming the new mantra, dowry became the perfect instrument for upward material mobility." A study done by a policy think-tank, the Institute of Development and Communication, states, "the quantum of dowry exchange may still be greater among the upper classes, but 80 percent of dowry deaths and 80 percent of dowry harassment occurs in the middle and lower stratas."

The article goes on to state, "So complete is the discrimination among women that the gender bias is extended even toward the guilty. In a bizarre trend, the onus of murder is often put on the women to protect the men. Sometimes it is by consent. Often, old mothers-in-law embrace all the blame to bail out their sons and husbands."

Despite every stigma, dowry continues to be the signature of marriage. Says Rainuka Dagar, "It is taken as a normative custom and dowry harassment as a part of family life."

Divorce

Divorce is not a viable option.

Divorce is rare - it is a considered a shameful admission of a woman's failure as a wife and daughter-in-law. In 1990, divorced women made up a miniscule 0.08 percent of the total female population.

Maintenance rights of women in the case of divorce are weak. Although both Hindu and Muslim law recognize the rights of women and children to maintenance, in practice, maintenance is rarely set at a sufficient amount and is frequently violated.

Both Hindu and Muslim personal laws fail to recognize matrimonial property. Upon divorce, women have no rights to their home or to other property accumulated during marriage; in effect, their contributions to the maintenance of the family and accumulation of family assets go unrecognized and unrewarded.

Inheritance

Women's rights to inheritance are limited and frequently violated.

In the mid-1950s the Hindu personal laws, which apply to all Hindus, Buddhists, Sikhs and Jains, were overhauled, banning polygamy and giving women rights to inheritance, adoption and divorce. The Muslim personal laws differ considerably from that of the Hindus, and permit polygamy. Despite various laws protecting women's rights, traditional patriarchal attitudes still prevail and are strengthened and perpetuated in the home.

Under Hindu law, sons have an independent share in the ancestral property. However, daughters' shares are based on the share received by their father. Hence, a father can effectively disinherit a daughter by renouncing his share of the ancestral property, but the son will continue to have a share in his own right. Additionally, married daughters, even those facing marital harassment, have no residential rights in the ancestral home.

Even the weak laws protecting women have not been adequately enforced. As a result, in practice, women continue to have little access to land and property, a major source of income and long-term economic security. Under the pretext of preventing fragmentation of agricultural holdings, several states have successfully excluded widows and daughters from inheriting agricultural land.

Women in Public Office

Panchayat Raj Institutions

The highest national priority must be the unleashing of woman power in governance. That is the single most important source of societal energy that we have kept corked for half a century. —Mani Shankar Aiyar, journalist, India Today

Through the experience of the Indian Panchayat Raj Institutions (PRI) 1 million women have actively entered political life in India. The 73rd and 74th Constitutional Amendment Acts, which guarantee that all local elected bodies reserve one-third of their seats for women, have spearheaded an unprecedented social experiment which is playing itself out in more than 500,000 villages that are home to more than 600 million people. Since the creation of the quota system, local women-the vast majority of them illiterate and poor-have come to occupy as much as 43% of the seats, spurring the election of increasing numbers of women at the district, provincial and national levels. Since the onset of PRI, the percentages of women in various levels of political activity have risen from 4-5% to 25-40%.

According to Indian writer and activist Devaki Jain, "the positive discrimination of PRI has initiated a momentum of change. Women's entry into local government in such large numbers, often more than the required 33.3 %, and their success in campaigning, including the defeat of male candidates, has shattered the myth that women are not interested in politics, and have no time to go to meetings or to undertake all the other work that is required in political party processes...PRI reminds us of a central truth: power is not something people give away. It has to be negotiated, and sometimes wrested from the powerful."

Contrary to fears that the elected women would be rubber stamp leaders, the success stories that have arisen from PRI are impressive. A government-financed study, based on field work in 180 villages in the states of Uttar Pradesh, Rajasthan and Madhya Pradesh, and coordinated by the Center for Women's Development Studies in New Delhi, has found that a full two-thirds of elected women leaders are actively engaged in learning the ropes and exercising power. Says Noeleen Heyzer, executive director of UNIFEM, "This is one of the best innovations in grass-roots democracy in the world."

Women leaders in the Panchayati Raj are transforming local governance by sensitizing the State to issues of poverty, inequality and gender injustice. Through the PRI, they are tackling issues that had previously gone virtually unacknowledged, including water, alcohol abuse, education, health and domestic violence. According to Sudha Murali, UNICEF Communications Officer in Andhra Pradesh, women are seeing this power as a chance for a real change for them and for their children and are using it to demand basic facilities like primary schools and health care centres.

The PRI has also brought about significant transformations in the lives of women themselves, who have become empowered, and have gained self-confidence, political awareness and affirmation of their own identity. The panchayat villages have become political training grounds to women, many of them illiterate, who are now leaders in the village panchayats. Says Sudha Pillai, joint secretary in India's Ministry for Rural Development, "It has given something to people who were absolute nobodies and had no way of making it on their own. Power has become the source of their growth."

By asserting control over resources and officials and by challenging men, women are discovering a personal and collective power that was previously unimaginable. This includes women who are not themselves panchayat leaders, but who have been inspired by the work of their sisters; "We will not bear it," says one woman. Once we acquire some position and power, we will fight it out...The fact that the Panchayats will have a minimum number of women [will be used] for mobilizing women at large." It is this critical mass of unified and empowered women which will push forward policies that enforce gender equity into the future.

An observation by Deepak Tiwari in This Week, India's No.1 Weekly News Magazine, displays the promising future made possible by the PRI. He notes, "'Learning politics' is the latest fad for young village girls, who dream of joining the growing band of women panchayat representatives, 164,060 at last count, in the state."

Conclusion

As UN Secretary General Kofi Annan has stated, "Gender equality is more than a goal in itself. It is a precondition for meeting the challenge of reducing poverty, promoting sustainable development and building good governance."

This recognition is currently missing in India. Transforming the prevailing social discrimination against women must become the top priority, and must happen concurrently with increased direct action to rapidly improve the social and economic status of women. In this way, a synergy of progress can be achieved.

As women receive greater education and training, they will earn more money.

As women earn more money - as has been repeatedly shown - they spend it in the further education and health of their children, as opposed to men, who often spend it on drink, tobacco or other women.

As women rise in economic status, they will gain greater social standing in the household and the village, and will have greater voice. As women gain influence and consciousness, they will make stronger claims to their entitlements - gaining further training, better access to credit and higher incomes - and command attention of police and courts when attacked.

As women's economic power grows, it will be easier to overcome the tradition of "son preference" and thus put an end to the evil of dowry. As son preference declines and acceptance of violence declines, families will be more likely to educate their daughters, and age of marriage will rise.

For every year beyond 4th grade that girls go to school, family size shrinks 20%, child deaths drop 10% and wages rise 20%. As women are better nourished and marry later, they will be healthier, more productive, and will give birth to healthier babies. Only through action to remedy discrimination against women can the vision of India's independence - an India where all people have the chance to live health and productive lives-be realized.

Land and Property Rights

In most Indian families, women do not own any property in their own names, and do not get a share of parental property. Due to weak enforcement of laws protecting them, women continue to have little access to land and property. In fact, some of the laws discriminate against women, when it comes to land and property rights.

The Hindu personal laws of mid-1956s (applied to Hindus, Buddhists, Sikhs and Jains) gave women rights to inheritance. However, the sons had an independent share in the ancestral property, while the daughters' shares were based on the share received by their father. Hence, a father could effectively disinherit a daughter by renouncing his share of the ancestral property, but the son will continue to have a share in his own right. Additionally, married daughters, even those facing marital harassment, had no residential rights in the ancestral home. After amendment of Hindu laws in 2005, now women in have been provided the same status as that of men. In 1986, the Supreme Court of India ruled that Shah Bano, an old divorced Muslim woman was eligible for maintenance money. However, the decision was vociferously opposed by fundamentalist Muslim leaders, who alleged that the court was interfering in their personal law. The Union Government subsequently passed the Muslim Women's (Protection of Rights Upon Divorce) Act. Similarly, the Christian women have struggled over years for equal rights of divorce and succession. In 1994, all the churches, jointly with women's organisations, drew up a draft law called the Christian Marriage and Matrimonial Causes Bill. However, the government has still not amended the relevant laws.

Crimes against Women

Police records show high incidence of crimes against women in India. The National Crime Records Bureau reported in 1998 that the growth rate of crimes against women would be higher than the population growth rate by 2010. Earlier, many cases were not registered with the police due to the social stigma attached to rape and molestation cases. Official statistics show that there has been a dramatic increase in the number of reported crimes against women.

Sexual Harassment

Half of the total number of crimes against women reported in 1990 related to molestation and harassment at the workplace. Eve teasing is a euphemism used for sexual harassment or molestation of women by men. Many activists blame the rising incidents of sexual harassment against women on the influence of "Western culture". In 1987, The Indecent Representation of Women (Prohibition) Act was passed to prohibit indecent representation of women through advertisements or in publications, writings, paintings, figures or in any other manner. In 1997, in a landmark judgement, the Supreme Court of India took a strong stand against sexual harassment of women in the workplace. The Court also laid down detailed guidelines for prevention and redressal of grievances. The National Commission for Women subsequently elaborated these guidelines into a Code of Conduct for employers.

Dowry

In 1961, the Government of India passed the Dowry Prohibition Act, making the dowry demands in wedding arrangements illegal. However, many cases of dowry-related domestic violence, suicides and murders have been reported. In the 1980s, numerous such cases were reported.

In 1985, the Dowry Prohibition (maintenance of lists of presents to the bride and bridegroom) rules were framed. According to these rules, a signed list of presents given at the time of the marriage to the bride and the bridegroom should be maintained. The list should contain a brief description of each present, its approximate value, the name of whoever has given the present and his/her relationship to the person. However, such rules are hardly enforced.

A 1997 report claimed that at least 5,000 women die each year because of dowry deaths, and at least a dozen die each day in 'kitchen fires' thought to be intentional. The term for this is "bride burning" and is criticized within India itself. Amongst the urban educated, such dowry abuse has reduced considerably.

Child Marriage

Child marriage has been traditionally prevalent in India and continues to this day. Historically, young girls would live with their parents till they reached puberty. In the past, the child widows were condemned to a life of great agony, shaving heads, living in isolation, and shunned by the society. Although child marriage was outlawed in 1860, it is still a common practice.

According to UNICEF's "State of the World's Children-2009" report, 47% of India's women aged 20–24 were married before the legal age of 18, with 56% in rural areas. The report also showed that 40% of the world's child marriages occur in India.

Female Infanticides and Sex Selective Abortions

India has a highly masculine sex ratio, the chief reason being that many women die before reaching adulthood. Tribal societies in India have a less masculine sex ratio than all other caste groups. This, in spite of the fact that tribal communities have far lower levels of income, literacy and health facilities. It is therefore suggested by many experts, that the highly masculine sex ratio in India can be attributed to female infanticides and sex-selective abortions.

All medical tests that can be used to determine the sex of the child have been banned in India, due to incidents of these tests being used to get rid of unwanted female children before birth. Female infanticide (killing of girl infants) is still prevalent in some rural areas. The abuse of the dowry tradition has been one of the main reasons for sex-selective abortions and female infanticides in India.

Trafficking

The Immoral Traffic (Prevention) Act was passed in 1956. However many cases of trafficking of young girls and women have been reported. These women are either forced into prostitution, domestic work or child labour.

Other Concerns

Health

The average female life expectancy today in India is low compared to many countries, but it has shown gradual improvement over the years. In many families, especially rural ones, the girls and women face nutritional discrimination within the family, and are anaemic and malnourished.

The maternal mortality in India is the second highest in the world. Only 42% of births in the country are supervised by health professionals. Most women deliver with help from women in the family who often lack the skills and resources to save the mother's life if it is in danger. According to UNDP Human Development Report (1997), 88% of pregnant women (age 15-49) were found to be suffering from anaemia.

Family Planning

The average woman in rural areas of India has little or no control over her reproductivity. Women, particularly women in rural areas, do not have access to safe and self-controlled methods of contraception. The public health system emphasises permanent methods like sterilisation, or long-term methods like IUDs that do not need follow-up. Sterilization accounts for more than 75% of total contraception, with female sterilisation accounting for almost 95% of all sterilisations.

6

Culture and Anarchy

Culture (from the Latin *cultura* stemming from *colere*, meaning "to cultivate") is a term that has various meanings. For example, in 1952, Alfred Kroeber and Clyde Kluckhohn compiled a list of 164 definitions of "culture" in *Culture: A Critical Review of Concepts and Definitions*. However, the word "culture" is most commonly used in three basic senses:

- Excellence of taste in the fine arts and humanities, also known as high culture
- An integrated pattern of human knowledge, belief, and behaviour that depends upon the capacity for symbolic thought and social learning
- The set of shared attitudes, values, goals, and practices that characterizes an institution, organization or group

When the concept first emerged in eighteenth- and nineteenth-century Europe, it connoted a process of cultivation or improvement, as in agriculture or horticulture. In the nineteenth century, it came to refer first to the betterment or refinement of the individual, especially through education, and then to the fulfillment of national aspirations or ideals. In the mid-nineteenth century, some scientists used the term "culture" to refer to a universal human capacity. For the German nonpositivist sociologist, Georg Simmel, culture referred to "the cultivation of individuals through the agency of external forms which have been objectified in the course of history".

Language and Culture

The connection between culture and language has been

noted as far back as the classical period and probably long before. The ancient Greeks, for example, distinguished between civilized peoples and bárbaros "those who babble", i.e. those who speak unintelligible languages. The fact that different groups speak different, unintelligible languages is often considered more tangible evidence for cultural differences than other less obvious cultural traits.

Indeed, the origin of language, understood as the human capacity of complex symbolic communication, and the origin of complex culture is often thought to stem from the same evolutionary process in early man. Linguists and evolutionary anthropologists suppose that language evolved as early humans began to live in large communities which required the use of complex communication to maintain social coherence. Language and culture then both emerged as a means of using symbols to construct social identity and maintain coherence within a social group too large to rely exclusively on pre-human ways of building community such as for example grooming. Since language and culture are both in essence symbolic systems, twentieth century cultural theorists have applied the methods of analyzing language developed in the science of linguistics to also analyze culture. Particularly the structural theory of Ferdinand de Saussure, which describes symbolic systems as consisting of signs (a pairing of a particular form with a particular meaning), has come to be applied widely in the study of culture. But also post-structuralist theories, that nonetheless still rely on the parallel between language and culture as systems of symbolic communication, have been applied in the field of semiotics. The parallel between language and culture can then be understood as analog to the parallel between a linguistic sign, consisting for example of the sound [kau] and the meaning "cow", and a cultural sign, consisting for example of the cultural form of "wearing a crown" and the cultural meaning of "being king". In this way it can be argued that culture is itself a kind of language. Another parallel between cultural and linguistic systems is that they are both systems of practice, that is they are a set of special ways of doing things that is constructed and perpetuated through social interactions. Children, for example, acquire language in the same way as they acquire the basic cultural norms of the society they grow up in – through interaction with older members of their cultural group.

However, languages, now understood as the particular set of speech norms of a particular community, are also a part of the larger culture of the community that speak them. Humans use language as a way of signalling identity with one cultural group and difference from others. Even among speakers of one language several different ways of using the language exist, and each is used to signal affiliation with particular subgroups within a larger culture. In linguistics such different ways of using the same language are called "varieties".

For example, the English language is spoken differently in the USA, the UK and Australia, and even within English-speaking countries there are hundreds of dialects of English that each signal a belonging to a particular region and/or subculture. For example, in the UK the cockney dialect signals its speakers' belonging to the group of lower class workers of east London. Differences between varieties of the same language often consist in different pronunciations and vocabulary, but also sometimes of different grammatical systems and very often in using different styles (e.g. cockney Rhyming slang or Lawyers' jargon). Linguists and anthropologists, particularly sociolinguists, ethnolinguists and linguistic anthropologists have specialized in studying how ways of speaking vary between speech communities.

A community's ways of speaking or signing are a part of the community's culture, just as other shared practices are. Language use is a way of establishing and displaying group identity. Ways of speaking function not only to facilitate communication, but also to identify the social position of the speaker. Linguists call different ways of speaking language varieties, a term that encompasses geographically or socioculturally defined dialects as well as the jargons or styles of subcultures. Linguistic anthropologists and sociologists of language define communicative style as the ways that language is used and understood within a particular culture.

The differences between languages does not consist only in differences in pronunciation, vocabulary or grammar, but also in different "cultures of speaking". Some cultures for example have elaborate systems of "social deixis", systems of signalling social distance through linguistic means. In English, social deixis is shown mostly though distinguishing between addressing some people by first name and others by surname, but also in titles such as "Mrs.", "boy", "Doctor" or "Your Honour", but in other languages such systems may be highly complex and codified in the entire grammar and vocabulary of the language.

In several languages of east Asia, for example Thai, Burmese and Javanese, different words are used according to whether a speaker is addressing someone of higher or lower rank than oneself in a ranking system with animals and children ranking the lowest and gods and members of royalty as the highest. Other languages may use different forms of address when speaking to speakers of the opposite gender or in-law relatives and many languages have special ways of speaking to infants and children. Among other groups, the culture of speaking may entail *not speaking* to particular people, for example many indigenous cultures of Australia have a taboo against talking to one's in-law relatives, and in some cultures speech is not addressed directly to children. Some languages also require different ways of speaking for different social classes of speakers, and often such a system is based on gender differences, as in Japanese and Koasati.

Anarchy

Anarchy may refer to any of the following:

- "No rulership or enforced authority."
- "A social state in which there is no governing person or group of people, but each individual has absolute liberty (without the implication of disorder)."
- "Absence of government; a state of lawlessness due to the absence or inefficiency of the supreme power; political disorder."
- "Absence or non-recognition of authority and order in any given sphere."
- "Acting without waiting for instructions or official permission... The root of anarchism is the single impulse to do it yourself: everything else follows from this."

Cases of Anarchy after the Collapse of a State

English Civil War

The tumult of the English Civil War (1641–1651) led to the term to be taken up in political philosophy. Anarchy was one of the issues at the Putney Debates of 1647:.

Thomas Rainsborough: I shall now be a little more free and open with you than I was before. I wish we were all true-hearted, and that we did all carry ourselves with integrity. If I did mistrust you I would not use such asseverations. I think it doth go on mistrust, and things are thought too readily matters of reflection, that were never intended. For my part, as I think, you forgot something that was in my speech, and you do not only yourselves believe that some men are inclining to anarchy, but you would make all men believe that. And, sir, to say because a man pleads that every man hath a voice by right of nature, that therefore it destroys by the same argument all property — this is to forget the Law of God. That there's a property, the Law of God says it; else why hath God made that law, Thou shalt not steal? I am a poor man, therefore I must be oppressed: if I have no interest in the kingdom, I must suffer by all their laws be they right or wrong. Nay thus: a gentleman lives in a country and hath three or four lordships, as some men have (God knows how they got them); and when a Parliament is called he must be a Parliament-man; and it may be he sees some poor men, they live near this man, he can crush them — I have known an invasion to make sure he hath turned the poor men out of doors; and I would fain know whether the potency of rich men do not this, and so keep them under the greatest tyranny that was ever thought of in the world. And therefore I think that to that it is fully answered: God hath set down that thing as to propriety with this law of his, Thou shalt not steal. And for my part I am against any such thought, and, as for yourselves, I wish you would not make the world believe that we are for anarchy.

Oliver Cromwell: I know nothing but this, that they that are the most yielding have the greatest wisdom; but really, sir, this is not right as it should be. No man says that you have a mind to anarchy, but that the consequence of this rule tends to anarchy, must end in anarchy; for where is there any bound or limit set if you take away this limit, that men that have no interest but the interest of breathing shall have no voice in elections? Therefore I am confident on 't, we should not be so hot one with another.

As people began to theorize about the English Civil War, "anarchy" came to be more sharply defined, albeit from differing political perspectives:

- 1651 – Thomas Hobbes (*Leviathan*) describes the natural condition of mankind as a war of all against all, where man lives a brutish existence. "For the savage people in many places of America, except the government of small families, the concord whereof dependeth on natural lust, have no government at all, and live at this day in that brutish manner." Hobbes finds three basic causes of the conflict in this state of nature: competition, diffidence and glory, "The first maketh men invade for gain; the second, for safety; and the third, for reputation". His first law of nature is that "that every man ought to endeavour peace, as far as he has hope of obtaining it; and when he cannot obtain it, that he may seek and use all helps and advantages of war". In the state of nature, "every man has a right to every thing, even to then go for one another's body" but the second law is that, in order to secure the advantages of peace, "that a man be willing, when others are so too... to lay down this right to all things; and be contented with so much liberty against other men as he would allow other men against himself". This is the beginning of contracts/covenants; performing of which is the third law of nature. "Injustice," therefore, is failure to perform in a covenant; all else is just.
- 1656 – James Harrington (*The Commonwealth of Oceana*) uses the term to describe a situation where the people use force to impose a government on an economic base composed of either solitary land ownership (absolute monarchy), or land in the ownership of a few (mixed monarchy). He distinguishes it from commonwealth, the situation when both land ownership and governance shared by the population at large, seeing it as a temporary situation arising from an imbalance

between the form of government and the form of property relations

French Revolution

Thomas Carlyle, Scottish essayist of the Victorian era known foremost for his widely influential work of history, *The French Revolution*, wrote that the French Revolution was a war against both aristocracy *and* anarchy:

Meanwhile, we will hate Anarchy as Death, which it is; and the things worse than Anarchy shall be hated more! Surely Peace alone is fruitful. Anarchy is destruction: a burning up, say, of Shams and Insupportabilities; but which leaves Vacancy behind. Know this also, that out of a world of Unwise nothing but an Unwisdom can be made. Arrange it, Constitution-build it, sift it through Ballot-Boxes as thou wilt, it is and remains an Unwisdom,— the new prey of new quacks and unclean things, the latter end of it slightly better than the beginning. Who can bring a wise thing out of men unwise? Not one. And so Vacancy and general Abolition having come for this France, what can Anarchy do more? Let there be Order, were it under the Soldier's Sword; let there be Peace, that the bounty of the Heavens be not spilt; that what of Wisdom they do send us bring fruit in its season!— It remains to be seen how the quellers of Sansculottism were themselves quelled, and sacred right of Insurrection was blown away by gunpowder: wherewith this singular eventful History called French Revolution ends.

Armand II, duke of Aiguillon came before the National Assembly (French Revolution) in 1789 and shared his views on the anarchy: I may be permitted here to express my personal opinion. I shall no doubt not be accused of not loving liberty, but I know that not all movements of peoples lead to liberty. But I know that great anarchy quickly leads to great exhaustion and that despotism, which is a kind of rest, has almost always been the necessary result of great anarchy. It is therefore much more important than we think to end the disorder under which we suffer. If we can achieve this only through the use of force by authorities, then it would be thoughtless to keep refraining from using such force.

Armand II was later exiled because he was viewed as being opposed to the revolution's violent tactics.

Professor Chris Bossche commented on the role of anarchy in the revolution: In The French Revolution, the narrative of increasing anarchy undermined the narrative in which the revolutionaries were striving to create a new social order by writing a constitution.

Jamaica 1720

Sir Nicholas Lawes, Governor of Jamaica, wrote to John Robinson, the Bishop of London, in 1720:

"As to the Englishmen that came as mechanics hither, very young and have now acquired good estates in Sugar Plantations and Indigo& co., of course they know no better than what maxims they learn in the Country. To be now short & plain Your Lordship will see that they have no maxims of Church and State but what are absolutely anarchical."

In the letter Lawes goes on to complain that these "estated men now are like Jonah's gourd" and details the humble origins of the "creolians" largely lacking an education and flouting the rules of church and state. In particular, he cites their refusal to abide by the Deficiency Act, which required slave owners to procure from England one white person for every 40 enslaved Africans, thereby hoping to expand their own estates and inhibit further English/Irish immigration. Lawes describes the government as being "anarchical, but nearest to any form of Aristocracy". "Must the King's good subjects at home who are as capable to begin plantations, as their Fathers, and themselves were, be excluded from their Liberty of settling Plantations in this noble Island, for ever and the King and Nation at home be deprived of so much riches, to make a few upstart Gentlemen Princes?"

Spain 1936

After General Francisco Franco declared war on the Spanish government in 1936 (Spanish Civil War) the government lost control over much of Spain. Resistance to the rebels was often organized through the confederation of anarcho-syndicalist trade unions, the *Confederación Nacional del Trabajo* (CNT) and the Iberian Anarchist Federation, the *Federación Anarquista Ibérica* (FAI). The Spanish Revolution occurred almost immediately after the failed coup of Franco, leading to the formation of worker's collectives all over Republican Spain. This has been hailed as the best example of a functioning anarchist system. The government was subsequently defeated by Franco, leading to almost 40 years of Francoist dictatorship in Spain.

Albania 1997

In the mid-1990s, Albania was becoming a liberalized economy after years under a controlled economy; the rudimentary financial system became dominated by Ponzi schemes, and government officials endorsed a series of pyramid investment funds. Many Albanians, approximately two-thirds of the population, invested in them. By 1997 the inevitable end came, and the people of Albania, who had lost $1.2 billion (out of a small population of 3 million), took their protest to the streets where uncontained rioting, fueled by their discontent at the state's failure to protect them from the fraud, led to the toppling of the government and the country descended into anarchy in which some 2,000 people were killed. Beginning in February, thousands of citizens gathered daily, demanding reimbursement by the government, which they suspected of profiting from the schemes. By March 1997, the protests had turned violent in the south, especially around the port city of Vlora, where numerous residents armed themselves with weapons looted from army barracks. On March 2, president Sali Berisha declared a state of emergency, but rioting and destruction spread throughout the country, gripping the capital, Tirana, for two weeks. Although the government quelled revolts in the north, the government and military establishments began to scatter and anarchy swept across the country, the southern half of Albania falling under the control of rebels and criminal gangs.

Somalia

Before the Islamic Courts Union took control, large parts of southern Somalia were effectively functioning without a central government. However, an economic survey by the World Bank found that distribution of wealth in the country was more equitable, and the extent of extreme poverty was lower than that found in nominally more stable West African nations. According to the same paper, although southern Somalia was effectively operating without a federal government before the rise to prominence of the Islamic Courts Union, it was not an anarchist society in the sense that society was more or less chaotic than organized non-coercively. Despite this, a libertarian think tank reported that living standards in Somalia increased – in absolute terms, relative to the pre-Somali Civil War era, and relative to other nations in Africa – during this period. Economist Peter Leeson attributes the rather astounding increase in economic activity since the rise of statelessness to the security in life, liberty and property provided by Somali customary law — the Xeer — in most parts of Somalia, which insures for a relative free market.

The Transitional Federal Government, internationally recognized as the government of Somalia, is allied with the Islamic Courts Union and the Alliance for the Re-liberation of Somalia, and backed by the United Nations, the African Union and the United States. It is currently battling various insurgent groups to regain control of the southern half of the country and restore national institutions.

List of Ungoverned Communities

- Icelandic Commonwealth (930 - 1262, CE)
- Gaelic Ireland
- Libertatia (late 17th century)
- The Free Territory (January 1919 – August 1921)
- Shinmin Free Province (1929–1932)
- Anarchist Catalonia, Spain, (July 21, 1936 -- June 14, 1937)
- Anarchist Aragon (October 6, 1936 – August 10, 1937)
- Freetown Christiania, Denmark, (September 26, 1971–2004).

Political Philosophy

Anarchism

Anarchists are those who advocate the absence of the state, arguing that common sense would allow people to come together in agreement to form a functional society allowing for the participants to freely develop their own sense of morality, ethics or principled behaviour. The rise of anarchism as a philosophical movement occurred in the mid 19th century, with its idea of freedom as being based upon political and economic self-rule. This occurred alongside the rise of the nation-state and large-scale industrial state capitalism or state-sponsored corporatism, and the political corruption that came with their successes.

Although anarchists share a rejection of the state, they differ about economic arrangements and possible rules that would prevail in a stateless society, ranging from no ownership, to complete common ownership, to supporters of private property and capitalist free market competition. For example, some forms of anarchism, such as that of anarcho-collectivism, anarcho-communism or anarcho-syndicalism not only seek rejection of the state, but also other systems which they perceive as authoritarian, which include capitalism, capitalist markets, and title-based property ownership. In opposition, a political philosophy known as free-market anarchism, contemporary individualist anarchism or anarcho-capitalism, argues that a society without a state is a free market capitalist system that is voluntarist in nature. The word "anarchy" is often used by non-anarchists as a pejorative term, intended to connote a lack of control and a negatively chaotic environment. However, anarchists still argue that anarchy does not imply nihilism, anomie, or the total absence of rules, but rather an anti-statist society that is based on the spontaneous order of free individuals in autonomous communities.

Anthropology

Some anarchist anthropologists, such as David Graeber and Pierre Clastres, consider societies such as those of the Bushmen, Tiv and the Piaroa to be anarchies in the sense that they explicitly reject the idea of centralized political authority.

Some more recent anthropologists, such as Marshall Sahlins and Richard Borshay Lee, have repudiated the idea of hunter-gatherer societies being a source of scarcity and brutalization; describing them as "affluent societies".

The evolutionary psychologist Steven Pinker writes:

Adjudication by an armed authority appears to be the most effective violence-reduction technique ever invented. Though we debate whether tweaks in criminal policy, such as executing murderers versus locking them up for life, can reduce violence by a few percentage points, there can be no debate on the massive effects of having a criminal justice system as opposed to living in anarchy. The shockingly high homicide rates of pre-state societies, with 10 to 60 percent of the men dying at the hands of other men, provide one kind of evidence. Another is the emergence of a violent culture of honour in just about any corner of the world that is beyond the reach of law...The generalization that anarchy in the sense of a lack of government leads to anarchy in the sense of violent chaos may seem banal, but it is often over-looked in today's still-romantic climate.

Some authors, such as Montague David Eder, question this view of evolution, where humanity was able to reinvent itself in the last ten thousand years, to better fulfil its needs.

Myth of Progress

Some 20th century authors refer to the "Myth of Progress" to challenge the Idea of Progress, especially the assumption that the human condition will inevitably improve. In 1932 English physician Montague David Eder wrote: "The myth of progress states that civilization has moved, is moving, and will move in a desirable direction. Progress is inevitable..... Philosophers, men of science and politicians have accepted the idea of the inevitability of progress." Eder argues that the advancement of civilization is leading to greater unhappiness and loss of control in the environment.

Sociologist P. A. Sorokin argued, "The ancient Chinese, Babylonian, Hindu, Greek, Roman and most of the medieval thinkers supporting theories of rhythmical, cyclical or trendless move-ments of social processes were much nearer to reality than the present proponents of the linear view."

Philosopher Karl Popper emphasized the inadequacies of the Idea of Progress as a scientific explanation of social phenomena. More recently, Kirkpatrick Sale, a self-proclaimed neo-luddite author, wrote exclusively about progress as a myth, in an essay entitled "Five Facets of a Myth".

Iggers (1965) says the great failing of the prophets of progress was that they underesti-mated the extent of man's destructiveness and irrationality. The failing of the critics of the Idea of Progress, he adds, came in misunderstanding the role of ra-tionality and morality in human behaviour.

Some Anarcho-primitivists believe that this concept is used to justify the values of modern industrial society and move individuals further from their natural necessities. John Zerzan has noted the existence of tribal societies with less violence than "advanced" societies. Zerzan and Theodore Kaczynski have talked about other forms of violence against the individual in advanced societies, generally expressed by the term "social anomie", that result from the system of monopolized security. These authors do not dismiss the fact that humanity is changing while adapting to its different social realities, but consider the situation anomalous. The two results are (1) that we either disappear or (2) become something very different from what we have come to value in our nature. It has been suggested that this shift towards civilization, through domestication, has caused an increase in diseases, labor, and psychological disorders. In contrast, Pierre Clastres maintains that violence in primitive societies is a natural way for each community to maintain its political independence, while dismissing the state as a natural outcome of the evolution of human societies.

Social Relation

Social Relations takes as its focus the relationships between people and their social world. It assumes that people are engaged in and shaped by multiple relationships, events and influences. Human experience and behaviour is therefore explored, not only by taking a range of social and psychological factors into account but also, importantly, by paying close attention to the meanings and interpretations that people attach to their diverse experiences.

The concept of 'the individual' can by definition exist only in relational terms. A person constructs a sense of identity in relation to family, other people, cultural practices, gender, social class, social/political systems, sexuality, geographic location and physical and mental abilities. It is therefore necessary to engage in learning as a cultural activity and to appreciate connections between individuals and the social, political and cultural structures that impact upon them. Significantly, Social Relations foregrounds people's lived experience and recognises that this experience is in continual process. In this way, it invites engagement with relevant topical issues and relationships. Similarly, the experiences and meanings that 'the learner' has (and therefore brings to any human interaction) also become a valuable resource for exploration and insight into the dimensions of human relationships.

Social Relations is a multi disciplinary approach that draws on several theoretical methodologies in its analysis. While all of the disciplines that have typically contributed to the 'humanities' offer important insights about human beings and their behaviours and needs, those that primarily concern themselves with the complexities of human behaviour are psychology, sociology and anthropology. These are therefore especially important within a Social Relations framework, as they each focus from different angles on how people organise and make meaning of their world and their relationships within it. Exploring the ways in which such relationships are produced, sustained and transformed is vitally important in establishing meaningful communication with groups and individuals. Social Relations provides a dynamic framework within which to gain rich insight and understanding about people and the social and emotional landscape of their lives.

Social Relations has particular relevance for people whose professional careers require a broad understanding of human behaviour and social relationships. Learning undertaken within this framework enhances people's personal relationships; their workplace relations with peers, managers and customers; and their engagement and sense of belonging with the community. It is an approach that is extremely useful for promoting understanding of particular social and cultural issues and local contexts.

Socialization

Socialization is a term used by sociologists, social psychologists, anthropologists, politicians and educationalists to refer to the process of inheriting norms, customs and ideologies. It may provide the individual with the skills and habits necessary for participating within their own society; a society itself is formed through a plurality of shared norms, customs, values, traditions, social roles, symbols and languages. Socialization is thus 'the means by which social and cultural continuity are attained'.

Socialization, however, is not a normative term: it describes a *process* which may or may not affect the reflexive agent, and which may or may not lead to desirable, or 'moral', outcomes. Individual views on certain issues, such as race or economics, may be socialized (and to that extent *normalized*) within a society. Many socio-political theories postulate that socialization provides only a partial explanation for human beliefs and behaviours; that agents are not 'blank slates' predetermined by their environment.

Scientific research provides strong evidence that people are shaped by both social influences *and* their hard-wired biological makeup. Genetic studies have shown that a person's environment interacts with their genotype to influence behavioural outcomes, whilst the linguistic theory of generative grammar demonstrates how something such as the capacity for learning changes throughout one's lifetime.

Socialization is the primary means by which human infants begin to acquire the skills necessary to perform as a functioning member of their society, and is the most influential learning processes one can experience.

Although cultural variability is manifest in the actions, customs, and behaviours of whole social groups (societies), the most fundamental expression of culture is found at the individual level. This can expression can only occur after an individual has been socialized by its parents, family, extended family and extended social networks. This reflexive process of both learning and teaching is the how cultural and social characteristics attain continuity.

To "socialise" may also mean simply to associate or mingle with people socially. In American English, "socialized" has mistakenly come to refer, usually in a pejorative sense, to the ownership structure of socialism or to the expansion of the welfare state. Traditionally, socialists and Marxists both used the term "socialization of industry" to refer to the reorganization of institutions so that the workers are all owners (cooperatives) and to refer to the implementation of workplace democracy.

Types of Socialization

Primary Socialization

Primary socialization occurs when a child learns the attitudes, values and actions appropriate to individuals as members of a particular culture. For example if a child saw his/her mother expressing a discriminatory opinion about a minority group, then that child may think this behaviour is acceptable and could continue to have this opinion about minority groups.

Secondary Socialization

Secondary socialization refers to the process of learning what is appropriate behaviour as a member of a smaller group within the larger society. It is usually associated with teenagers and adults, and involves smaller changes than those occurring in primary socialization. eg. entering a new profession, relocating to a new environment or society.

Developmental Socialization

Developmental socialization is the process of learning behaviour in a social institution or developing your social skills.

Anticipatory Socialization

Anticipatory socialization refers to the processes of socialization in which a person "rehearses" for future positions, occupations, and social relationships.

Resocialization

Resocialization refers to the process of discarding former behaviour patterns and accepting new ones as part of a transition in one's life. This occurs throughout the human life cycle (Schaefer & Lamm, 1992: 113). Resocialization can be an intense experience, with the individual experiencing a sharp break with their past, and needing to learn and be exposed to radically different norms and values. An example might be the experience of a young man or woman leaving home to join the military, or a religious convert internalizing the beliefs and rituals of a new faith. An extreme example would be the process by which a transsexual learns to function socially in a dramatically altered gender role.

Organizational Socialization

Organizational socialization is the process whereby an employee learning the knowledge and skills necessary to assume his or her organizational role. As newcomers become socialized, they learn about the organization and its history, values, jargon, culture, and procedures. They also learn about their work group, the specific people they work with on a daily basis, their own role in the organization, the skills needed to do their job, and both formal procedures and informal norms. Socialization functions as a control system in that newcomers learn to internalize and obey organizational values and practices.

Agents/Units of Socialization

In the social sciences, institutions are the structures and mechanisms of social order and cooperation governing the behaviour of a set of individuals within a given human collectivity. Institutions are identified with a social purpose and permanence, transcending individual human lives and intentions, and with the making and enforcing of rules governing cooperative human behaviour. Types of institution include:

- The Family
- Religion
- Education
- Economic systems
- Legal systems
- Penal systems
- Psychiatric hospitals and Asylums
- Mass media and News media
- Organizations Art and Culture
- Language.

Media and Socialization

Theorists like Parsons and textbook writers like Ely Chinoy (1960) and Harry M. Johnson (1961) recognized that socialization didn't stop when childhood ends. They realized that socialization continued in adulthood, but they treated it as a form of specialized education. Johnson (1961), for example, wrote about the importance of inculcating members of the US Coastguard with a set of values to do with responding to commands and acting in unison without question.Later scholars accused these theorists of socialization of not recognizing the importance of the mass media which, by the middle of the twentieth century were becoming more significant as a social force. There was concern about the link between television and the education and socialization of children – it continues today – but when it came to adults, the mass media were regarded merely as sources of information and entertainment rather than moulders of personality. According to these

Some sociologists and theorists of culture have recognized the power of mass communication as a socialization device. Dennis McQuail recognizes the argument:

> ... the media can teach norms and values by way of symbolic reward and punishment for different kinds of behaviour as represented in the media. An alternative view is that it is a learning process whereby we all learn how to behave in certain situations and the expectations which go with a given role or status in society. Thus the media are continually offering pictures of life and models of behaviour in advance of actual experience. —McQuail 2005: 494)

Gender Socialization and Gender Roles

Henslin (1999:76) contends that "an important part of socialization is the learning of culturally defined gender roles." Gender socialization refers to the learning of behaviour and attitudes considered appropriate for a given sex. Boys learn to be boys and girls learn to be girls. This "learning" happens by way of many different agents of socialization. The family is certainly important in reinforcing gender roles, but so are one's friends, school, work and the mass media. Gender roles are reinforced through "countless subtle and not so subtle ways" (1999:76).

Racial Socialization

Racial socialization has been defined as "the developmental processes by which children acquire the behaviours, perceptions, values, and attitudes of an ethnic group, and come to see themselves and others as members of the group". The existing literature conceptualizes racial socialization as having multiple dimensions. Researchers have identified five dimensions that commonly appear in the racial socialization literature: cultural socialization, preparation for bias, promotion of mistrust, egalitarianism, and other. Cultural socialization refers to parenting practices that teach African American children about their racial history or heritage and is also referred to as pride development. Preparation for bias refers to parenting practices focused on preparing African American children to be aware of, and cope with, discrimination. Promotion of mistrust refers to the parenting practices of socializing children to be wary of people from other races. Egalitarianism refers to socializing children with the belief that all people are equal and should be treated with a common humanity.

Cultural Assimilation

Cultural assimilation is a socio-political response to demographic multi-ethnicity that supports or promotes the assimilation of ethnic minorities into the dominant culture. It is opposed to affirmative philosophy (for example, multiculturalism) which recognizes and seeks to maintain differences.

The term assimilation is often used with regard to immigrants and various ethnic groups who have settled in a new land. New customs and attitudes are acquired through contact and communication. The transfer of customs is not simply a one-way process. Each group of immigrants contributes some of its own cultural traits to its new society. Assimilation usually involves a gradual change and takes place in varying degrees; full assimilation occurs when new members of a society become indistinguishable from older members.

Cultural Influence

A group (a state or an ethnicity) can spontaneously adopt a different culture due to its political relevance, or to its perceived superiority. The first is the case of the Latin language and culture, that were gradually adopted by most of the subjugated people. The second is the case of subjugated, but older and richer culture, which see itself imitated by the new masters, e.g. the victorious Roman Republic adopted more from the Hellenistic cultures than it imposed in most domains, except such Roman specialties as law and the military.

Assimilation of Immigrants

Immigrant assimilation is a complex process in which an immigrant fully integrates themselves into a new country. Social scientists rely on four primary benchmarks to assess immigrant assimilation: socioeconomic status, geographic distribution, second language attainment, and intermarriage. William A.V. Clark defines immigrant assimilation "as a way of understanding the social dynamics of American society and that it is the process that occurs spontaneously and often unintended in the course of interaction between majority and minority groups".

It has been found that between 1880 and 1920, the United States took in roughly 24 million immigrants. This increase in immigration can be attributed to many historical changes. Later, during the cold war from the 1960s through the 1980s and the disintegration of the Soviet Union in the late 1980s, over 1.8 million Jews (including some non-Jewish family members) emigrated from the former Soviet Union. The major destination countries were Israel (about 1.1 million), the United States (over 400,000), Germany (about 130,000), and Canada (about 30,000). The beginning of the twenty-first century has also marked a massive era of immigration, and sociologists are once again trying to make sense of the impact that immigration has on society and the impact it has on immigrants themselves.

Theoretical Explanations

Researchers have attempted to explain the assimilation rate for post 1965 immigrants in the United States with experiences of immigrants who entered the United States between 1880 and 1920. Many of the methods and theories that are used to assess immigrant assimilation today are derived from earlier immigrant studies. One of the leading theories in understanding immigrant assimilation came from William I. Thomas and Florian Znaniecki whom published "The Polish Peasant in Europe and America". William I. Thomas and Florian Znaniecki's study on Polish immigrants (1880–1910) assessed how these immigrants built an institutional community in the United States during the Napoleonic War. Another influence on immigrant assimilation came from Robert Park, Ernest Burgess, and William I. Thomas, in which they trained graduate students to study the experiences of immigrants in Chicago. Robert Park, Ernest Burgess, and William I. Thomas provided these graduate students with theoretical tools such as Park's theory on collective behaviour. The third theory on immigrant assimilation comes from Gordon's book, *Assimilation in American life*. Gordon highlighted the generational change in immigrant groups, it states that the first generation or foreign born were less assimilated and less exposed to American life than their American-born children (the second generation), and their grandchildren (third-generation) were more like the American mainstream than their parents.

Theoretical Models to Immigrant Assimilation

The first, classic and new assimilation model sees immigrants and native-born people following a "straight-line" or a convergence. This theory sees immigrants becoming more similar over time in norms, values, behaviours, and characteristics. This theory also expects those immigrants residing the longest in the host population, as well as the members of later generations, to show greater similarities with the majority group than immigrants who have spent less time in the host society. The second, racial or ethnic disadvantage model states that immigrant's chances to assimilate are "blocked". An example of this model would be discrimination and institutional barriers to employment and other opportunities. The third, the segmented assimilation model theorizes that structural barriers, such as poor urban schools, cut off access to employment and other opportunities—obstacles that often are particularly severe in the case of the most disadvantaged members of immigrant groups, and such impediments can lead to stagnant or downward mobility, even as the children of other immigrants follow divergent paths toward classic straight-line assimilation.

Core Measurements to Immigrant Assimilation

Researchers have assessed that assimilation exists among immigrants because we can measure assimilation on four primary benchmarks. These core measurable aspects of immigrant assimilation that were formulated to study European immigrants to the United States are still the starting points for understanding current immigrant assimilation. These measurable aspects of assimilation are socioeconomic status, spatial concentration, language attainment, and intermarriage.

1. *Socioeconomic Status* is defined by educational attainment, occupation, and income. By measuring socioeconomic status researchers want to find out if immigrants eventually catch up to native-born people in terms of human capital characteristics.
2. *Spatial Concentration* is defined by geography or residential patterns. The spatial residential model (based on theories of Park) proposed by Massey states that increasing socioeconomic attainment, longer residence in the U.S, and higher generational status lead to decreasing residential concentration for a particular ethnic group.
3. *Language Attainment* is defined as the ability to speak English and the loss of the individual's mother tongue. The three-generation model of language assimilation states that the first generation makes some progress in language assimilation but remains dominant in their native tongue, the second generation is bilingual, and the third-generation only speaks English.
4. *Intermarriage* is defined by race or ethnicity and occasionally by generation. High rates of intermarriage are considered to be an indication of social integration because it reveals intimate and profound relations between people of different groups, intermarriage reduces the ability of families to pass on to their children a consistent ethnic culture and thus is an agent of assimilation. Intermarriage came under particular scrutiny by the Jewish community in the early-mid 20th century as Jewish leaders more and more often turned to social scientists to explain why Judaism was a typically endogamic religion. Although intermarriage was viewed as a firm base from which to begin an argument for assimilation, it was also seen as a way to gradually ease the transition into their new culture. Julius Draschler, a graduate student at Columbia University, believed that as long as people are allowed to maintain some differences, such as the Jewish practice of only marrying another Jew, they will delay

the inevitable while simultaneously enriching the nation in the process of their slow assimilation. While Draschler acknowledged that assimilation was the ultimate endpoint for all American groups, he hoped to prove through his intermarriage studies that, the more gradual the process, the better. Such need to justify (or vilify) the intermarriage practice became increasingly important after the 1950s as Jews (as well as other typically endogamic cultures, such as African-Americans) began to engage in more exogamic relationships.

Immigrant Name Changing as a Form of Assimilation

While the changing of immigrant names is not one of the 4 measurable benchmarks for assimilation outlined by early sociologists, it nonetheless represents a clear abandonment of the old as new immigrants are absorbed into the fabric of society. It is often believed that, due to language barriers, or the lack of training and sensitivity by government officials, names were often changed, without consent, by inspectors on Ellis Island. This general misconstruction of the facts is refuted in an article released by the Immigration and Naturalization Service, claiming that inspectors did not personally take names, instead inventorying the passengers using manifestos created by the shipping companies themselves.

As a matter of fact, many immigrants changed their names willingly. It's suggested by the Immigration and Naturalization Service that most name blunders were likely the fault of the origin, and not the destination. Donna Przecha, a published and well-known expert in genealogy, suggests a number of alternative explanations for name changing, one of which was a need for employment. A huge surplus of labor began to immigrate to the United States, many of whom were unskilled, with names that were often difficult to pronounce. Employers were not bound by the same anti-discriminatory legislature that they are now, and tended to gravitate towards individuals with more American names. Comfort and fitting in was also a heavy motivator behind the changing of names. Many, if not most, US immigrants in the mid 1900's planned to make the United States their new home, permanently. Given this fact, it should come as no surprise that many immigrants welcomed the impending assimilation brought on by their host country. Eager to begin their new lives, many did as much as they could to become "American" as quickly as possible, particularly children. Of course, simplicity was yet another factor in the abandonment of old titles. As immigrants poured in from various European countries, many found their names to be difficult to pronounce and/or spell for many Americans, such as those names with many syllables, or with a large number of Z's.

Policies on Immigrant Assimilation

When considering immigrant assimilation it is important to consider why immigrants migrate. One reason immigrants migrated was the 1986 Immigration Reform and Control Act (IRCA), which legalized 2.3 million formerly undocumented Mexican Immigrants. This Act freed these newly legalized immigrants from the fear of being apprehended, and many of these immigrants moved to states beyond the nearest U.S-Mexican border.

Modifications for Assessing Immigrant Assimilation

Studies on immigrant assimilation in the 19th century and 20th century conclude that immigrants had a hard time catching up to the same human capital characteristics as native-born people in the 19th century, but studies in the 20th century suggest that immigrants eventually catch up to native born people. Timothy J. Hatton explains this puzzle on immigrant assimilation in the 19th century and in the 20th century. He explores how recent studies have been producing misleading results between the two. Hatton focuses his research on the specification of the earnings function.Hatton argues that that specification of the earnings function should be improved in two ways. First, immigrants who arrived as children should be treated separately from those who arrived as adults. Second, specification of the earnings function should be better approximate to the true shape of age-earnings profiles. Hatton points out that with these modifications, the patterns of immigrant earnings which have emerged make more sense with those of the 20th century and with traditional views on immigrant assimilation in the 19th century.

Owning a Home and Immigrant Assimilation

Owning a home can be seen as a step into assimilation. William A.V. Clark explores this link in his book "Immigrants and the American Dream Remarking the Middle Class". Clark is aware that the process of assimilation is more than just being able to purchase a home. He argues that "homeownership" is one of the steps of assimilation, it is becoming part of the community and a neighborhood, and being a part of the daily activities that take place in a community.

Naturalization and Immigrant Assimilation

Other than marriage, Citizenship is one of the most significant factors in assimilation. The immigration debate focuses not only the number of immigrants, who should be admitted, and who should be allowed to be admitted but also the processes of incorporation and, most importantly, how citizenship should be extended and to whom. For example, should it be extended to those who arrive illegally? Allowing for naturalization of immigrants can create tension in assimilation. On one hand, those who favor the admission of immigrants input that these new residents will help build and enrich the American democratic process. However, others argue that the nature and legitimacy of the nation may be challenged and perhaps even threatened.

New Immigrant Gateways and Immigrant Assimilation

Although it is changing, the overwhelming majority of immigrants still settle in traditional gateway states such as Florida, New York, California, Illinois, Texas, and Massachusetts. It has found that immigrants settle in traditional gateways where there are large populations of foreign-born people. Walters and Jimenez have illustrated the changes in the geographic distribution and the rates of growth of immigration in the United States. They show the number of foreign-born individuals in states where the foreign-born population grew by a factor of two or more between 1990 and 2000. Walters and Jimenez found that the largest percentage growth in the foreign-born population, was found in either the Midwest or the South in additional none of the traditional gateways were included in this large percentage growth. Walters and Jimenez noted that a reason these traditional gateways did not have an increase at the same rate of the new gateways was because, new gateways did not have many immigrants to begin with. Walters and Jimenez have argued that this new change in geography could possibly change the way researchers assess immigrant assimilation. They argue that these new gateways are unique and they propose that immigrant assimilation may be different from the experiences of immigrants in more traditional gateways in at least three ways. First, the long history of immigration in these established gateways means that the place of immigrants in terms of class, racial, and ethnic hierarchies in these traditional gateways are more structured or established on the other hand these new gateways do not have much immigration history therefore the place of immigrants in terms of class, racial, and ethnic hierarchies is less defined and immigrants may have more influence to define their position. Second, the size of new gateways may influence immigrant assimilation. Having a smaller gateway may influence the level of segregation among immigrants and native-born people. Third, the difference in institutional arrangements may influence immigrant assimilation. Traditional gateways unlike new gateways have many institutions set up to help immigrants which include legal-aid, bureaus, social organizations. Finally, Walters and Jimenez have only speculated that these differences may influence immigrant assimilation and the way researchers should assess immigrant assimilation.

Culture Shock

Culture shock is the difficulty people have adjusting to a new culture that differs markedly from their own.

The shock of moving to a foreign country often consists of distinct phases, though not everyone passes through these phases and not everyone is in the new culture long enough to pass through all five. There are no fixed symptoms ascribed to culture shock as each person is affected differently.

Honeymoon Phase

During this period the differences between the old and new culture are seen in a romantic light, wonderful and new. For example, in moving to a new country, an individual might love the new foods, the pace of the life, the people's habits, the buildings and so on. During the first few weeks most people are fascinated by the new culture.

They associate with the nationals that speak their language and are polite to the foreigners. This period is full of observations and new discoveries. Like many honeymoons this stage eventually ends. "When an individual sets out to study, live or work in a new country, he or she will invariably experience difficulties with language, housing, friends, school, work..."

Negotiation Phase

After some time (usually three months but it may be sooner or later depending on the individual), differences between the old and new culture become apparent and may create anxiety. That sense of excitement will eventually give way to new and unpleasant feelings of frustration and anger as you continue to have unfavorable encounters that strike you as strange, offensive, and unacceptable. These reactions [...] are typically centred on the formidable language barrier as well as stark differences in: public hygiene; traffic safety; the type and quality of the food [...].

Adjustment Phase

Again, after some time (usually 6 – 12 months), one grows accustomed to the new culture and develops routines. One knows what to expect in most situations and the host country no longer feels all that new. One becomes concerned with basic living again, and things become more "normal". One starts to develop problem-solving skills for dealing with the culture, and begins to accept the culture ways with a positive attitude. The culture begins to make sense, and negative reactions and responses to the culture are reduced.

Mastery Phase

In the mastery stage assignees are able to participate fully and comfortably in the host culture. Mastery does not mean total conversion, and people are capable of not adopting some aspects of the host culture. It is often referred to as the biculturalism stage.

General Note

Culture Shock can not only occur after a honeymoon phase, but directly upon arrival in the country. You may immediately begin to miss your home country, even things you didn't like about it, and miss your home foods, family, friends, etc. It is not advisable to sleep excessively, isolate yourself, or have anger towards your host people. You should write, spend time with the host family, or people, and try to adjust yourself to the culture- including eating even if you are not hungry, sleeping at normal times- not when you feel you should, and adjusting yourself to the time change (if applicable).]]

Reverse Culture Shock

Reverse Culture Shock (a.k.a. "Re-entry Shock", or "own culture shock") may take place — returning to one's home culture after growing accustomed to a new one can produce the same effects as described above. This results from the psychosomatic and psychological consequences of the readjustment process to the primary culture. The affected person often finds this more surprising and difficult to deal with than the original culture shock.

Outcomes

There are three basic outcomes of the Adjustment Phase:

- Some people find it impossible to accept the foreign culture and integrate. They isolate themselves from the host country's environment, which they come to perceive as hostile, withdraw into a "ghetto" and see return to their own culture as the only way out. These "Rejectors" also have the greatest problems re-integrating back home after return.
- Some people integrate fully and take on all parts of the host culture while losing their original identity. They normally remain in the host country forever. This group is sometimes know as "Adopters".
- Some people manage to adapt the aspects of the host culture they see as positive, while keeping some of their own and creating their unique blend. They have no major problems returning home or relocating

elsewhere. This group can be thought to be somewhat cosmopolitan.

Culture shock has many different effects, time spans, and degrees of severity. Many people are handicapped by its presence and don't recognize what is bothering them.

Transition Shock

Culture shock is a subcategory of a more universal construct called transition shock. Transition shock is a state of loss and disorientation predicated by a change in one's familiar environment which requires adjustment. There are many symptoms of transition shock, some which include:

- excessive concern over cleanliness and health
- feelings of helplessness and withdrawal
- irritability
- glazed stare
- desire for home and old friends
- physiological stress reactions
- homesickness
- boredom
- withdrawal
- getting "stuck" on one thing
- excessive sleep
- compulsive eating/drinking/weight gain
- stereotyping host nationals
- hostility towards host nationals.

Hierarchy Makes you Sick

A hierarchy is an arrangement of items (objects, names, values, categories, etc.) in which the items are represented as being "above," "below," or "at the same level as" one another. Abstractly, a hierarchy is simply an ordered set or an acyclic graph.

A hierarchy can link entities either directly or indirectly, and either vertically or horizontally. The only direct links in a hierarchy, in so far as they are hierarchical, are to one's immediate superior or to one of one's subordinates, although a system that is largely hierarchical can also incorporate alternative hierarchies. Indirect hierarchical links can extend "vertically" upwards or downwards via multiple links in the same direction, following a path.

All parts of the hierarchy which are not linked vertically to one another nevertheless can be "horizontally" linked through a path by traveling up the hierarchy to find a common direct or indirect superior, and then down again. This is akin to two co-workers or colleagues; each reports to a common superior, but they have the same relative amount of authority.

Terminology

Hierarchies have their own special vocabulary. These terms are easiest to understand when a hierarchy is diagrammed.

The generic hierarchy uses the following terms:

- Object: one entity (e.g., a person, department or concept) or element of arrangement or member of a set
- System: the entire set of objects that are being arranged hierarchically (e.g., an administration)
- Dimension: another word for "system" from on-line analytical processing (e.g. cubes)
- Member: an (element or object) in a (system or dimension) at any (level or rank)
- Rank: the relative value, worth, complexity, power, importance, authority, level etc. of an object
- Level: a set of objects with the same rank OR importance
- Ordering: the arrangement of the (ranks or levels)
- Hierarchy: the arrangement of a particular set of (ranks or levels) i.e. multiple hierarchies are possible per (dimension or system)
- Collection: all of the objects at one level
- Superior: a higher level or an object ranked at a higher level (parent or ancestor)
- Subordinate: a lower level or an object ranked at a lower level (Child or descendent)
- Hierarch, the top level of the hierarchy, usually consisting of one object or member of a dimension

- Peer: an object with the same rank (and therefore at the same level)
- Neighbour: the adjacent level/ranking (the immediate superior and immediate inferior)
- Interaction: the relationship between an object and its direct superior or subordinate (i.e. a superior/inferior pair)
    - a direct interaction occurs when one object is on a level exactly one higher or one lower than the other (i.e., on a tree, the two objects have a line between them)
- Distance: the minimum number of connections between two objects, i.e., one less than the number of objects that need to be "crossed" to trace a path from one object to another
- Span: a qualitative description of the width of a level when diagrammed, i.e., the number of subordinates an object has (N.B., while hierarchies are commonly studied using graph theory, the general terminology used is different, and words such as "direct" may have different general meanings).

Most hierarchies use a more specific vocabulary pertaining to their subject, but the idea behind them is the same. For example, with data structures, objects are known as nodes, superiors are called parents and subordinates are called children. In a business setting, a superior is a supervisor/boss and a peer is a colleague.

Degree of Branching

Degree of branching refers to the number of direct subordinates or children an object has (equivalent to the number of vertices a node has). Hierarchies can be categorized based on the "maximum degree", the highest degree present in the system as a whole. Categorization in this way yields two broad classes: *linear* and *branching.*

In a linear hierarchy, the maximum degree is 1. In other words, all of the objects can be visualized in a lineup, and each object (excluding the top and bottom ones) has exactly one direct subordinate and one direct superior. Note that this is referring to the *objects* and not the *levels*; every hierarchy has this property with respect to levels, but normally each level can have an infinite number of objects. An example of a linear hierarchy is the hierarchy of life.

In a branching hierarchy, one or more objects has a degree of 2 or more (and therefore the maximum degree is 2 or higher). For many people, the word "hierarchy" automatically evokes an image of a branching hierarchy. Branching hierarchies are present within numerous systems, including organizations and classification schemes. The broad category of branching hierarchies can be further subdivided based on the degree.

A flat hierarchy is a branching hierarchy in which the maximum degree approaches infinity, i.e., with a wide span. Most often, systems intuitively regarded as hierarchical have at most a moderate span. Therefore, a flat hierarchy is often not viewed as a hierarchy at all at first blush. For example, diamonds and graphite is a flat hierarchy of numerous carbon atoms which can be further decomposed into subatomic particles.

An overlapping hierarchy is a branching hierarchy in which at least one object has two parent objects. For example, a graduate student can have two co-supervisors to whom they report directly and equally, and who have the same level of authority within the university hierarchy (i.e., they have the same position or tenure status

History of the Term

The first use of the English word "hierarchy" cited by the Oxford English Dictionary was in 1880, when it was used in reference to the three orders of three angels as depicted by Pseudo-Dionysius the Areopagite (5th–6th centuries). Pseudo-Dionysius used the related Latin word (*hierarchia*) both in reference to the celestial hierarchy and the ecclesiastical hierarchy. His term is derived from the Greek term "1åñáñ÷ßá" meaning "rule by priests" and Dionysius is credited with first use of it as an abstract noun. Since hierarchical churches, such as the Roman Catholic and Eastern Orthodox churches, had tables of organization that were "hierarchical" in the modern sense of the word (traditionally with God as the pinnacle or head of the hierarchy), the term came to refer to similar organizational methods in secular settings.

Visualization

A hierarchy is typically depicted as a pyramid, where the height of a level represents that level's status and width of a level represents the quantity of items at that level relative to the whole. For example, the few Directors of a company could be at the apex, and the base could be thousands of people who have no subordinates. These pyramids are typically diagrammed with a tree or triangle diagram (but note that not all triangle/pyramid diagrams are hierarchical), both of which serve to emphasize the size differences between the levels. An example of a triangle diagram appears to the right. An organizational chart is the diagram of a hierarchy within an organization, and is depicted in tree form below.

Informal Representation

In plain English, a hierarchy can be thought of as a set in which:

1. No element is superior to itself, and
2. One element, the *hierarch*, is superior to all of the other elements in the set.

The first requirement is also interpreted to mean that a hierarchy can have no circular relationships; the association between two objects is always transitive. The second requirement asserts that a hierarchy must have a leader or root that is common to all of the objects.

Mathematical Representation

Mathematically, in its most general form, a hierarchy is a partially ordered set or *poset*. The system in this case is the entire poset, which is constituted of elements. Within this system, each element shares a particular unambiguous property. Objects with the same property value are grouped together, and each of those resulting levels is referred to as a class. "Hierarchy" is particularly used to refer to a poset in which the classes are organized in terms of increasing complexity.

Subsumptive Containment Hierarchy

A *subsumptive* containment hierarchy is a classification of objects from the general to the specific. Other names for this type of hierarchy are "compositional hierarchy", "taxonomic hierarchy" and "IS-A hierarchy". The last term describes the relationship between each level—a lower-level object "is a" member of the higher class.

The taxonomical structure outlined above is a subsumptive containment hierarchy, as are all systematic naming schemes. Using again the example of Linnaean taxonomy, it can be seen that an object that is part of the level *Mammalia* "is a" member of the level *Animalia*; more specifically, a human "is a" primate, a primate "is a" mammal, and so on. A subsumptive hierarchy can also be defined abstractly as a hierarchy of "concepts". For example, with the Linnaean hierarchy outlined above, an entity name like *Animalia* is a way to group all the species that fit the conceptualization of an animal.

Compositional Containment Hierarchy

A *compositional* containment hierarchy is an ordering of the parts that make up a system—the system is "composed" of these parts. Most engineered structures, whether natural or artificial, can be broken down in this manner.

The compositional hierarchy that every person encounters at every moment is the hierarchy of life. Every person can be reduced to organ systems, which are composed of organs, which are composed of tissues, which are composed of cells, which are composed of molecules, which are composed of atoms. In fact, the last two levels apply to all matter, at least at the macroscopic scale. Moreover, each of these levels inherit all the properties of their children.

In this particular example, there are also *emergent properties*—functions that are not seen at the lower level (e.g., cognition is not a property of neurons but is of the brain)—and a scalar quality (molecules are bigger than atoms, cells are bigger than molecules, etc.). Both of these concepts commonly exist in compositional hierarchies, but they are not a required general property.

These *level hierarchies* are characterized by bi-directional causation. *Upward causation* involves lower-level entities causing some property of a higher level entity; children entities may interact to yield parent entities, and parents are composed at least partly by their children. *Downward causation* refers to the effect that the incorporation of entity x into a higher-level entity can have on *x*'s properties and interactions. Furthermore, the entities found at each level are *autonomous*.

Contexts and Applications

Almost every system within the world is arranged hierarchically. By their common definitions, every nation has a government and every government is hierarchical. Socioeconomic systems are stratified into a social hierarchy (the social stratification of societies), and all systematic classification schemes (taxonomies) are hierarchical. Most organized religions, regardless of their internal governance structures, operate as a hierarchy under God. Many Christian denominations have an autocephalous ecclesiastical hierarchy of leadership.

Families are viewed as a hierarchical structure in terms of cousinship (e.g., first cousin once removed, second cousin, etc.), ancestry (as depicted in a family tree) and inheritance (succession and heirship). All the requisites of a well-rounded life and lifestyle can be organized using Maslow's hierarchy of human needs. Learning must often follow a hierarchical scheme—to learn differential equations one must first learn calculus; to learn calculus one must first learn elementary algebra; and so on. Even nature itself has its own hierarchies, as demonstrated in numerous schemes such as Linnaean taxonomy, the organization of life, and biomass pyramids. Hierarchies are so infused into daily life that they are viewed as trivial.

While the above examples are often clearly depicted in a hierarchical form and are classic examples, hierarchies exist in numerous systems where this branching structure is not immediately apparent. For example, all postal code systems are necessarily hierarchical. Using the Canadian postal code system, the top level's binding concept is the "postal district", and consists of 18 objects (letters). The next level down is the "zone", where the objects are the digits 0–9. This is an example of an overlapping hierarchy, because each of these 10 objects has 18 parents. The hierarchy continues downward to generate, in theory, 7,200,000 unique codes of the format *A0A 0A0*. Most library classification systems are also hierarchical. The Dewey Decimal System is regarded as infinitely hierarchical because there is no finite bound on the number of digits can be used after the decimal point.

Organizations

Organizations can be structured using a hierarchy. In an organizational hierarchy, there is a single person or group with the most power and authority, and each subsequent level represents a lesser authority. Most organizations are structured in this manner, including governments, companies, militia and organized religions. The units or persons within an organization are depicted hierarchically in an organizational chart.

In a reverse hierarchy, the conceptual pyramid of authority is turned upside-down, so that the apex is at the bottom and the base is at the top. This model represents the idea that members of the higher rankings are responsible for the members of the lower rankings.

Organizational Hierarchy

A hierarchical organization is an organizational structure where every entity in the organization, except one, is subordinate to a single other entity. This arrangement is a form of a hierarchy. In an organization, the hierarchy usually consists of a singular/group of power at the top with subsequent levels of power beneath them. This is the dominant mode of organization among large organizations; most corporations, governments, and organized religions are hierarchical organizations with different levels of management, power or authority. For example, the broad, top-level overview of the general organization of the Catholic Church consists of the Pope, then the Cardinals, then the Archbishops, and so on.

Members of hierarchical organizational structures chiefly communicate with their immediate superior and with their immediate subordinates. Structuring organizations in this way is useful partly because it can reduce the communication overhead by limiting information flow; this is also its major limitation.

Visualization

A hierarchy is typically visualized as a pyramid, where the height of the ranking or person depicts their power status and the width of that level represents how many people or business divisions are at that level relative to the whole—the highest-ranking people are at the apex, and there are very few of them; the base may include thousands of people who have no subordinates).

These hierarchies are typically depicted with a tree or triangle diagram, creating an organizational chart or organigram. Those nearest the top have more power than those nearest the bottom, and there being fewer people at the top then at the bottom. As a result, superiors in a hierarchy generally have higher status and command greater rewards than their subordinates.

Common Models

All governments and most companies have similar structures. Traditionally, the monarch was the pinnacle of the state. In many countries, feudalism and manorialism provided a formal social structure that established hierarchical links at every level of society, with the monarch at the top.

In modern post-feudal states the nominal top of the hierarchy still remains the head of state, which may be a president or a constitutional monarch, although in many modern states the powers of the head of state are delegated among different bodies. Below the head, there is commonly a senate, parliament or congress, which in turn often delegate the day-to-day running of the country to a prime minister. In many democracies, the people are considered to be the notional top of the hierarchy, over the head of state; in reality, the people's power is restricted to voting in elections.

In business, the business owner traditionally occupied the pinnacle of the organization. In most modern large companies, there is now no longer a single dominant shareholder, and the collective power of the business owners is for most purposes delegated to a board of directors, which in turn delegates the day-to-day running of the company to a managing director or CEO. Again, although the shareholders of the company are the nominal top of the hierarchy, in reality many companies are run at least in part as personal fiefdoms by their management; corporate governance rules are an attempt to mitigate this tendency.

Criticism and Alternatives

In the work of diverse theorists such as William James (1842-1910), Michel Foucault (1926-1984) and Hayden White, important critiques of hierarchical epistemology are advanced. James famously asserts in his work "Radical Empiricism" that clear distinctions of type and category are a constant but unwritten goal of scientific reasoning, so that when they are discovered, success is declared. But if aspects of the world are organized differently, involving inherent and intractable ambiguities, then scientific questions are often considered unresolved. A hesitation to declare success upon the discovery of ambiguities leaves heterarchy at an artificial and subjective disadvantage in the scope of human knowledge. This bias is an artifact of an aesthetic or pedagogical preference for hierarchy, and not necessarily an expression of objective observation.

Hierarchies and hierarchical thinking has been criticized by many people, including Susan McClary and one political philosophy which is vehemently opposed to hierarchical organization: anarchism is generally opposed to hierarchical organization in any form of human relations. Heterarchy is the most commonly proposed alternative to hierarchy and this has been combined with responsible autonomy by Gerard Fairtlough in his work on Triarchy theory.

Amidst constant innovation in information and communication technologies, hierarchical authority structures are giving way to greater decision-making latitude for individuals and more flexible definitions of job activities and this new style of work presents a challenge to existing organizational forms, with some research studies contrasting traditional organizational forms against groups that operate as online communities that are characterized by personal motivation and the satisfaction of making one's own decisions.

Computer Graphic Imaging (CGI)

Within most CGI and computer animation programs is the use of hierarchies. On a 3D model of a human, the chest is a parent of the upper left arm, which is a parent of the lower left arm, which is a parent of the hand. This is used in modeling and animation of almost everything built as a 3D digital model.

Hierarchical Verbal Alignment

In some languages, such as Cree and Mapudungun, subject and object on verbs are distinguished not by different subject and object markers, but via a hierarchy of persons.

In this system, the three (or four with Algonquian languages) persons are placed in a hierarchy of salience. To distinguish which is subject and which object, *inverse markers* are used if the object outranks the subject.

In music, the structure of a composition is often understood hierarchically, and in the (1985) Generative Theory of Tonal Music, by composer Fred Lerdahl and linguist Ray Jackendoff). The sum of all notes in a piece is understood to be an all-inclusive surface, which can be reduced to successively more sparse and more fundamental types of motion. The levels of structure that operate in Schenker's theory are the foreground, which is seen in all the details of the musical score; the middle ground, which is roughly a summary of an essential contrapuntal progression and voice-leading; and the background or Ursatz, which is one of only a few basic "long-range counterpoint" structures that are shared in the gamut of tonal music literature.

The pitches and form of tonal music are organized hierarchically, all pitches deriving their importance from their relationship to a tonic key, and secondary themes in other keys are brought back to the tonic in a recapitulation of the primary theme. Susan McClary connects this specifically in the sonata-allegro form to the feminist hierarchy of gender in her book *Feminine Endings*, even pointing out that primary themes were often previously called "masculine" and secondary themes "feminine."

Ethics, Behavioral Psychology, Philosophies of Identity

In ethics, various virtues are enumerated and sometimes organized hierarchically according to certain brands of virtue theory.

In all of these random examples, there is an asymmetry of 'compositional' significance between levels of structure, so that small parts of the whole hierarchical array depend, for their meaning, on their membership in larger parts.

In the work of diverse theorists such as William James (1842–1910), Michel Foucault (1926–1984) and Hayden White, important critiques of hierarchical epistemology are advanced. James famously asserts in his work "Radical Empiricism" that clear distinctions of type and category are a constant but unwritten goal of scientific reasoning, so that when they are discovered, success is declared. But if aspects of the world are organized differently, involving inherent and intractable ambiguities, then scientific questions are often considered unresolved.

Feminists, Marxists, anarchists, communists, critical theorists and others, all of whom have multiple interpretations, criticize the hierarchies commonly found within human society, especially in social relationships. Hierarchies are present in all parts of society: in businesses, schools, families, etc. These relationships are often viewed as necessary. However, feminists, Marxists, critical theorists and others analyze hierarchy in terms of the values and power that it arbitrarily assigns to one group over another.

7

Process of Indian Social Stratification

History of Social Relations in India

Caste and Gender Equations in Indian History

No aspect of Indian history has excited more controversy than India's history of social relations. Western indologists and Western-influenced Indian intellectuals have seized upon caste divisions, untouchability, religious obscurantism, and practices of dowry and sati as distinctive evidence of India's perennial backwardness. For many Indologists, these social ills have literally come to define India - and have become almost the exclusive focus of their writings on India.

During the colonial period, it served the interests of the British (and their European cohorts) to exaggerate the democratic character of their own societies while diminishing any socially redeeming features of society in India (and other colonized nations). Social divisions and inequities were a convenient tool in the arsenal of the colonizers. On the one hand, tremendous tactical gains could be achieved by playing off one community against the other. On the other hand, there were also enormous psychological benefits in creating the impression that India was a land rife with uniquely abhorrent social practices that only an enlightened foreigner could attempt to reform. India's social ills were discussed with a contemptuous cynicism and often with a willful intent to instill a sense of deep shame and inferiority.

Strong elements of such colonial imagery continue to dominate the landscape of Western Indology. A liberal, dynamic West embracing universal human values is posed against an obdurate and unchanging East clinging to odious social values and customs.

It is little wonder, therefore, that India's intellectuals have been unable to either fully understand the historic dynamics and context which gave life to these social practices or find effective solutions for their cure. Many historians and social activists appear to have tacitly accepted the notion that caste divisions in society are a uniquely Indian feature and that Indian society has been largely unchanged since the writing of the *Manusmriti* which provides formal sanction to such social inequities.

But caste-like divisions are neither uniquely Indian nor has Indian society been as socially stagnant as commonly believed. In all non-egalitarian societies where wealth and political power were unequally distributed, some form of social inequity appeared and often meant hereditary privileges for the elite and legally (or socially) sanctioned discrimination against those considered lower down in the social hierarchy.

In fact, caste-like divisions are to be found in the history of most nations - whether in the American continent, or in Africa, Europe or elsewhere in Asia. In some societies, caste-like divisions were relatively simple, in others more complex. For instance, in Eastern Africa some agricultural societies were divided between land-owning and landless tribes (or clans) that eventually took on caste-like characteristics. Priests and warriors enjoyed special privileges in the 15th C. Aztec society of Mexico as did the Samurais (warrior nobles) and priests of medieval Japan. Notions of purity and defilement were also quite similar in Japanese society and members of society who carried out "unclean" tasks were treated as social outcasts - just as in India.

Amongst the most stratified of the ancient civilizations was the Roman Civilization where in addition to state-sanctioned slavery, there were all manner of caste-like inequities coded into law. Even in the Christian era, European feudalism provided all manner of hereditary privileges for the knights and landed barons (somewhat akin to India's Rajputs and Thakurs) and amongst the royalty, arranged marriages and dowry were just as common as in India. Discrimination against the artisans was also commonplace throughout Europe, and as late as the 19th century - artisans in Germany had to go through a separate court system to seek legal redress. They were not permitted to appeal to courts that dealt with the affairs of the nobility and the landed gentry. (For instance, Beethoven wrote numerous letters to German judicial authorities pleading that he not be treated as a second-class citizen - that as Germany's pre-eminent composer he deserved better treatment.) A common pattern that seems to emerge from a study of several such ancient and medieval societies is that priests and warriors typically formed an elite class in most medieval societies and social privileges varied according to social rank; in settled agriculture based societies, this was usually closely related to ownership of land.

For instance, we find no evidence of caste-like discrimination in societies where land was collectively owned and jointly cultivated, or where goods and services were exchanged within the village on the basis of barter, and there was no premium assigned to any particular type of work. All services and all forms of human labor were valued equally. Such village communes may have once existed throughout India and some appear to have survived until quite recently - especially in the hills, (such as in parts of Himachal and the North East, including Assam and Tripura), but also in Orissa and parts of Central India. In such societies, we also see little evidence of gender discrimination.

In India, caste and gender discrimination appear to become more pronounced with the advent of hereditary and authoritarian ruling dynasties, a powerful state bureaucracy, the growth of selective property rights, and the domination of Brahmins over the rural poor in *agrahara* villages. But this process was neither linear nor always irreversible. As old ruling dynasties were overthrown, previously existing caste equations and caste hierarchies were also challenged and modified.

In many parts of India this process may have taken several centuries to crystallize and caste rigidity may be a much more recent phenomenon than has been commonly portrayed. The impression that caste divisions were always strictly enforced, or that there were no challenges to caste rigidity does not seem to square with a dispassionate examination of the Indian historical record. It should also be emphasized that caste-distinctions were not the only way, or even the most egregious way in which social inequities manifested themselves in older societies. In ancient Greece and Rome, the institution of slavery was at least as cruel a practice, if not worse. (It is therefore quite ironic how the slave-owning Greek states are revered by Western intellectuals as the world's first "democratic" societies but ancient India is denigrated for it's incomprehensible social ills.) Levels and degree of caste discrimination in India have varied with time and there has been both upward and downward mobility of castes and social groups. Going by the strictures outlined in the *Manusmriti,* one might conclude that caste distinctions were set in stone, rigidly enforced and the possibilities of caste mobility completely circumscribed. But a closer examination of the historical record suggests otherwise.

Already in the Upanishadic period there were tensions between Brahmins and Kshatriyas, and there are explicit parables in the Upanishadic texts illustrating how an enlightened Kshatriya was able to exceed a Brahmin in spiritual wisdom and philosophical knowledge. In the Mahabharatha, there are references to a Brahmin warrior suggesting that caste categories were not entirely inflexible.

There is also criticism of parasitism amongst Brahmins in some of the texts from the Upanishadic period, and social commentators emphasized how those who reneged on their social obligations were undeserving of their caste privileges.

This is an important point because it suggests that there was an implied social contract that involved both privileges and social obligations. The monarch might have enjoyed immense power and prestige, and exacted numerous rights over the common people, but also had the obligation to defend the people - to protect them from invaders, to dispense justice in an unprejudiced manner and assist in the development and preservation of irrigation facilities and roads. Failure to meet such expectations could and did lead to revolts, and dynasties rose and fell within a matter of few generations.

Challenges to Brahminical Hegemony and Caste-rigidity

In the Upanishads, there is also recognition that conceptions of god could be quite varied, that Brahminical rituals were not essential to spiritual release, and that individuals might choose different deities or methods of worship. This ecumenical outlook facilitated the growth of alternative viewpoints not only in the realm of religious practice but also on norms of how society ought to be structured.

Social challenges to absolute monarchical rule and the immense power of the priestly class probably led to a crescendo during the Buddhist period when Brahmin hegemony received challenges from several quarters - from radical atheists such as the *Lokayatas,* from Jain agnostics, and heterodox Hindus and Buddhists who wanted to reconstruct society on a less discriminatory and more humane basis.

Although it would be wrong to romanticize the Buddhists as being completely against caste distinctions {since there is evidence that they accepted caste distinctions in society outside their *sanghas* (communes)}, Buddhists along with other social critics undoubtedly played a powerful role in ensuring that caste was not the sole or even the dominant factor in shaping Indian society of that period. This is borne out by how so many ruling clans arose from a non-Kshatriya (and also non-Brahmin) background. The Nandas, the Mauryas, the Kalingas and the Guptas are just some of the more illustrious of India's ruling dynasties that did not arise from a Kshatriya background.

(Of course, once some of these clans established themselves as ruling dynasties, they took on the Kshatriya mantle, and over time, the radical changes that accompanied their ascent to power gave way to social conservatism and a decaying of the radical currents that had contributed to their rise to power).

It is also worth noting that the classical four varna division of Hindu society (as described in the *Manusmriti)* does not appear to have had much practical significance if one were to go by the accounts of the Greek chronicler, Megasthenes. In his accounts of Mauryan India. Megasthenes appears to list a seven fold social order in which he differentiates between the priest and the philosopher (who he ranked much above the priest, and who could have been a Brahmin, Jain or Buddhist) and also gives special attention to court bureaucrats such as record keepers, tax collectors and judicial officials. He also ascribed to the peasantry a higher status than might be inferred from the *Manusmriti* and noted with amazement how the peasantry was left unharmed during battles.

According to Megasthenes, philosophers - whether Brahmins or Jain/Buddhist monks also had obligations in terms of offering advice to the ruler in matters of public policy, agriculture, health and culture. Repeated failure to provide sound counsel could lead to a loss of privileges - even exile or death. Thus, although many Brahmins may have held on to their privileges by being shameless sycophants - others made significant contributions in the realm of science, philosophy and culture. Social mobility was possible since learning was not an exclusive preserve of the Brahmins and both the Buddhist and Jain sanghas admitted people from different social backgrounds and also admitted women. (Jyotsna Kamat points to a Karnataka inscription from 1187 A.D. that suggests that Jain nuns enjoyed the same amount of freedom as their male counterparts.) The more advanced *sanghas* enforced a separate quorum for women to ensure that a largely male gathering may not take decisions that did not meet with the approval of the women members of the *sangha*.

Over time, it appears that the *sanghas* degenerated, losing their intellectual vitality and egalitarian spirit allowing the Brahmins to gradually consolidate their power and influence in the Gangetic plain. But even as late as the 6th-7th C, Gupta-period inscriptions describing land grants in Bengal appear to corroborate Megasthenes' view of how Indian society was structured. Social rank of senior court administrators (who may have risen from different caste backgrounds) invariably exceeded the rank of ordinary village priests.

(In Orissa, Rajasthan and parts of Central and Southern India, this pattern prevailed till even later. Moreover, as society headed towards caste-ossification, it was the court administrators who after acquiring hereditary caste status, became the most privileged agents in society. In some instances, these administrative castes simply merged with other privileged castes such as Brahmin or Kshatriya, or else they were treated as equivalent, and the historic distinctions between then became blurred or obscured.)

In a sampling of Gupta period land grant decrees, it is intriguing that caste identities are omitted more often than explicitly included. Had caste been as important or dominant a social category, one might expect otherwise. Some of the most important figures appear to be officials involved in tax collection and land measurement. Various ranks of officials are mentioned without any explicit mention of their caste. Villagers are also frequently named without reference to their cast. Only occasionally, there are references to villagers who are also mentioned as being Brahmins. Some of the land grant records indicate that before land grants were made, certain categories of villagers - perhaps those considered more important - were consulted by the higher officials. Although Brahmins are mentioned in the list of those consulted, there are equal references to other categories of villagers such as *kutumbins* and *mahattaras* who may have been village officials or important landholders in the village. {Vishwa Mohan Jha describes the *kutumbins* and *mahattaras* as *varna/jati* nuetral categories (i.e. caste-independent categories) that included Brahmins and non-Brahmins alike.}

Other references point to consultative committees that included the chief artisan, the chief scribe, the merchant and the guild-president cf the town. It also appears that administrative changes led to the creation of new posts, the merger or elimination of older posts, and changes in ranks of various officials over time. An examination of the land grant decrees over a space of three centuries (5th-7th C Bengal) points to such changes and others - such as changes in procedures, or changes in the constitution of consultative committees, perhaps to reflect changing political alliances or changes in the economic status of different groups of townspeople and villagers.

In a land allotment plate from Paschimbagh (Bengal) Brahmins are mentioned as tax payers, and the status of ordinary Brahmins does not seem at all exceptional. For instance, it points to a teacher or a Vedic scholar as being entitled to 10 *patakas* of land, but other Brahmins were entitled to only 2 *patakas* - a share less than that of a *Kayastha* (record-keeper) or *Vaidya* (medical practitioner). Carpenters, smiths and artisans were also put far above other service communities in terms of their share of land.

The Paschimbagh inscription also describes the grant of plots of land to florists, potters, carpenters, masons, blacksmiths and sweepers for serving a *matha (*monastery*)* indicating that when land was granted for a temple or monastery, priests were not the exclusive beneficiaries of land grants. (Two Bhaumakara charters from Talcher/Dhenkanal in Orissa similiarly refer to donations of land for a Buddhist temple, and allocations for its maintenance.)

A study of land grants from 12th C Rajasthan (Pali) and Karnataka (Kalikatti) suggests that land grants had a limited life tenure even when initially decreed to be for life or for perpetuity. Beneficiaries of land grants were subject to transfers, and grants to a particular beneficiary were transferred to another beneficiary five or ten years later. It also appears that the beneficiaries were selected based on administrative rank rather than any particular caste-affiliation.

It is also not at all apparent that administrative rank was limited by birth. In Orissa, there is explicit evidence to the contrary. Ordinary peasants were able to rise up in the ranks of the military, and it is likely that a similar situation prevailed in the administrative ranks. Mayadhar Mansinha suggests that a combination of factors such as training, merit and personal determination played a role, (in addition to social standing and political connections) in determining rank and promotions. In Karnataka, there is evidence that some of the chief administrators were women.

Brahminical Ascendance

Nevertheless, the seeds for a more privileged role for the Brahmins were also being sown through the process of land grants to Brahmins. In some instances, thousands of Brahmins were granted rights to hitherto uncultivated land. In other cases, Brahmins were appointed as the local representatives of the state authorities in what are described as *agrahara* villages where Brahmins presided over small peasants, who in Bihar were mostly landless sharecoppers or bonded labourers. These *agrahara* villages were typically small villages and sattelites of bigger villages that included members of several castes and bigger land-holders. In Bihar, such *agrahara* villages proliferated and it is quite likely that in such *agraharas* oppressive social relations and some of the most egregious patterns of caste-centred discrimination and exploitation may have developed.

(While early Gupta period records indicate the existence of rural consultative councils that mediated between the rulers and the artisans and peasants, it seems that such consultative councils became less important or were phased out with the growth of the *agraharas*. Thereafter, the Brahmins became the sole intermediaries between the village and the state, and over time, this may have enabled the Brahmins to exercise social and political hegemony over other inhabitants of the village. It also appears that the greatest incidence of the practice of untouchability occurs in conjunction with the growth in the power and authority of the Brahmins in such villages.)

But these developments took time to spread elsewhere in India, first spreading to Bengal and eastern UP, and very gradually elsewhere in India. However, this pattern was not necessarily replicated in identical form throughout India and some parts of India virtually escaped this trend. In *agrahara* villages in other parts of India, Brahmins did take on the role of local administrators and tax collectors, but the status of the small peasantry was not always as miserable as in Bihar. The degree of exploitation and oppression appears to be related to the extent of alienation from land-ownership.

For example, evidence for Brahmin domination in Kalikatti, Southern Karnataka emerges after the 13th C. when villagers were instructed to pay taxes to the Brahmin assignees, leading to constant tensions and disputes, but without dramatic changes in the overall status of the tax-paying villagers.

Although Brahminization was an important factor in leading to caste ossification, it was not necessarily the sole or even the most important factor in the mix. The impact of the Islamic invasions, colonization by the British and ecological changes played an equally crucial if not decisive role in many instances.

For instance, in Orissa, the ossification of the bureaucracy and its conversion into a group of privileged and exclusive castes appears to take place after the 14th-15th C. when we begin to see a general decline in its overseas trade due to the silting up of its rivers. At the same time, we see the growth of Brahminical hegemony in the realm of religion and military defeats at the hands of the Mughal armies led by Raja Man Singh of Jaipur. All these factors may have played a role in destroying the vibrancy of Oriya society and encouraging caste conservatism.

Impact of the Islamic Invasions

Unfortunately, many social historians have studiously ignored the effect of such external factors in the shaping of social relations in India. But we know that the Islamic invasions led to monumental changes in the political and cultural life of the sub-continent and especially so in the Gangetic plain - so it would be exceedingly odd if the invasions had no impact on the social structure of Indian society. While some social analysts have tried to analyze Hindu society during the period of Islamic rule as though it had been untouched by the Islamic invasions and left to stagnate in a cocoon of its own making, others have succumbed to illusory simplifications such as Islam was an egalitarian faith whereas Hinduism had caste divisions.

Because Islam first arose in those parts of the world where settled agriculture was not possible - i.e. in the desert sands of the Arabian peninsula - social divisions had not yet emerged in quite the same way that they had in long settled agricultural societies like India. For the warring nomadic tribes of the desert, Islam may have been a tool for the upward mobility of clans that may have earlier survived on petty thievery and by raiding the wealth of settled urban societies (and later for those who joined the ranks of the military in the Islalmic states), the upward mobility of some came at the expense of enormous human rights violations against others. In the hands of expansionist conquerors, Islam became more an instrument of devastation and terror rather than a vehicle for social equality or social justice.

Taken in its entirety, the period of Islamic rule in India cannot be seen as furthering social equity or social harmony in the subcontinent. As a faith-based ideological system Islam could at best guarantee equality before "God" - i.e. equality after death. However, a closer study of the Quran dispels even such notions, for even amongst believers, there is gender discrimination and rank based on the "quality" and "type" of service provided to the Islamic cause. In any case, on earth, the plight of Muslim converts depended more on social realities, on political equations - than on the abstract and remote promise of equality offered by Islam.

During times of heavy political and economic oppression, the only option for the poor was complete and total submission to the will of "God" which in effect meant sacrificing all their autonomy in favor of the clergy, (who rarely challenged political authority), and more often than not, were largely beholden to the rulers who chose to support and promote them. When the clergy did resist political authority, it often tended towards social conservatism and reaction rather than social progress.

By and large, social inequities widened with the onset of Islamic rule in the sub-continent. Land revenue records clearly indicate that with few exceptions (as in Kashmir and Bengal for a time), Islamic rulers taxed the peasantry at significantly higher rates. If the average rate of taxation during the pre-Islamic period varied between 10% to a maximum of 20% - averaging around 15-16%, it had increased to 33% or even more under the Mughals. *(Note that even the Manusmriti limited the tax rate on the peasantry to one-sixth - about 16%).*

While all Islamic rulers may not have insisted on the discriminating *jaziya,* many of the earlier invaders insisted upon it, and more than one court chronicler of the Delhi Sultanate describes the violent means taken to suppress peasant rebellions and extract the high taxes from the crushed peasantry. Urban revolts were also not uncommon and the Arab chronicler Ibn Batuta mentions how such rebellions were suppressed with great cruelty. Punishment for those who rebelled could mean loss of adults (particularly young women) and children to slavery, massacres or forced evacuations of entire villages and small towns, pillage and destruction of places of learning, of temples and other symbols of cultural identification, and denial of job opportunities in the courts. In the early centuries of Islamic rule, the distrust of the locals was so intense that virtually all the important administrative positions were kept in the hands of foreigners.

(Romila Thapar has pointed out that prior to the Islamic invasions, Hindu rulers also invaded or pillaged the temples of their rivals, especially since these temples were repositories of great wealth. She has also indicated that the management of some of these rich temples was extremely corrupt. Plunder of temple wealth was definitely a factor in the destruction of such temples during raids and attacks by Islamic invaders and conquerors. However, during the Islamic invasions, this practice accelerated both in frequency and intensity.

It should also be noted that not all temples were storehouses of great wealth or under the management of corrupt Brahminical trusts. The majority of temples had considerable cultural significance for the local populations and many were built and maintained by non-Brahminical cults. For instance, in Bundelkhand, Rajasthan, Madhya Pradesh and Orissa, there are a sizable number of surviving temples that not only escaped the path of the Islamic invaders, but were obviously left untouched in local battles between rival Hindu kings. There are even scattered remains from the Gupta period. But in the Gangetic plain, virtually nothing from the region's pre-Islamic past has survived. Clearly, there were important political dimensions to the destruction of Northern India's cultural wealth. One might speculate that the political subjugation of a reluctant and possibly even hostile population required the physical elimination of cultural symbols that instilled pride and self-confidence, and thus threatened the authority of the alien rulers.

In any case, the smashing of facial features, genitalia and breasts on sculpted figures has no parallel to earlier practices. There is also little evidence that those defeated in battle were killed or enslaved on the scale of what happened during the Islamic invasions.)

For instance, the Afghanistan region (which once had a sizeable Hindu and Buddhist population) acquired the reputation of being a land where Hindus were slaughtered and hence took the name Hindu-Kush, and references to wanton destruction occur with boastful regularity in the records of the triumphant conquerors. However, in the Gangetic plain the Hindu population was essential in maintaining the tax base for the rulers and therefore, it was only necessary to break the autonomy of the Hindu population and crush their resistance to higher taxation. This was largely achieved through the almost complete destruction of older centres of culture and learning, burning of libraries such as in Nalanda and Vikramshila, the widespread conversion of Buddhists to Islam, and violent acts of reprisal against those who resisted.

One of the most deleterious effects of the Islamic invasions on social relations in India was the practice of slavery, which was introduced on a scale hitherto unseen in the subcontinent. Unlike the societies of the East, slavery appears to have played an important role almost throughout the history of the Western world and the Quran has passages that endorse the practice of slavery. During the Islamic period, in sub-Saharan Africa, slaves labored in the salt mines and copper mines and served as a vital link in the trans-Saharan trade routes acting as porters where camels and donkeys could not go.

Scott Levi (Univ. of Wisconsin) points to judicial documents of medieval Samarqand (and other Central Asian sources) that disclose the presence there of many thousands of Indian slaves throughout the medieval period. A number of Indian sources make it clear that, from the early Ghaznavid raids to the Mughal period, hundreds of thousands (if not millions over the centuries) of men, women and children were marched over to the slave markets in Iran and Central Asia, i.e. beyond the northwest frontier of India, and out of the reach of their familial support systems.

(Although state sanctioned slavery came to an end with the dawn of the Christian era in Europe, a slave-owning replica of ancient Rome arose in the American South, and slaves were employed throughout the Caribbean and South America. The Portuguese were notorious for their slave-markets in India. Even as slavery was banned in Europe, the European trading companies made huge profits from the slave trade. Slavery was not a practice confined to the Islamic parts of the world.)

The practice of slavery probably led to the growth in the custom of *Jauhar* and *Sati* amongst the military castes. Prior to the Islamic invasions, there are very few records to indicate that such practices were widely followed. But the onslaught of the Islamic invaders had led to a complete breakdown in the implementation of war ethics. Whereas in earlier wars, it was required of both sides to protect the peasantry, to leave women, children and the elderly at peace, and there were injunctions against the enslavement of prisoners or of harming those who surrendered in battle - the invaders had few if any compunctions in unleashing all manner of torments on the defeated population. In such an environment, it is not surprising that for the proud Rajput societies, the act of *jauhar,* or mass suicide was a more honorable option.

(It should be noted that such acts of mass or individual suicide are not unknown elsewhere in the world. Sometimes these acts were voluntary (as was usually emphasized in the Indian tradition), at other times they were entirely coerced. Amongst the Vikings, it was customary for a warrior's young concubines to join the funeral pyres of dead Viking warriors. In ancient Nubia (upper Sudan and lower Egypt) there are records of mass suicide upon the death of a warrior king and Nubian burials of warriors indicate practices quite similiar to *Jauhar / Sati.* There are also parallels in the Japanese tradition of *Harakiri*'(suicide for honour) or *Sepukku* amongst the *Samurai* - warrior nobles of Japan. Voluntary suicide of widows (although rare) also took place in China during the reign of the Qing dynasty. There are also records of the Celts and the Romans practicing human sacrifice. Amongst the Aztecs of the 15th C, the custom of human sacrifice of the defeated does not appear to have any voluntary character, and was seen as a legitimate rite in the celebration of a victory in war.

Western feminist indologists who see the practice of Sati as a unique form of gender oppression peculiar to India might note that in the Christian world, the scourge of witch-burning was a far more dangerous threat to the lives of women. The mere charge of being a "witch" could lead to public hanging, and the Salem-witch trials in America were part of a long chain of witch-burnings that took place throughout Christian Europe and carried over into New England)

Nevertheless, Islamic rule in India did not prevail entirely without benefits for specific social classes who chose to collaborate with the invaders. Trading communities probably benefited from the installation of Islamic rulers whose policies of lower taxes on trade, and state support of local traders and financiers was in their interest. Scott Levi suggests that from the end of the thirteenth century, and throughout much of the Delhi Sultanate period, the Muslim nobility were dependent upon heavily capitalized indigenous banking firms (identified in the Tarikh-i Firuz Shahi as *'Sahs'* and *'Multanis'*). These domestic financiers loaned seeds and other necessary inputs to peasants and village-artisans and manufacturers (such as textile weavers) in return for a share of the produce. The rest they bought in cash, and a part of that cash was then recovered by the state treasuries through taxation.

It should also be noted that, (by and large), Islamic rulers born and raised in India relied less on violence and sheer terror, but sought alliances with sections of the local population, especially with those amongst the Hindu elite who were willing to collaborate. Although some of these alliances were coerced, others led to tangible material benefits for the royal collaborators.

Alliances were forged through marriage, or simply from political convenience. Military alliances with Hindu rulers were crucial in maintaining the power of many Islamic rulers. After Akbar, the Mughals relied heavily on the Jaipur and Bikaner Rajputs, who in return were given rights to a share of the taxes extracted from the Gangetic plain. And although Hindus were numerically discriminated in jobs at the courts, by skillfully playing off different caste communities against one another, the Mughals were able to win over a section of the Hindus in maintaining their position of political preeminence.

Hence, it would be wrong to see the many centuries of Islamic rule in India purely from the prism of religious antagonisms. But it would be equally wrong to see the long period of rule by Islamic-identified rulers (even those that were born in India) as entirely benevolent or benign, or no different from the rule of earlier Hindu kings. Since most were heavier taxers, the distance between the ruling elites and the peasant and artisan masses tended to widen and there were other aspects of Islamic rule (particularly during the rule of the more oppressive Sultanates) that limited social mobility.

For many of the Islamic rulers, the Brahmin dominated *agraharas* were highly suited to efficient tax collection and the might of the Sultanates came down very heavily on social challenges that weakened the ability of the state to collect taxes. The fear of enslavement and the denial of equal access to job opportunities in the Sultanate courts led to Hindu society becoming extremely inward-looking in large parts of the plains. With opportunities for jobs in the administrative ranks shrinking, caste loyalties were in all likelihood strengthened, not weakened. Thus, rather than shake up the caste system as some might expect, Islamic rule (by foreign invaders who distrusted the locals) may have actually helped in its crystallization. Neither is there any evidence that Islamic rule helped end the practice of untouchability.

(In fact, the problems of untouchability and caste-discrimination are especially notable in states like UP and Bihar where Islamic rule held complete sway for five centuries. In Sindh and Western Punjab, where almost the entire population was converted to Islam, it is important to observe that janitorial workers were never converted, and to this date remain a highly oppressed and discriminated group. There is also evidence that Muslims developed their own versions of caste. Romila Thapar points out how foreign-origin Muslims such as Syeds, Sheiks and Ashrafs kept themselves consciously apart from Muslims who came from artisan and peasant backgrounds. Language was another divider. In Bijapur district, the elite Muslims spoke Urdu whereas the ordinary Muslims spoke Kannada. Zarina Bhatty in an essay on *"Social stratification among Muslims"* describes caste differentiation amongst Ashraf and non-Ashraf Muslims and notions of impurity that closely parallel caste cleavages and attitudes in Hindu society. Sandra Mackey in the *Caste/Class System in Iran* describes patterns of social differentiation remarkably similiar to India's.)

Over time, Islamic rule in India created a much stronger and more unified elite, which made it more difficult for the ordinary masses to resist regressive social changes, particularly in the realm of philosophical choice, religious pluralism, regional and local autonomy in matters of religion, gender equity, freedom of sexual expression and sexual orientation. For instance, prior to the arrival of Islam, women enjoyed greater freedom of movement and dress. 11th C chronicler of Indian life, *Al-Biruni* expresses puzzlement at how the Hindu men (of Punjab) took the advice of the women "in all consultations and emergencies". But in a matter of few centuries, Islamic notions of gender separation and sexual prudery had infected Hindu households as well. A weaker version of the *Purdah* system and a more conservative dress code became the custom even in Hindu homes, especially so amongst those of the trading community that had frequent contacts with Muslims.

Although in sime passages, the Quran states that their ought to be no compulsion in matters of religion, in other passages, the Quran leaves no doubt that force and coercion are acceptable in furthering Islamic practice. Consequently, the practice of Islam conformed more to the passages advicating force and coercion. In Mali, the Tunisian chronicler Ibn Batuta noted that children who were neglectful in learning the Quran were put in chains until they had it memorized. Regarding India, he commented how newly converted peasants had a very lackadaisical attitude towards attending regular prayers and how the Imams had to cane non-attendees to force attendance. He also describes how he personally led a battle against the reluctance of women to cover their breasts in the Maldives.

In the Indian tradition, moral codes concerning dress were more in keeping with the natural environment. Clothes were light and simple, consistent with the generally hot climate. And in matters of religion, there was greater diversity, and much more personal choice. It was often up to the devotee to visit a temple at a time of his or her choosing. Which deity to worship involved an element of local choice and different *jatis* might worship different deities. Local versions of the epics such as the *Ramayana* and the *Krishna-Leela* were popularized and recent research points to hundreds of different versions in circulation. Unlike in Islam, pilgrimages were undertaken under less pressure and with greater individual volition. *Al-Biruni* also noted how the Hindus were remarkably flexible and willing to change customs and traditions they no longer felt to be relevant or essential.

(Although notions of *Dharma* played an important role in determining the boundaries for social conduct, these varied with time and were also adapted to suit the individual needs and preferences of different regions and localities.)

Pluralism in Indian History

In religions that paid tremendous stress on "revealed truth" (such as Christianity or Islam) there have always been strong tendencies towards dogmatic rigidity. But even at the peak of their influence, India's Brahmins were never quite able to impose any comparable sort of rigid uniformity in the practice of Hinduism on a national (let alone, international) scale. In some localities, the lower castes did without the Brahmins entirely while elsewhere, especially in the South, or in Central India and Orissa - Brahmins often felt obliged to give due deference to dissenting and heterodox cults, and incorporated their belief systems into mainstream Hinduism.

T.K Venkatasubramaniam describes how in Tamil Nadu, Brahmins begin to play an important role in politics and society only after the 7th C., when the Pallavas began to challenge the authority of the previous ruling clans such as the Chera, Chola and Pandya. Because the Pallavas did not rise from an aristocratic background, they used the Brahmins to validate their right to rule through a combination of persuasion and coercion.

At that time, Tamil Nadu was a hotbed of a variety of non-Brahminical traditions, (such as Buddhist, Jain and many others) - hence, a synthesis of these different traditions took place between the 7th and the 11th centuries. Vajrayana Buddhism, Shaivite Tantrism and Hata-Yoga were amongst the trends that became integrated. The Bhakti tradition in which the devotee is held in a higher status than the Brahmin had it's impact as did the ideals of the Siddhis whose supreme ideal was freedom, perfect health and immortality - all to be gained on this earth through magic and yoga. The Kalamukas, Pasupatas and Kapalikas were popular practitioners of Yogic and Tantric cults - the latter helped assimilate the ecstatic tribal cults of earlier times. This was also the period when the androgyne forms of the Hindu gods (the *Ardhanarishwara*) became popularized.

The existence of these numerous cults was partly an expression of the struggle for social equality and freedom from exploitation, but for some, it was also a means for accessing greater social privileges. The Brahmins of Tamil Nadu (along with the rulers) attempted to manage these social tensions through co-option, philosophical accommodation and synthesis.

In Andhra, folk religions played a powerful role in mediating Brahminical influences, and a vibrant example of the deep penetration of folk influences in popular religion is to be seen in the sculpted array of folkloric panels in the temple of Srisailam (sponsored by the Vijayanagar rulers in the 14th-15th C.). In neighbouring Karnataka, the Bhakti ideal and Jain influences put their stamp on prevailing religious practices.

Religion in India thus developed in a much more organic fashion than is commonly realized, and it was never completely divorced from popular inputs. Both male and female deities drew followers, and while goddesses were sometimes displayed in demonic warrior roles, gods were sometimes displayed with feminine qualities. In the Yogini temples, all the deities were women and although today, there are only a handful of surviving Yogini temples, (mostly in Orissa and Madhya Pradesh) it is not unlikely that many more may have been in existence.

In the 8th-10th C Pratihara era temples, men and women were sculpted in identical heights and proportions - perhaps implying that male domination had not yet fully come to pass. Tantric ideas on sexual liberation found their way into the grand temples not only of Khajuraho and Konarak but also in temples in Rajasthan, the Jabalpur and Raipur regions, in Telengana and elsewhere in the South. Unlike Islam where entry into mosques was curtailed for women, and separate *zenana* areas were constructed, restraints on the entry of women in temples were not commonplace. Contrary to the suppression of female sexuality in the Semitic religious streams, temple architecture from the 11th-13th C appears to revel in the eroticism of both genders - and there are even displays of same-gender interaction.

In this relatively liberal atmosphere, philosophy continued to flourish and while some tendencies drifted towards religious idealism, others emphasized the rational and worldly. The slow but steady record of scientific progress up to the 12th-13th C points to the toleration that atheist, agnostic and rational currents may have enjoyed in Indian society in contrast to the violence meted out towards "heretics" and disbelievers in medieval Europe and the Middle East. Religion in India developed in a relatively secular atmosphere where all manner of religious variations coexisted with the abstract and all-inclusive monotheism articulated in the Upanishads and later emulated in the various Bhakti streams of worship.

At the grassroots level, these relatively more liberal tendencies had their impact on the practice of Islam as well. Sufism, the worship of *pirs* (saints), the practice of the *Urs* were attempts at forging some sort of a compromise.

(Romila Thapar points to peasant and artisan Muslims of Bijapur who continued to celebrate Hindu festivals. To this day, Muslim peasants of Northern Karnataka celebrate Islamic festivals with folk dances that have Hindu origins - quite unlike the orthodox practice of these festivals where singing and dancing might be frowned upon. Such hybrid Muslim communities exist elsewhere in India too.)

But in the Madrasahs, (with few exceptions) conservatism and orthodoxy were the norm; attempts at providing a secular education never really took off, and over time this had a distinctly illiberal effect on how social relations matured in the sub-continent.

The Sikh Renaissance

Just prior to British rule, Mughal rule had virtually collapsed and power had gone into the hands of Sikh rulers in the North and the Maratha kings in much of Central and Southern India. The Sikhs had been at the forefront of powerful social reforms as they fought against the intolerable burden of high taxes imposed by the Mughals. Gender equality received particular attention from the early Sikh Gurus as did caste discrimination. During the time of Guru Gobind Singh - women not only participated as warriors but they also led some of the battles, and 40% of the spiritual leadership came from the ranks of women.

However once the Sikhs became rulers, the egalitarian currents in the Sikh tradition became successively dissipated. Upper caste converts to Sikhism retained their caste identification, and *Gurudwaras* became divided between those for the upper and lower castes. Nevertheless, the peasantry did win some concessions and the *Gurudwaras* institutionalized charitable practices on a scale unmatched in previous eras. Overall, the century that preceded colonization was a period of growing social ferment in India, but as British colonial rule tightened, it was to put a great damper on the pace of social reforms.

The British Colonial Era

Although some versions of Indian history ascribe to the early colonial administrators a penchant for social reform, it should be noted that the colonial "reformers" were at best aligning themselves with active indigenous reform currents. They were not usually the initiators or great crusaders for social reform as is frequently portrayed.

In any case, after 1857, the cynical strategy of divide and conquer not only impacted relations between Hindus and Muslims, but also aggravated caste tensions. But even independently of conscious attempts by British administrators to inflame caste tensions, the ruination of the Indian economy alone led to a disastrous degradation in social relations.

The Zamindari system particularly disenfranchised the peasantry whose status dropped dramatically in comparison to those castes who were able to find a foothold in the new administration, or find some employment in the new colonial cities. The enormous burden of high taxes led to unprecedented levels of indebtedness and the privileging of the money-lending castes. The economic devastation caused by the Mahalwari system of taxation in the Awadh region led to higher levels of gender discrimination, and an increase in coercion in matters related to dowry. Differential access to modern education and jobs in the colonial administration increased the distance between the favored castes - and the Indian masses. (The favored castes naturally included Brahmins, Kshatriyas and Banias, but also other important administrative castes such as Kayasthas. Large land owning castes such as Mehtas and Reddis were also favored, as were Marathas, Jatts and other castes who had risen during the decline of Mughal rule.)

It was also the British who resurrected the *Manusmriti* and used it to frame the "Hindu Civil Code". Prior to colonization, the *Manusmriti* was nothing more than an obscure text, long-forgotten and rarely used to determine what was acceptable social practice. The *Manusmriti* came in very handy in social control. Because the numerical presence of the Britishers in India was not substantial, the Britishers had to rule largely by proxy. It was important that their agents did not face resistance or rebellion, even in the social realm. Owing to it's repressive and highly divisive character, the *Manusmriti* helped in preventing both individual and collective resistance to local authorities, who were typically upper caste and often Brahmin. That the *Manusmriti* represented an archaic and outdated social code didn't matter. It fit in very well with the British colonial project.

It was also convenient in providing ideological cover for repressive legal steps the British wanted to take anyway. For instance it didn't hurt that the *Manusmriti* advocated laws that legitimized gender discrimination or attacked same-gender relationships. Such attitudes were then equally prevalent in Europe and it made it easier to disenfranchise women in matters of inheritance or introduce legal injunctions against same-gender sexual relations (as was the case in Britain during the 18th C.).

Changes in Caste Equations

Historians who have attempted to draw a straight line between the *Manusmriti* and post-independence India are clearly unfamiliar with those patterns of Indian history that contradict such a linear view. While some of the social evils of modern India may have ancient roots, many others have a fairly recent history. And even those that may have ancient precedence were modulated and modified as a result of numerous struggles for social equality that have taken place throughout Indian history. For example, after independence one could find temples built in the late 18th or 19th century that restricted entry to dalits and menstruating women. But it is not at all clear if such strictures were widespread prior to colonization. Research indicates that during the Pratihara period, caste categories were relatively flexible and popular temples were constructed by those considered low-caste. Temple construction was often a way of gaining social respect and upward mobility. Restrictions on temple entry most likely reached a peak during the British period partly because only the upper castes had the means to build temples, and also because the control of existing temples passed into the hands of trusts who were hand-picked by the British, and were given free license (possibly even encouraged) to promote discriminatory practices. The iron hand of the colonial state made it much more difficult to challenge such reactionary tendencies.

"The original caste: power, history and hierarchy in South Asia", in McKim Marriott, ed. "India through Hindu Categories" "Under colonialism, caste was appropriated, and in many respects reinvented, by the British" "Paradoxically, colonialism seems to have created much of what is now accepted as Indian 'tradition', including an autonomous caste structure with the Brahman clearly at the head" "Caste, as it is still portrayed in much current anthropological literature, is a colonial construction, reminiscent only in some ways of the social forms that preceded colonial intervention"

Economic factors were also crucial in determining caste rank and caste relationships. In periods of intense economic exploitation, caste discrimination intensified, and the reverse took place in periods of economic expansion. For instance, most historians are in agreement that the Gupta period was a period of rising prosperity and also a period of increasing social mobility. Improvements in agricultural productivity led to concomitant improvements in the social rank of the cultivators.

Similiarly, (though much later) there is evidence for the rise in status of the *telis* - cooking oil manufacturers and traders whose earlier low caste status did not fit with their growing economic importance, and were thus granted a higher caste rank. Besides, all through Indian history, phony lineages for non-Kshatriya rulers were constructed to create the aura of continuity and legitimacy. Hence, the mere existence of a document like the Manusmriti should not cause serious social scientists to jump to broad conclusions without greater scrutiny and dispassionate analysis of the Indian historical record.

It is also important not to judge an older society by modern standards. Social relations cannot be entirely separated from how productive activities are carried out and what the level of available technology makes socially possible. In today's world, the widespread availability of printed matter, of computers and other means to store and develop knowledge systems makes the older systems of learning and skill-preservation largely redundant. But in older times, the artisans guild system helped in the development and preservation of specialized knowledge and perfection of important manufacturing skills. In India, artisans guilds were closely correlated to *jati* or caste. It was not only the Brahmins and upper castes who favored hereditary continuity, but skilled carpenters, weavers, metalworkers, painters and numerous categories of other artisans also saw certain benefits in maintaining their *jati* identities. While the artisan castes often fought for greater social equality - the complete breakdown of caste identities was never a serious option except for those at the very bottom of the caste totem pole.

The caste system survived not just because it was enforced by the legal writ of an elite class, but as much because it served a social purpose in an era in which it was difficult if not impossible to organize the educational and productive activities of society in a more flexible and democratic way.

Other forms of Social Discrimination

In addition, societies that may not have overtly practised a caste system (such as Europe in the Christian era) may have yet prevented egalitarian social interaction and free social mobility through other means. The virtual annihilation and isolation of Native American communities by Christian invaders and immigrants is a striking and tragic example of systematic social exclusion.

While slavery in America was a thoroughly cruel and demeaning practice, the abolition of slavery did not end injustices against African Americans or other non-European immigrants. For instance, until the passing of the civil rights act - discrimination against African Americans and other nationalities such as Chinese, Indian and Mexican were enshrined in law. Inter-racial marriages were banned in many states and the mere charge of taking an interest in a Caucasian woman could lead to the lynching of Afro-American men in the South. Early Chinese and Indian immigrants were paid substantially less than the prevailing wages, were not allowed to bring wives and family members into the country, and prevented from owning property. Even workers guilds and trade unions discriminated against non-European immigrant workers.

(The evidence from the richest of the world's capitalist countries suggests that both overt and covert forms of social inequality continues to this day. For instance, many elected Presidents in the US (including Clinton, Bush and Reagan) can trace their lineage to the British royal family, implying that the old ruling classes continue to enjoy special access to power. In Britain, hereditary privileges are enshrined in the constitution for the monarchy, as well as other members of the nobility. The House of Lords is another vestige of the old system that privileges certain elites. The 'old-boys' network, exclusive college sororities and fraternities are another way in which the elite are usually able to arrange privileged and differential access to jobs and business opportunities.

At the other end of the social spectrum, African Americans in the US remain a highly discriminated group. Although comprising less than 10% of the US population, they make up almost fifty percent of prisoners on death row and a similarly high percentage of jail inmates. Numerous studies have pointed to highly discriminatory practices in how African Americans are arrested (much more frequently), charged (with much lower thresholds of incriminating evidence) and sentenced (to much longer prison terms) relative to Caucasian Americans. In California, there are more African Americans in jails than in universities. The unemployment rate amongst African Americans in some US cities is as high as 50% whereas the average rate of unemployment is less than 5% in the country as a whole.)

Discrimination in the Modern World

While in India, caste continues to be an important category leading to grave social inequities, national origin and race have become important factors in how inequality is propagated in much of the modern world. Racial and national discrimination was at the core of how colonial rulers justified their exploitation of the colonies. The colonial system was unique in how human exploitation reached a level of intensity unseen in human history and enabled the creation of exploitative patterns across vast oceans and geographical territories. The legacy of this economic devastation lives on in how negative social practices from older eras continue to survive not only in India but in much of Africa and other colonized nations.

The legacy of colonialism also shows up in how there is no equal work for equal pay across nations. Even accounting for differences in purchasing power, the income and ability to consume for a doctor, engineer, skilled industrial worker or service worker in the US, Europe or Japan is often five to ten times greater than say in India or Bangladesh or Kenya or Indonesia.

While it is undeniable that the task of democratization of Indian society is incomplete, that caste and gender discrimination continue to cause grave harm, that Adivasis and Dalits still face all manner of trials and tribulations, and that all such social inequities need to be fought with continued vigour - India's social evils cannot be analyzed or eliminated in isolation of other necessary changes. It is important that the process of how social relations become shaped in a certain way be better understood. While battles for social equality need widespread support, their ultimate success may be determined as much by how India's economy develops.

All through human history, property-less classes have suffered social discrimination of one kind or another. Economic disparities remain a serious contributor to social inequities today. Any social system that is based on unequal access to economic assets - (whether they be land, raw materials, industrial or commercial wealth) will inevitably lead to some form of social discrimination and inequity. Victims of older forms of discrimination will either continue to be victimized, or simply become victims of new forms of discrimination.

For that reason, the challenge for countries like India is not only to fight against all instances of social discrimination, but to also struggle for greater economic equality - not only within India, but also in terms of India's equality with the rest of the world.

8

Caste Stratification in Indian Society

The Indian caste system describes the system of social stratification and social restrictions in India in which social classes are defined by thousands of endogamous hereditary groups, often termed *jatis* or castes. Within a jati, there exist exogamous groups known as gotras, the lineage or clan of an individual.

In a handful of sub-castes such as Shakadvipi, endogamy within a gotra is permitted and alternative mechanisms of restricting endogamy are used (e.g. banning endogamy within a surname).

The Indian caste system involves four castes and outcasted social groups. Although generally identified with Hinduism, the caste system was also observed among followers of other religions in the Indian subcontinent, including some groups of Muslims and Christians. Caste barriers have mostly broken down in large cities, though they persist in rural areas of the country, where 72% of India's population resides.

None of the Hindu scriptures endorses caste-based discrimination, and the Indian Constitution has outlawed caste-based discrimination, in keeping with the secular, democratic principles that founded the nation.

Nevertheless, the caste system, in various forms, continues to survive in modern India because of a combination of political factors and social perceptions and behaviour.

History

The history of the Indian caste system dates back to the Vedic period.

Possible Genetic Origin

The origin of the caste system as it is today is still obscure. There is significant disagreement regarding whether or not castes are genetically distinct, and whether genetic differences between groups might partly explain their origin.

A 1995 study by Joanna L. Mountain et al. of Stanford University concluded that there was "no clear separation into three genetically distinct groups along caste lines", although "an inferred tree revealed some clustering according to caste affiliation".

A 2001 genetic study, led by Michael Bamshad of University of Utah, found that the genetic affinity of Indians to Europeans is proportionate to caste rank, the upper castes being most similar to Europeans, whereas lower castes are more like Asians. The researchers believe that the Indo-European speakers entered India from the Northwest, admixing with or displacing the proto-Dravidian speakers. Subsequently they may have established a caste system and placed themselves primarily in higher castes. The study concludes that the Indian castes "are most likely to be of proto-Asian origin with West Eurasian admixture resulting in rank-related and sex-specific differences in the genetic affinities of castes to Asians and Europeans.". Because the Indian samples for this study were taken from a single geographical area, it remains to be investigated whether its findings can be safely generalized.

A 2002-03 study by T. Kivisild et al. concluded that the "Indian tribal and caste populations derive largely from the same genetic heritage of Pleistocene southern and western Asians and have received limited gene flow from external regions since the Holocene." A 2006 genetic study by the National Institute of Biologicals in India, testing a sample of men from 32 tribal and 45 caste groups, concluded that the Indians have acquired very few genes from Indo-European speakers.

According to a 2006 study by Ismail Thanseem et al. of Centre for Cellular and Molecular Biology (India) "the vast majority (>98%) of the Indian maternal gene pool, consisting of Indo-European and Dravidian speakers, is genetically more or less uniform", while the invasions after the late Pleistocene settlement might have been mostly male-mediated.

The study concluded that the "lower caste groups might have originated with the hierarchical divisions that arose within the tribal groups with the spread of Neolithic agriculturalists, much earlicr than the arrival of Aryan speakers", and "the Indo-Europeans established themselves as upper castes among this already developed caste-like class structure within the tribes."

The study indicated that the Indian caste system may have its roots much before the arrival of the Indo-Aryan immigrants; a rudimentary version of the caste system may have emerged with the shift towards cultivation and settlements, and the divisions may have become more well-defined and intensified with the arrival of Indo-Aryans.

A study conducted by the Centre for Cellular and Molecular Biology in 2009 (in collaboration with Harvard Medical School, Harvard School of Public Health and the Broad Institute of Harvard and MIT) analyzed half a million genetic markers across the genomes of 132 individuals from 25 ethnic groups from 13 states in India across multiple caste groups.

The study concludes, based on the impossibility of identifying any genetic indicators across caste lines, that castes in South Asia grew out of traditional tribal organizations during the formation of Indian society, and was not the product of any mythical Aryan Invasion and subjugation of Dravidian people.

Hindu Scriptures

The caste system as we know today is not from the classical Hindu system.According to classical Hindu system, the society was divided into four "Varnas" (classes or categories), purely based on profession and not by birth.

1. Brahmins – the clergy, teacher, religious authority
2. Kshatriya – the warriors, administrators, political authority
3. Vaisyas – the merchants, farmers, the business persons
4. Shudras – the servants, labours.

The Varna system was originally evolved for the classification of human duties in a healthy society. The system allowed free movement within the Varnas. So a Brahmin's son can be a Khatriya or Vaisya. The caste system practiced today is not mentioned anywhere in any of the Hindu scriptures.

Although the Hindu scriptures contain some passages that can be interpreted to sanction the caste system, they also contain indications that the caste system is not an essential part of the Hindu religion, and both sides in the debate are able to find sections in scriptures that support their views.

The most ancient scriptures—the *Shruti* texts, or Vedas, place very little importance on the caste system, mentioning caste only sparingly and descriptively (i.e., not prescriptive). Indeed, the only verse in the *Rigveda* which mentions all four *varnas* is 10.90, the *Purushasûkta*. The other *varnas*, the *Brahma* (i.e. Brahmins) and *Rajanya* (i.e. Kshatriyas) are mentioned separately in some other verses in the *Rigveda* (e.g. RV 10.80.1) and the other Vedas, and rarely in the Upanishads. Some—definitely including most *Smriti* texts—have interpreted these as *prescribing* the division of society in the four *varnas*. A hymn from the Rig Veda seems to indicate that one's caste is not necessarily determined by that of one's family:

Rig Veda 9.112.3

—I am a bard, my father is a physician, my mother's job is to grind the corn.

In the Vedic period, there also seems to no discrimination against the Shudras (which later became an ensemble of the so-called low-castes) on the issue of hearing the sacred words of the Vedas and fully participating in all religious rights, something which became totally banned in the later times.

Later scriptures such as *Bhagavad Gita* and *Manusmriti* state that the four varnas are created by God. However, at the same time, the Gita says that one's varna is to be understood from one's personal qualities and one's *karma* (work), not one's birth. Some scholars believe that, in its initial period, the caste system was flexible and it was merit and job based. One could migrate from one caste to other caste by changing one's profession. This view is supported by records of sages who became Brahmins. For example, the sage Vishwamitra belonged to a Kshatriya caste, and only later became recognized as a great Brahmin sage, indicating that his caste was not determined by birth. Similarly, Valmiki, once a low-caste robber, became a great sage. Veda Vyasa, another sage, was the son of a fisherwoman. Vasishtha was a shudra and he became sage later.

Manusmriti, dated between 200 B.C.E. and 100 A.D., contains some laws that codified the caste system. The Manu Smriti belongs to a class of books that are geared towards ethics, morals, and social conduct - NOT religion. The content of these texts reflects the thinking of philosophers (like Manu) belonging to that age regarding issues pertaining to ethics, morals and social conduct. In this non-religious text (the Manu Smriti), the sage Manu explains that society is like the human body, where all body parts are required to function optimally in order to ensure the optimal function of society as a whole. He divided this metaphoric body into 4 main constituent parts: Head, Arms, Torso, Legs. The head of a body is required for thinking, planning, and decision making. Thus the metaphoric head of society (the Brahmins) were also responsible for these things. The arms of a body are responsible for protection of the body. Thus the arms of society were the Kshatriyas who were responsible for protection of the society. The torso of the body is responsible for consumption, production, and to hold society together as a whole. Thus, the Vaishya class was likened to the torso and constituted of the peasants, farmers, merchants, etc. Finally, the legs of a body are what carry the entire body altogether without which the body can make no movement or progress. These legs are the hardest physically working part of the body. The Shudra class of labourers was likened to the legs and was responsible for most physical labor jobs.

In this way, the entire body of society was complete and functional. No part of the body (society) was intended to be superior to another, just as all parts of the human body are equally important for optimal function. There was no hierarchy intended. This societal superiority/inferiority interpretation was a product of our flawed human nature which is to belittle those whom we believe are doing more menial work than we are. It was the tendency to think “Well, I'm a Brahman, and you're just a Shudra so I'm better or higher than you are” that caused the belief that Brahmans are the highest and Shudras are the lowest. Again, an unintentional twisting of the original caste system which was nothing more than a system of equal division of social responsibilities amongst all citizens to begin with.

Furthermore, the caste a person belongs to was traditionally inherited. However, it should be noted that these castes were not permanent and inherited only. Study of the Gita and other ancient texts allows one to understand that an individual's "caste" is largely determined by his character and nature. This is reflected in the Gita when Krishna explains to Arjun that the moment he ceases to perform the duties of a Kshatriya, he will no longer remain one. Also, in his book, "The Holy Science" (less commonly known as "Kaivalya Darshanam"), Swami Sri Yukteshwar Giri explains that an individual's caste is largely determined by the nature of one's Chitta (the deepest, purest conscious state of the unliberated soul). The nature of one's Chitta (and essentially any desire other than that for unity with God) is expressed in the desires and tendencies of man. Therefore, one ignorant of spirituality and able to comprehend only the physical world would be in a dark state of mind prevalent in the Kali Yuga that would correspond with the Shudra caste. As one's spiritual awareness grows lifetime upon lifetime, his natural caste (as opposed to the caste assigned by default from birth) climbs "upward" (spiritually, not socially or materialistically - and no, this does not imply that Brahman's are superior to anyone, just as a saint does not consider himself to be superior to anyone else, simply because he's in the later stages of spiritual evolution)

Emergence of Rigid Caste Structures

Megasthenes, the Greek ambassador to Chandragupta Maurya's court in India classified people of India into seven classes: philosophers, peasants, herdsmen, craftsmen and traders, soldiers, government officials and councilors.

In its later stages, the caste system is said to have become rigid, and caste began to be inherited rather than acquired by merit. In the past, members of different castes would not partake in various activities, such as dining and religious gatherings, together. In addition, the performance of religious rites and rituals were restricted to Brahmins, who were the designated priesthood. The "Pandaram" priests are an example of an order of Dravidian tamil priests, based in Nepal and South India. The Pandaram maintain the same tradition as the Brahmin priests, including the use of the Sanskrit language (traditionally reserved for the Brahmins) for the rituals. While they are not generally as well trained as the Brahmin priests, they are highly respected within their community and are addressed with reverence.

According to the Manusmriti, every caste belongs to one of the four varnas (Brahmin, Kshtriya, Vaishya, and Shudra). However, there have been many disputes about the varna of many castes, such as castes being considered Kshatriya by some scholars, while described as Shudra by others. While texts such as the Manusmriti attempted to rationalize ambiguous castes by placing them in varna-sankaras (i.e. mixed varna), the fact remains that Indian society was, and is, composed of numerous geographically diversified but endogamous groups. With many occupational groups practicing endogamy within a particular region, as well as numerous sub-divisions within the four main castes, a more complex system of subcastes and jatis is evident. The jatis have broken up into clans like Agarwal, Iyer, etc.

Mobility Across the Castes

The view of the caste system as "static and unchanging" has been disputed by many scholars. For instance, sociologists such as Bernard Buber and Marriott McKim describe how the perception of the caste system as a static and textual stratification has given way to the perception of the caste system as a more processual, empirical and contextual stratification. Other sociologists such as Y.B Damle have applied theoretical models to explain mobility and flexibility in the caste system in India.. According to these scholars, groups of lower-caste individuals could seek to elevate the status of their caste by attempting to emulate the practices of higher castes.

Some scholars believe that the relative ranking of other castes was fluid or differed from one place to another prior to the arrival of the British.

The distinctions, particularly between the Brahmans and the other castes, were in theory sharper, but in practice it now appears that social restrictions were not so rigid. Brahmans often lived off the land and founded dynasties. Most of the groups claiming Kshatriya status had only recently acquired it. The conscious reference to being Kshatriya, a characteristic among Rajputs, is a noticeable feature in post-Gupta politics.

The fact that many of these dynasties were of obscure origin suggests some social mobility: a person of any caste, having once acquired political power, could also acquire a genealogy connecting him with the traditional lineages and conferring Kshatriya status. A number of new castes, such as the Kayasthas (scribes) and Khatris (traders), are mentioned in the sources of this period. According to the Brahmanic sources, they originated from intercaste marriages, but this is clearly an attempt at rationalizing their rank in the hierarchy. Many of these new castes played a major role in society. The hierarchy of castes did not have a uniform distribution throughout the country. Flexibility in caste laws permitted very low-caste religious clerics such as Valmiki to compose the Ramayana, which became a central work of Hindu scripture.

According to some psychologists, mobility across broad caste lines may have been "minimal", though sub-castes (jatis) may change their social status over the generations by fission, relocation, and adoption of new rituals..

Sociologist M. N. Srinivas has also debated the question of rigidity in Caste. In an ethnographic study of the Coorgs of Karnataka, he observed considerable flexibility and mobility in their caste hierarchies. He asserts that the caste system is far from a rigid system in which the position of each component caste is fixed for all time. Movement has always been possible, and especially in the middle regions of the hierarchy. It was always possible for groups born into a lower caste to "rise to a higher position by adopting vegetarianism and teetotalism" i.e. adopt the customs of the higher castes. While theoretically "forbidden", the process was not uncommon in practice. The concept of sanskritization, or the adoption of upper-caste norms by the lower castes, addressed the actual complexity and fluidity of caste relations.

Historical examples of mobility in the Indian Caste System among Hindus have been researched. There is also precedent of certain Shudra families within the temples of the Shrivaishava sect in South India elevating their caste.

Historical Advantages of the Caste System

Historically, the caste system offered several advantages to the population of the Indian subcontinent. While Caste is nowadays seen by instances that render it anachronistic, in its original form the caste system served as an important instrument of order in a society in which mutual consent rather than compulsion ruled; where the ritual rights as well as the economic obligations of members of one caste or sub-caste were strictly circumscribed in relation to those of any other caste or sub-caste; where one was born into one's caste and retained one's station in society for life; where merit was inherited, where equality existed within the caste, but inter-caste relations were unequal and hierarchical. A well-defined system of mutual interdependence through a division of labour created security within a community.

1. Preservation of order in society through the use of institutional stratification of social groups.
2. Integration of foreigners and invading forces into Indian culture by assigning a caste to them (a process that historian Jawaharlal Nehru referred to as "Indianization"): India has faced repeated invasions from outside the region, dating back to the Macedonian invasion by Alexander the Great. Most invaders were swiftly assimilated into ancient Indian society by assigning them specific castes. Examples include the Kambojas, believed to be of Indo-Scythian descent, who were retroactively assigned a social position in the Manusmriti.
3. The Varna system, with its normative interpretation as a division of labor, had and continues to have a heavy bias towards spiritual evolution. The deep religious proclivities and the urge for spiritual uplift had induced the people to search for simpler and effective ways to achieve the spiritual goal which led to innovations like the Bhakti movement which had a powerful impact on the socio-cultural-spiritual life of the people even at mass level without distinctions of caste or class or other

social differences. It is these deeply run cultural roots which caused an abiding following for Hinduism even in the face of unrelenting assaults by other religions and had in fact continued to influence the lives of people even after their conversion to other faiths. Thus, the caste system can be said to have preserved ancient cultural values in Indian society.

4. The caste system played an influential role in shaping economic activities. The caste system functioned much like medieval European guilds, ensuring the division of labour, providing for the training of apprentices and, in some cases, allowing manufacturers to achieve narrow specialisation. For instance, in certain regions, producing each variety of cloth was the speciality of a particular sub-caste.
5. Philosophers argue that the majority of people would be comfortable in stratified endogamous groups and have been in ancient times. Membership in a particular caste, with its associated narrative, history and genealogy would instill in its members a sense of group accomplishment and cultural pride. Such sentiments are routinely expressed by the Marathas, for instance.

British Rule

The caste system had been a fascination of the British since their arrival in India. Coming from a society that was divided by class, the British attempted to equate the caste system to the class system. As late as 1937 Professor T. C. Hodson stated that: "Class and caste stand to each other in the relation of family to species. The general classification is by classes, the detailed one by castes. The former represents the external, the latter the internal view of the social organization." The difficulty with definitions such as this is that class is based on political and economic factors, caste is not. In fairness to Professor Hodson, by the time of his writing, caste had taken on many of the characteristics that he ascribed to it and that his predecessors had ascribed to it but during the 19th century caste was not what the British believed it to be. It did not constitute a rigid description of the occupation and social level of a given group and it did not bear any real resemblance to the class system. However, this will be dealt with later in this essay. At present, the main concern is that the British saw caste as a way to deal with a huge population by breaking it down into discrete chunks with specific characteristics. Moreover, as will be seen later in this paper, it appears that the caste system extant in the late 19th and early 20th century has been altered as a result of British actions so that it increasingly took on the characteristics that were ascribed to by the British.

One of the main tools used in the British attempt to understand the Indian population was the census. Attempts were made as early as the beginning of the 19th century to estimate populations in various regions of the country but these, as earlier noted, were methodologically flawed and led to grossly erroneous conclusions. It was not until 1872 that a planned comprehensive census was attempted. This was done under the direction of Henry Beverely, Inspector General of Registration in Bengal. The primary purpose given for the taking of the census, that of governmental preparedness to deal with disaster situations, was both laudable and logical. However, the census went well beyond counting heads or even enquiring into sex ratios or general living conditions. Among the many questions were enquiries regarding nationality, race, tribe, religion and caste. Certainly none of these things were relevant to emergency measures responses by the government. Further, neither the notion of curiosity nor planned subterfuge on the part of the administration suffices to explain their inclusion in the census. On the question of race or nationality it could be argued that these figures were needed to allow analyses of the various areas in an attempt to predict internal unrest. However, there does not appear to have been any use made of the figures from that perspective. With regard to the information on religion and caste, the same claim could be made but once again there does not appear to have been any analyses done with the thought of internal disturbance in mind. Obviously there had to be some purpose to the gathering of this data since due to the size of both the population and the territory to be covered, extraneous questions would not have been included due to time factors. Therefore, there must have been a reason of some sort for their inclusion. That reason was, quite simply, the British belief that caste was the key to understanding the people of India. Caste was seen as the essence of Indian society, the system through which it was possible to classify all of the various groups of indigenous people according to their ability, as reflected by caste, to be of service to the British.

Caste was seen as an indicator of occupation, social standing, and intellectual ability. It was, therefore necessary to include it in the census if the census was to serve the purpose of giving the government the information it needed in order to make optimum use of the people under its administration. Moreover, it becomes obvious that British conceptions of racial purity were interwoven with these judgements of people based on caste when reactions to censuses are examined. Beverly concluded that a group of Muslims were in fact converted low caste Hindus. This raised howls of protest from representatives of the group as late as 1895 since it was felt that this was a slander and a lie.H. H. Risely, Commissioner of the 1901 census, also showed British beliefs in an 1886 publication which stated that race sentiment, far from being:

> a figment of the intolerant pride of the Brahman, rests upon a foundation of fact which scientific methods confirm, that it has shaped the intricate grouping of the caste system, and has preserved the Aryan type in comparative purity throughout Northern India.

Here is a prime example of the racial purity theories that had been developing throughout the 19th century. Here also is the plainest explanation for the inclusion of the questions on race, caste and religion being included with the censuses. Thus far this essay has dwelt almost entirely with British actions to the exclusion of any mention of Indian actions and reactions. This should not be taken to mean that the Indians were passive or without input into the process. Any change within a society requires the participation of all the groups if it is to have any lasting effect. The Indian people had a very profound effect on the formulation of the census and their analysis. However, Indian actions and reaction must be considered within the context of Indian history and Indian culture in the same way that British actions must be considered within British cultural context. For this reason, it has been necessary to postpone consideration of Indian reactions and contributions to the British activities until the next section of this essay which will then be followed by a more in depth examination of the development of British attitudes. Finally, the results of the combination of both Indian and British beliefs will be examined with a view to reaching a consensus on how they affected the compilation of and conclusions reached through the censuses.

The word caste is not a word that is indigenous to India. It originates in the Portuguese word casta which means race,breed, race or lineage. However, during the 19th century, the term caste increasingly took on the connotations of the word race. Thus, from the very beginning of western contact with the subcontinent European constructions have been imposed on Indian systems and institutions.

To fully appreciate the caste system one must step away from the definitions imposed by Europeans and look at the system as a whole, including the religious beliefs that are an integral part of it. To the British, viewing the caste system from the outside and on a very superficial level, it appeared to be a static system of social ordering that allowed the ruling class or Brahmins, to maintain their power over the other classes. What the British failed to realize was that Hindus existed in a different cosmological frame than did the British. The concern of the true Hindu was not his ranking economically within society but rather his ability to regenerate on a higher plane of existence during each successive life.

Varna and Jati

According to the ancient Hindu scriptures, there are four "varnas". The Bhagavad Gita says varnas are decided based on Guna and Karma. Manusmriti and some other shastras name four varnas: the Brahmins (teachers, scholars and priests), the Kshatriyas (kings, warriors and administrators), the Vaishyas (agriculturists and traders), and Shudras (service providers, labourers).

This theoretical system postulated Varna categories as ideals and explained away the reality of thousands of endogamous Jatis actually prevailing in the country as being the result of historical mixing among the "pure" Varnas – *Varna*

Sankara. All those who did not subscribe to the norms of the Hindu society, including foreigners, tribals, nomads and certain criminals, were considered contagious and untouchables. Another group excluded from the main society was called Parjanya or Antyaja. This group of people formerly called "untouchables", now self-described as the Dalits, was considered either the lowest among the Shudras or outside the Varna system altogether. Passages from scriptures such as Manusmriti indicate that the varna system was originally non-hereditary.

Several critics of Hinduism state that the caste system is rooted in the varna system mentioned in the ancient Hindu scriptures. However, many groups, such as ISKCON, consider the modern Indian caste system and the varna system two distinct concepts. Many European administrators from the colonial era incorrectly regarded the Manusmriti as the "law book" of the Hindus, and thus concluded that the caste system is a part of Hinduism, an assertion that is now rejected by most scholars, who state that it is a social practice, not a religious belief. Manusmriti was a work of reference for some Brahmins of north India, especially in Bengal, and was largely unknown in southern India.

Although many Hindu scriptures contain passages that can be interpreted to sanction the caste system, they also contain indications that the caste system is not an essential part of Hinduism. The Vedas placed no importance on the caste system, mentioning caste only once (in the Purush Sukta), almost in passing, out of tens of thousands of verses. Most Vedic scholars believe even this to be a subsequent and artificial insertion; B. R. Ambedkar concluded after a thorough study that this is a much later interpolation, and gave strong evidence to support his conclusion. In the Vedic period, there was no prohibition against anyone, including the Shudras, listening to the Vedas or participating in any religious rite.

In *Early Evidence for Caste in South India*, George L. Hart stated that "the earliest Tamil texts show the existence of what seems definitely to be caste, but which antedates the Brahmins and the Hindu orthodoxy". He believes that the origins of the caste system can be seen in the "belief system that developed with the agricultural civilization", and was later profoundly influenced by "the Brahmins and the Brahmanical religion".

These early Tamil texts also outline the concept of equality. Saint Valluvar has stated "pirapokkum ella uyirkkum", which means "all are equal at birth". Likewise, Saint Auvaiyaar has stated that there are only two castes in the world: those who contribute negatively and those who contribute positively. From these statements, it can be inferred that the caste system is a socio-economic class system.

Caste and Social Status

Traditionally, although the political power lay with the Kshatriyas, historians portrayed the Brahmins as custodians and interpreters of Dharma, who enjoyed much prestige and many advantages.

Fa Hien, a Buddhist pilgrim from China, visited India around 400 AD. "Only the lot of the Chandals he found unenviable; outcastes by reason of their degrading work as disposers of dead, they were universally shunned... But no other section of the population were notably disadvantaged, no other caste distinctions attracted comment from the Chinese pilgrim, and no oppressive caste 'system' drew forth his surprised censure.". In this period kings of Sudra and Brahmin origin were as common as those of Kshatriya *varna* and caste system was not wholly prohibitive and repressive.

The castes did not constitute a rigid description of the occupation or the social status of a group. Since British society was divided by class, the British attempted to equate the Indian caste system to their own social class system. They saw caste as an indicator of occupation, social standing, and intellectual ability. Intentionally or unintentionally, the caste system became more rigid during the British Raj, when the British started to enumerate castes during the ten year census and codified the system under their rule.

The Harijans, or the people outside the caste system, had the lowest social status. The Harijans, earlier referred to as *untouchables* by some, worked in what were seen as unhealthy, unpleasant or polluting jobs. In the past, the Harijans suffered from social segregation and restrictions, in addition to extreme poverty. They were not allowed temple worship with others, nor water from the same sources. Persons of higher castes would not interact with them. If somehow a member of a higher caste came into physical or social contact with an untouchable, the member of the higher caste was defiled, and had to bathe thoroughly to purge him or herself of the impurity. Social discrimination developed even among the Harijans; sub-castes among Harijans, such as the *dhobi* and *nai*, would not interact with lower-order Bhangis, who were described as "outcastes even among outcastes".

Sociologists have commented on the historical advantages offered by a rigid social structure as well as its drawbacks. While caste is now seen as anachronistic, in its original form the caste system served as an instrument of order in a society where mutual consent rather than compulsion ruled; where the ritual rights and the economic obligations of members of one caste or sub-caste were strictly circumscribed in relation to those of any other caste or sub-caste; where one was born into one's caste and retained one's station in society for life; where merit was inherited, where equality existed within the caste, but inter-caste relations were unequal and hierarchical. A well-defined system of mutual interdependence through a division of labour created security within a community. In addition, the division of labour on the basis of ethnicity allowed immigrants and foreigners to quickly integrate into their own caste niches. The caste system played an influential role in shaping economic activities, where it functioned much like medieval European guilds, ensuring the division of labour, providing for the training of apprentices and, in some cases, allowing manufacturers to achieve narrow specialisation. For instance, in certain regions, producing each variety of cloth was the speciality of a particular sub-caste. Additionally, some philosophers have argued that the majority of people would be comfortable in stratified endogamous groups, as they were in ancient times.

Caste Mobility

Some scholars believe that the relative ranking of other castes was fluid or differed from one place to another prior to the arrival of the British. Sociologists such as Bernard Buber and Marriott McKim describe how the perception of the caste system as a static and textual stratification has given way to the perception of the caste system as a more processual, empirical and contextual stratification. Other sociologists such as Y.B Damle have applied theoretical models to explain mobility and flexibility in the caste system in India. According to these scholars, groups of lower-caste individuals could seek to elevate the status of their caste by attempting to emulate the practices of higher castes. Flexibility in caste laws permitted very low-caste religious clerics such as Valmiki to compose the Ramayana, which became a central work of Hindu scripture. There is also precedent of certain Shudra families within the temples of the Sri Vaishnava sect in South India elevating their caste. The following is a list of changes in varNa cited in Hindu texts:

- Manu eldest son [Priyavrata] became king, a Kshatriya. Out of his ten sons seven became kings while three became Brahman. Their names were Mahavira, Kavi and Savana.
- Kavash –ailush was born to a Sudra and attained varn of a Rishi. He became mantra-drashta to numerous Vedic mantras in Rig-Veda 10th Mandal.
- Jabala's son [Satyakama] born from unknown father became Rishi by his qualities.
- [Matanga] became a Rishi after his birth in low Varna.

According to some psychologists, mobility across broad caste lines may have been "minimal", though sub-castes (jatis) may have changed their social status over the generations by fission, re-location, and adoption of new rituals.

Sociologist M. N. Srinivas has also debated the question of rigidity in Caste. In an ethnographic study of the Coorgs of Karnataka, he observed considerable flexibility and mobility in their caste hierarchies. He asserts that the caste system is far from a rigid system in which the position of each component caste is fixed for all time; instead, movement has always been possible, especially in the middle regions of the hierarchy. It was always possible for groups born into a lower caste to "rise to a higher position by adopting vegetarianism and teetotalism" i.e. adopt the customs of the higher castes. While theoretically "forbidden", the process was not uncommon in practice. The concept of sanskritization, or the adoption of upper-caste norms by the lower castes, addressed the complexity and fluidity of caste relations. The fact that many of the dynasties were of obscure origin suggests some social mobility: a person of any caste, having once acquired political power, could also acquire a genealogy connecting him with the traditional lineages and conferring Kshatriya status. A number of new castes, such as the Kayasthas (scribes) and Khatris (traders), are mentioned in the sources of this period. According to the Brahmanic sources, they originated from intercaste marriages, but this is clearly an attempt at rationalizing their rank in the hierarchy. Khatri appears to be unquestionably a Prakritised form of the Sanskrit Kshatriya. Many of these new castes played a major role in society. The hierarchy of castes did not have a uniform distribution throughout the country.

Reforms

There have been challenges to the caste system from the time of Buddha, Mahavira and Makkhali Gosala. Opposition to the system of varna is regularly asserted in the Yoga Upanisads and is a constant feature of Cinaacara tantrism, a Chinese-derived movement in Asom; both date to the medieval era. The Natha system, which was founded by Matsya-indra Natha and Go-rakca Natha in the same era and spread throughout India, has likewise been consistently opposed to the system of varna.

Many Bhakti period saints rejected the caste discriminations and accepted all castes, including untouchables, into their fold. During the British Raj, this sentiment gathered steam, and many Hindu reform movements such as Brahmo Samaj and Arya Samaj renounced caste-based discrimination. The inclusion of so-called untouchables into the mainstream was argued for by many social reformers.

Mahatma Gandhi called them "Harijans" (children of God) although that term is now considered patronizing and the term Dalit (*downtrodden*) is the more commonly used. Gandhi's contribution toward the emancipation of the untouchables is still debated, especially in the commentary of his contemporary Dr. B.R. Ambedkar, an untouchable who frequently saw Gandhi's activities as detrimental to the cause of upliftment of his people.

The practice of untouchability was formally outlawed by the Constitution of India in 1950, and has declined significantly since then, to the point of a society allowing former untouchables to take high political office, like former President K. R. Narayanan, who took office in 1997, and former Chief Justice K. G. Balakrishnan.

British Rule

The fluidity of the caste system was affected by the arrival of the British. Prior to that, the relative ranking of castes differed from one place to another. The castes did not constitute a rigid description of the occupation or the social status of a group.

The British attempted to equate the Indian caste system to their own class system, viewing caste as an indicator of occupation, social standing, and intellectual ability. During the initial days of the British East India Company's rule, caste privileges and customs were encouraged, but the British law courts disagreed with the discrimination against the lower castes. However, British policies of divide and rule as well as enumeration of the population into rigid categories during the 10 year census contributed towards the hardening of caste identities.

During the period of British rule, India saw the rebellions of several lower castes, mainly tribals that revolted against British rule. These were:

1. Halba rebellion (1774–79)
2. Bhopalpatnam Struggle (1795)
3. Bhil rebellion (1822–1857)
4. Paralkot rebellion (1825)
5. Tarapur rebellion (1842–54)
6. Maria rebellion (1842–63)
7. First Freedom Struggle (1856–57)
8. Bhil rebellion, begun by Tantya Tope in Banswara (1858)
9. Koi revolt (1859)
10. Gond rebellion, begun by Ramji Gond in Adilabad (1860)
11. Muria rebellion (1876)
12. Rani rebellion (1878–82)
13. Bhumkal (1910).

Modern Status of the Caste System

In some rural areas and small towns, the caste system is still very rigid. Caste is also a factor in the politics of India.

The Government of India has officially documented castes and sub-castes, primarily to determine those deserving reservation (positive discrimination in education and jobs) through the census. The Indian reservation system, though limited in scope, relies entirely on quotas. The Government lists consist of Scheduled Castes, Scheduled Tribes and Other Backward Classes:

Scheduled Castes (SC)

Scheduled castes generally consist of "Dalit". The present population is 16% of the total population of India (around 160 million). For example, the Delhi state has 49 castes listed as SC.

Scheduled Tribes (ST)

Scheduled tribes generally consist of tribal groups. The present population is 7% of the total population of India i.e. around 70 million.

Other Backward Classes (OBC)

The Mandal Commission covered more than 3000 castes under OBC Category and stated that OBCs form around 52% of the Indian population. However, the National Sample Survey puts the figure at 32%. There is substantial debate over the exact number of OBCs in India; it is generally estimated to be sizable, but many believe that it is lower than the figures quoted by either the Mandal Commission or the National Sample Survey. The caste-based reservations in India have led to widespread protests, such as the 2006 Indian anti-reservation protests, with many complaining of reverse discrimination against the forward castes (the castes that do not qualify for the reservation). Many view negative treatment of forward castes as socially divisive and equally wrong.

Caste System among Non-Hindus

In some parts of India, Christians are stratified by sect, location, and the castes of their predecessors, usually in reference to upper class Syrian Malabar Nasranis. Christians in Kerala are divided into several communities, including Syrian Christians and the so-called "Latin" or "New Rite" Christians.

Syrian Christians derive status within the caste system from the tradition that they are converted Namboodiris and Jews, who were evangelized by St. Thomas. Writers Arundhati Roy and Anand Kurian have written personal accounts of the caste system at work in their community. Syrian Christians, especially Knanaya Christians, tend to be endogamous and not to intermarry with other Christian castes.

The Latin Rite Christians were among the scheduled castes in the coastal belt of Kerala, where fishing was the primary occupation. They were actively converted by missionaries in the 16th and 19th centuries. These missionary activities were carried out by Western Latin Rite missionaries who did not understand the significance of the caste system in India; mone of the Syrian churches had participated in such activities among the scheduled castes of India because they were aware of the prejudices of the caste system. The government of India later granted this group OBC status. Very rarely are there intermarriages between Syrian Christians and Latin Rite Christians

Anthropologists have noted that the caste hierarchy among Christians in Kerala is much more polarized than the Hindu practices in the surrounding areas, due to a lack of jatis. Also, the caste status is kept even if the sect allegiance is switched (i.e. from Syrian Catholic to Syrian Orthodox).

In the Indian state of Goa, mass conversions were carried out by Portuguese Latin missionaries from the 16th century onwards. The Hindu converts retained their caste practices. The continued maintenance of the caste system among the Christians in Goa is attributed to the nature of mass conversions of entire villages, as a result of which existing social stratification was not affected. The Portuguese colonists, even during the Goan Inquisition, did not do anything to change the caste system. Thus, the original Hindu Brahmins in Goa now became Christian *Bamons* and the Kshatriya became Christian noblemen called *Chardos*. The Christian clergy became almost exclusively Bamon. Vaishyas who converted to Christianity became *Gauddos*, and Shudras became *Sudirs*. Finally, the

Dalits or "Untouchables" who converted to Christianity became *Maharas* and *Chamars*, the latter an appellation of the anti-Dalit ethnic slur *Chamaar*.

Units of social stratification, termed "castes" by many, have developed among Muslims in some parts of South Asia. Sources indicate that the castes among Muslims developed as the result of close contact with Hindu culture and Hindu converts to Islam. The Sachar Committee's report commissioned by the government of India and released in 2006 documents the continued stratification in Muslim society.

Among Muslims, those who are referred to as Ashrafs are presumed to have a superior status derived from their foreign Arab ancestry, while the Ajlafs are assumed to be converts from Hinduism, and have a lower status. In addition, the *Arzal* caste among Muslims was regarded by anti-caste activists like Ambedkar as the equivalent of untouchables. In the Bengal region of India, some Muslims stratify their society according to 'Quoms'. While many scholars have asserted that the Muslim castes are not as acute in their discrimination as those of the Hindus, some like Ambedkar argued that the social evils in Muslim society were "worse than those seen in Hindu society".

The Buddhists also had a caste system. In Sri Lanka, the Rodis might have been outcast by the Sri Lankan Buddhists due to the absence of *ahimsa* (*non-violence*), a central tenet of Buddhism, among their beliefs. The writer Raghavan notes, "That a form of worship in which human offerings formed the essential ritual would have been anathema to the Buddhist way of life goes without saying; and it needs no stretch of imagination that any class of people in whom the cult prevailed or survived even in an attenuated form would have been pronounced by the sangha (i.e. the Buddhist clergy) as exiles from the social order." Savarkar believed that the status of the backward castes (e.g. Chamar) that performed non-violence only worsened. When Ywan Chwang traveled to South India after the period of the Chalukyan Empire, he noticed that the caste system had existed among the Buddhists and Jains.

Jains also had castes in places such as Bihar. For example, in the village of Bundela, there were several *"jaats"* (*groups*) amongst the Jains. A person of one *"jaat"* cannot intermingle with a Jain or another *"jaat"*. They also could not eat with the members of other *"jaats"*.

The Sikh Gurus criticized the hierarchy of the caste system. While some castes were widely perceived as being better or higher than others (e.g. Brahmins being higher than others), they preached that all sections of society were valuable and that merit and hard-work were essential aspects of life. In the Shiromani Gurdwara Prabandhak Committee, out of 140 seats, 20 are reserved for low caste Sikhs. However, the quota system has attracted much criticism due to the lack of meritocracy, since merit is considered the single most important component of winning a seat.

Baha'i Faith has grown to prominence in India, since its philosophy of the unity of humanity attracted many of the lower castes.

Caste-related Violence

Caste-related violence and hate crimes in India have occurred despite the gradual reduction of casteism in the country.

According to a report by Human Rights Watch, "Dalits and indigenous peoples (known as Scheduled Tribes or adivasis) continue to face discrimination, exclusion, and acts of communal violence. Laws and policies adopted by the Indian government provide a strong basis for protection, but are not being faithfully implemented by local authorities."

Independent India has witnessed a considerable amount of violence and hate crimes motivated by caste. Various incidents of violence against Dalits, such as Kherlanji Massacre have been reported from many parts of India. Many violent protests by Dalits, such as the 2006 Dalit protests in Maharashtra, have also been reported.

Phoolan Devi, who belonged to the *Mallah* lower caste, was mistreated and raped by upper-caste Thakurs at a young age. She became a bandit and carried out violent robberies against upper-caste people. In 1981, her gang massacred twenty-two Thakurs, most of whom were not involved in her kidnapping or rape. Later, she became a politician and Member of Parliament.

Andhra Pradesh

This state is considered to be one of the most caste-crime infested places of India which has had many Dalit Massacres like Chundur Massacre, Neerukonda Massacre etc,.

Ranvir Sena

Ranvir Sena is an caste-supremacist fringe paramilitary group based in Bihar. The group is based amongst the higher-caste landlords, and carries out actions against the outlawed naxals in rural areas. It has committed violent acts against Dalits and other members of the scheduled caste community in an effort to prevent reforms aimed at their emancipation.

Tamil Nadu

The state of Tamil Nadu has witnessed several caste-based incidents both against Dalits and Brahmins. In 2000, three young men belonging to the Dalit undercaste were killed in the Cuddalore district of Tamil Nadu. This fuelled some localized violence in the caste-sensitive region, which has seen numerous caste-related incidents in which the majority of the victims have been Dalits. Six of the killings have been registered as murders under the Indian Penal Code and others as "Deaths under suspicious circumstances". No arrests have been made in these cases.

However, several Dalits have been arrested as *goondas* (hoodlums). The Chief minister of Tamil-Nadu, M. Karunanidhi, has been accused of having an "anti-Dalit" bias by the radical organization "Dalit Panthers of India". Theories concerning these crimes against Dalits range from "alcohol bootleggers opposing prohibition movements among Dalits" to "inter-caste relations between an Vanniya boy and a Dalit girl". Political parties sympathetic to the Dalits have protested against these incidents and have alleged systemic biases against Dalits in several parts of the country.

Bant Singh Case of Punjab

On the evening of January 5, 2006 Bant Singh, a poor Sikh Dalit, was attacked by unknown assailants. His injuries necessitated medical amputation. He alleges that this was in retaliation for actively working to secure justice for his daughter, who was gang raped by upper caste members of his village in Punjab five years earlier.

A 55-year-old Dalit Sikh woman, Sawinder Kaur has been tortured, stripped and tied to a tree in Ram Duali village of Punjab because her nephew eloped with a girl from the same community. The police arrested four persons for allegedly committing the crime on 9 September 2007.

In January, 1999 four members of the village panchayat of Bhungar Khera village in Abohar paraded a handicapped Dalit woman naked through the village. No action was taken by the police, despite local Dalit protests. It was only on July 20 that the four pancha yat members were arrested, after the State Home Department was compelled to order an inquiry into the incident.

A Dalit Sikh woman, Sukhwinder Kaur of Sumel Kheri village was molested and beaten up by an octroi contractor of Malaudh when she resisted his attempt to sexually exploit her.

Kherlanji Massacre

On September 29, 2006, four members of the Bhotmange family belonging to the Dalit underclass were slaughtered in Kherlanji, a small village in Bhandara district of Maharashtra. The women of the family, Surekha and Priyanka, were paraded naked in public, then allegedly gang-raped before being murdered. Although initially ascribed by the media and by the Human Rights Watch to upper castes, the criminal act was actually carried out by Kunbi caste (classified as Other Backward Classes by Government of India) farmers for having opposed the requisition of the Dalit land to have a road built over it.

On November 23, 2006, some members of the Dalit community in the nearby district of Chandrapur staged a protest regarding this incident.The protesters allegedly turned violent and threw stones. The police resorted to baton-charging the protestors to control the situation. Dalit leaders, however, denied that they had first resorted to violent and stated that they had been "protesting in peace".

2006 Dalit Protests in Maharashtra

In November-December 2006, the desecration of a Ambedkar statue in Kanpur (Uttar Pradesh) triggered violent protests by

Dalits in Maharashtra. Several people remarked that the protests were fueled by the Kherlanji Massacre. During the violent protests, the Dalit protestors set three trains on fire, damaged over 100 buses and clashed with police. At least four deaths and many more injuries were reported. Later, the Kanpur Police arrested a Dalit youth Arun Kumar Balmiki for desecrating the Ambedkar statue. According to the police, the youth had "admitted to having damaged the statue in a drunken state along with two friends". Earlier in a similar case, a Dalit youth was held for desecrating an Ambedkar statue in Gulbarga, Karnataka.

In response to these protests, Raj Thackeray drew attention to another incident in Kherlanji, in which a Dalit allegedly raped a girl and killed her. Thackeray demanded action on those responsible for the rape and the subsequent death of the girl, and also remarked that nobody helped the girl's family.

Rajasthan

In the Indian province of Rajasthan, between the years 1999 and 2002, crimes against Dalits average at about 5024 a year, with 46 killings and 138 cases of rape.

Punjab

On 25 May 2009, violence and rioting broke out when thousands of protesters took to the streets in almost all major towns and cities in the Indian state of Punjab after a dalit preacher, Sant Ramanand, was attacked in a temple in Vienna, Austria. He was among 16 people injured, including another preacher Sant Nirajnan Dass, and later died in hospital. Both the preachers were from a low-caste Sikh sect which has a large following in parts of Punjab and had travelled to Vienna to conduct a special service. Several high-caste Sikh groups had apparently opposed his presence and threatened violence. This happened after the preacher had reportedly made remarks about the Sikh groups.

Other Incidents

On September 1, 2007 some Yadavs poured steaming dal on a Dalit woman and her infant daughter, and beat up several other Dalits, for allowing their children to play in the premises of a temple at Shivayalay Mushari, on the outskirts of Patna.

Caste Politics

Caste is one among the major factors in politics of India. Independent India has seen intense debates over reverse discrimination, caste-based quotas and reservations. According to a report by Human Rights Watch, "Dalits and indigenous peoples (known as Scheduled Tribes or adivasis) continue to face discrimination, exclusion, and acts of communal violence. Laws and policies adopted by the Indian government provide a strong basis for protection, but are not being faithfully implemented by local authorities." B. R. Ambedkar and Jawaharlal Nehru had radically different approaches to caste, especially concerning constitutional politics and the status of untouchables. Since the 1980s, caste has become a major issue in the politics of India.

The Mandal Commission was established in 1979 to "identify the socially or educationally backward" and to consider the question of seat reservations and quotas for people to redress caste discrimination. In 1980, the commission's report affirmed the affirmative action practice under Indian law, whereby members of lower castes were given exclusive access to a portion of government jobs and slots in public universities. When V. P. Singh's administration tried to implement the recommendations of the Mandal Commission in 1989, massive protests were held in the country. Many alleged that the politicians were trying to cash in on caste-based reservations for purely pragmatic electoral purposes.

Many political parties in India have openly indulged in caste-based votebank politics. Parties such as Bahujan Samaj Party (BSP), the Samajwadi Party and the Janata Dal claim that they are representing the backward castes, and rely on OBC support, often in alliance with Dalit and Muslim support, to win elections. Remarkably, in what is called a landmark election in the history of India's biggest state of Uttar Pradesh, the Bahujan Samaj Party was able to garner a majority in the state assembly elections with the support of the brahmin community.

Criticism

Back in 1950s, B. R. Ambedkar had criticized the use of caste as a political plank. He anticipated the limitations of using caste as a political resource and instead, emphasized on eliminating the concept of caste from the society.

There has been criticism of the caste system from both within and outside of India. Criticism of the Caste system in Hindu society came both from the Hindu fold and Dalit.

Historical Criticism

Many bhakti period saints, including Nanak, Kabir, Caitanya, Dnyaneshwar, Eknath, Ramanuja and Tukaram, rejected all caste-based discrimination and accepted disciples from all the castes. Many Hindu reformers such as Swami Vivekananda believe that there is no place for the caste system in Hinduism. The 15th century saint Ramananda accepted all castes, including untouchables, into his fold. Most of these saints subscribed to the Bhakti movements in Hinduism during the medieval period that rejected casteism. Nandanar, a low-caste Hindu cleric, also rejected casteism and accepted Dalits.

Some other movements in Hinduism have also welcomed lower-castes into their fold, the earliest being the Bhakti movements of the medieval period. Early Dalit politics involved many reform movements; these arose primarily as a reaction to the advent of Christian missionaries in India and their attempts to convert Dalits, who were attracted to the prospect of escaping the caste system.

In the 19th Century, the Brahmo Samaj under Raja Ram Mohan Roy actively campaigned against untouchability and casteism. The Arya Samaj founded by Swami Dayanand also renounced discrimination against Dalits. Sri Ramakrishna Paramahamsa and his disciple Swami Vivekananda founded the Ramakrishna Mission that participated in the emancipation of Dalits. Upper-caste Hindus such as Mannathu Padmanabhan participated in movements to abolish untouchability against Dalits; Padmanabhan opened his family temple to Dalits for worship. Narayana Guru, a pious Hindu and an authority on the Vedas, also criticized casteism and campaigned for the rights of lower-caste Hindus within the context of Hinduism.

The first upper-caste temple to openly welcome Dalits into their fold was the Laxminarayan Temple in Wardha in the year 1928; the move was spearheaded by reformer Jamnalal Bajaj.

The caste system has also been criticized by many Indian social reformers. Some reformers, such as Jyotirao Phule and Iyothee Thass, argued that the lower caste people were the original inhabitants of India, who had been conquered in the ancient past by "Brahmin invaders." Mahatma Gandhi coined the term *Harijan*, a euphemistic word for untouchable, literally meaning *Sons of God*. B. R. Ambedkar, born in Hindu Dalit community, was a heavy critic of the caste system. He pioneered the Dalit Buddhist movement in India, and asked his followers to leave Hinduism, and convert to Buddhism. India's first Prime Minister, Jawaharlal Nehru, based on his own relationship with Dalit reformer Ambedkar, supported the eradication of untouchability for the benefit of the Dalit community. In 1936, the Maharaja proclaimed that "outcastes should not be denied the consolations and the solace of the Hindu faith". Even today, the Sri Padmanabhaswamy temple that first welcomed Dalits in the state of Kerala is revered by the Dalit Hindu community.

Contemporary Criticism

Some activists consider the caste system a form of racial discrimination. At the United Nations Conference Against Racism in Durban, South Africa in March 2001, participants condemned discrimination based on the caste system and tried to pass a resolution declaring caste as a basis for segregation and oppression a form of apartheid. However, no formal resolution was passed.

The alleged maltreatment of Dalits in India has been described by some authors as "India's hidden apartheid". Critics of the accusations point to substantial improvements in the position of Dalits in post-independence India, consequent to the strict implementation of the rights and privileges enshrined in the Constitution of India, as implemented by the Protection of Civil rights Act, 1955. They also note that India has had a Dalit president, K.R. Narayanan, and argue that the practise had disappeared in urban public life.

According to William A. Haviland, however:

Although India's national constitution of 1950 sought to abolish cast discrimination and the practice of untouchability, the caste system remains deeply entrenched in Hindu culture and is still widespread throughout southern Asia, especially in rural India. In what has been called India's "hidden apartheid", entire villages in many Indian states remain completely segregated by caste. Representing about 15 percent of India's population—or some 160 million people—the widely scattered Dalits endure near complete social isolation, humiliation, and discrimination based exclusively on their birth status. Even a Dalit's shadow is believed to pollute the upper classes. They may not cross the line dividing their part of the village from that occupied by higher castes, drink water from public wells, or visit the same temples as the higher castes. Dalit children are still often made to sit in the back of classrooms.

Sociologists Kevin Reilly, Stephen Kaufman and Angela Bodino, while critical of casteism, conclude that modern India does not practice any apartheid since there is no state-sanctioned discrimination. They write that casteism in India is presently "not apartheid. In fact, untouchables, as well as tribal people and members of the lowest castes in India benefit from broad affirmative action programmes and are enjoying greater political power." The Constitution of India places special emphasis on outlawing caste discrimination, especially the practice of untouchability.

Caste and Race

Allegations that caste amounts to race were addressed and rejected by B.R. Ambedkar, an advocate for Dalit rights and critic of untouchability. He wrote that "The Brahmin of Punjab is racially of the same stock as the Chamar of Punjab. The Caste system does not demarcate racial division. The Caste system is a social division of people of the same race",

Such allegations have also been rejected by sociologists such as Andre Béteille, who writes that treating caste as a form of racism is "politically mischievous" and worse, "scientifically nonsensical" since there is no discernible difference in the racial characteristics between Brahmins and Scheduled Castes. He states, "Every social group cannot be regarded as a race simply because we want to protect it against prejudice and discrimination".

The Indian government also rejects the claims of equivalency between caste and racial discrimination, pointing out that the caste issues are essentially intra-racial and intra-cultural.

Indian Attorney General Soli Sorabjee insisted that "[t]he only reason India wants caste discrimination kept off the agenda is that it will distract participants from the main topic: racism. Caste discrimination in India is undeniable but caste and race are entirely distinct".

Many scholars dispute the claim that casteism is akin to racism. Sociologist M. N. Srinivas has debated the question of rigidity in caste. Others have applied theoretical models to explain mobility and flexibility in the caste system in India. According to these scholars, groups of lower-caste individuals could seek to elevate the status of their caste by attempting to emulate the practices of higher castes.

In her book *Democracy and Authoritarianism in South Asia*, Pakistani-American sociologist Ayesha Jalal writes, "As for Hinduism, the hierarchical principles of the Brahmanical social order have always been contested from within Hindu society, suggesting that equality has been and continues to be both valued and practiced."

In India, some observers felt that the caste system must be viewed as a system of exploitation of poor low-ranking groups by more prosperous high-ranking groups. In many parts of India, land is largely held by high-ranking property owners of the dominant castes, who economically exploit low-ranking landless labourers and poor artisans.

Matt Cherry claims that karma underpins the caste system, which traditionally determines the position and role of every member of Hindu society. Caste determines an individual's place in society, the work he or she may carry out, and who he or she may marry and meet. According to him, Hindus believe that the karma of previous life will determine the caste an individual will be (re)born into.

On 29 March 2007, the Supreme Court of India, as an interim measure, stayed the law providing for 27% reservation for Other Backward Classes in educational institutions. This was done in response to a public interest litigation — Ashoka Kumar Thakur vs. Union of India. The Court held that the 1931 census could not be a determinative factor for identifying the OBCs for the purpose of providing reservation. The court also observed, "Reservation cannot be permanent and appear to perpetuate backwardness". However, the Supreme Court later upheld the reservation.

Genetic Analysis

There have been several studies examining caste members as discrete populations, examining the hypothesis that their ancestors have different origins. A 2002–03 study by T. Kivisild et al. concluded that the "Indian tribal and caste populations derive largely from the same genetic heritage of Pleistocene southern and western Asians and have received limited gene flow from external regions since the Holocene." Studies point to the various Indian caste groups having similar genetic origins and having negligible genetic input from outside south Asia. Because the Indian samples for this study were taken from a single geographical area, it remains to be investigated whether its findings can be safely generalized.

An earlier 1995 study by Joanna L. Mountain et al. of Stanford University had concluded that there was "no clear separation into three genetically distinct groups along caste lines", although "an inferred tree revealed some clustering according to caste affiliation". A 2006 study by Ismail Thanseem et al. of Centre for Cellular and Molecular Biology (India) concluded that the "lower caste groups might have originated with the hierarchical divisions that arose within the tribal groups with the spread of Neolithic agriculturalists, much earlier than the arrival of Aryan speakers", and "the Indo-Europeans established themselves as upper castes among this already developed caste-like class structure within the tribes." The study indicated that the Indian caste system may have its roots long before the arrival of the Indo-Aryans; a rudimentary version of the caste system may have emerged with the shift towards cultivation and settlements, and the divisions may have become more well-defined and intensified with the arrival of Indo-Aryans.

A 2006 genetic study by the National Institute of Biologicals in India, testing a sample of men from 32 tribal and 45 caste groups, concluded that the Indians have acquired very few genes from Indo-European speakers. More recent studies have also debunked the British claims that so-called Aryans and Dravidians have a racial divide. A study conducted by the

Centre for Cellular and Molecular Biology in 2009 (in collaboration with Harvard Medical School, Harvard School of Public Health and the Broad Institute of Harvard and MIT) analyzed half a million genetic markers across the genomes of 132 individuals from 25 ethnic groups from 13 states in India across multiple caste groups. The study establishes, based on the impossibility of identifying any genetic indicators across caste lines, that castes in South Asia grew out of traditional tribal organizations during the formation of Indian society, and was not the product of any Aryan invasion and subjugation of Dravidian people.

9

Sociology of Religion

Religion is the belief in and worship of a god or gods, or a set of beliefs concerning the origin and purpose of the universe. It is commonly regarded as consisting of a person's relation to God, gods, or spirits. Many religions have narratives, symbols, traditions and sacred histories associated with their deity or deities, that are intended to give meaning to life. They tend to derive morality, ethics, religious laws or a preferred lifestyle from their ideas about the cosmos and human nature.

The word *religion* is sometimes used interchangeably with *faith* or *belief system*, but religion differs from private belief in that it has a public aspect. Most religions have organized behaviours, including congregations for prayer, priestly hierarchies, holy places, and/or scriptures.

Academics studying the subject have defined religion into three broad categories: world religions, a term which refers to transcultural, international faiths, indigenous religions, which refers to smaller, culture-specific religious groups, and new religious movements, which refers to recently developed faiths.

The development of religion has taken different forms in different cultures. Some religions place greater emphasis on belief, while others emphasize practice. Some religions focus on the subjective experience of the religious individual, while others consider the activities of the community to be most important. Some religions claim to be universal, believing their laws and cosmology to be binding for everyone, while others are intended to be practiced only by one, localized group. Religion often makes use of meditation, music and art. In many places it has been associated with public institutions such as education, the family, government, and political power.

One of the more influential theories of religion today is social constructionism, which says that religion is a modern concept suggesting all spiritual practice and worship follows a model similar to Christianity; social constructionism suggests that religion, as a concept, has therefore been applied inappropriately to non-Western cultures.

Sociology of Religion

The sociology of religion concerns the role of religion in society; the practices, historical backgrounds, developments and universal themes of religion in society. There is particular emphasis on the recurring role of religion in all societies and throughout recorded history. The sociology of religion is distinguished from the philosophy of religion in that it does not set out to assess the validity of religious beliefs, though the process of comparing multiple conflicting dogmas may require what Peter L. Berger has described as inherent "methodological atheism". Whereas the sociology of religion broadly differs to theology in assuming the invalidity of the supernatural, theorists tend to acknowledge socio-cultural reification of religious practise.

Modern academic sociology *began* with the analysis of religion in Durkheim's 1897 study of suicide rates amongst Catholic and Protestant populations, a foundational work of social research which served to distinguish sociology from other disciplines, such as psychology. The works of Karl Marx and Max Weber emphasised the relationship between religion and the economic or social structure of society. Contemporary debates have centred on issues such as secularization, civil religion, and the cohesiveness of religion in the context of globalization and multiculturalism. The contemporary sociology of religion may also encompass the sociology of *irreligion* (for instance, in the analysis of Secular Humanist belief systems).

Typology of Religious Groups

According to one common typology among sociologists, religious groups are classified as ecclesias, denominations, sects, or cults (now more commonly referred to in scholarship as

NRMs). Note that sociologists give these words precise definitions which are different from how they are commonly used. Particularly the words 'cult' and 'sect' are used free from negative connotations by sociologists, even though the popular use of these words is often pejorative.

History and Relevance Today

The classical, seminal sociological theorists of the late 19th and early 20th century were greatly interested in religion and its effects on society. These theorists include Émile Durkheim, Max Weber, and Karl Marx. Like Plato and Aristotle from Ancient Greece, and enlightenment philosophers from the 17th through 19th centuries, the ideas posited by these sociologists continue to be addressed today. More recent prominent sociologists of religion include Peter Berger, Robert N. Bellah, Thomas Luckmann, Rodney Stark, Robert Wuthnow, Christian Smith, and Bryan R. Wilson.

The View of Religion in Classical Sociology

Durkheim, Marx, and Weber had very complex and developed theories about the nature and effects of religion. Durkheim and Weber specifically are often difficult to understand, especially in light of the lack of context and examples in their primary texts. Religion was considered to be an extremely important social variable in the work of all three:

Karl Marx

Despite his later influence, Karl Marx did not view his work as an ethical or ideological response to nineteenth-century capitalism (as most later commentators have). His efforts were, in his mind, based solely on what can be called applied science. Marx saw himself as doing morally-neutral sociology and economic theory for the sake of human development. As Christiano states, "Marx did not believe in science for science's sake...he believed that he was also advancing a theory that would...be a useful tool...[in] effecting a revolutionary upheaval of the capitalist system in favor of socialism." As such, the crux of his arguments was that humans are best guided by reason. Religion, Marx held, was a significant hindrance to reason, inherently masking the truth and misguiding followers. As we will later see, Marx viewed social alienation as the heart of social inequality. The antithesis to this alienation is freedom. Thus, to propagate freedom means to present individuals with the truth and give them a choice to accept or deny it. In this, "Marx never suggested that religion ought to be prohibited."

Central to Marx's theories was the oppressive economic situation in which he dwelt. With the rise of European industrialism, Marx and his colleague Friedrich Engels witnessed and responded to the growth of what he called "surplus value." Marx's view of capitalism saw rich capitalists getting richer and their workers getting poorer (the gap, the exploitation, was the "surplus value"). Not only were workers getting exploited, but in the process they were being further detached from the products they helped create. By simply selling their work for wages, "workers simultaneously lose connection with the object of labor and become objects themselves. Workers are devalued to the level of a commodity – a thing..." From this objectification comes alienation. The common worker is told he or she is a replaceable tool, alienated to the point of extreme discontent. Here, in Marx's eyes, religion enters. Capitalism utilises our tendency towards religion as a tool or ideological state apparatus to justify this alienation. Christianity teaches that those who gather up riches and power in this life will almost certainly not be rewarded in the next ("it is harder for a rich man to enter the Kingdom of Heaven than it is for a camel to pass through the eye of a needle...") while those who suffer oppression and poverty in this life, while cultivating their spiritual wealth, will be rewarded in the Kingdom of God. Thus Marx's famous line - "religion is the opium of the people", as it soothes them and dulls their senses to the pain of oppression.

Émile Durkheim

Émile Durkheim placed himself in the positivist tradition, meaning that he thought of his study of society as dispassionate and scientific. He was deeply interested in the problem of what held complex modern societies together. Religion, he argued, was an expression of social cohesion.

In the fieldwork that led to his famous *Elementary Forms of Religious Life*, Durkheim, a secular Frenchman, looked at anthropological data of Indigenous Australians. His underlying interest was to understand the basic forms of religious life for all societies. In *Elementary Forms*, Durkheim argues that the totems the aborigines venerate are actually expressions of their own conceptions of society itself. This is true not only for the aborigines, he argues, but for all societies.

Religion, for Durkheim, is not "imaginary," although he does deprive it of what many believers find essential. Religion is very real; it is an expression of society itself, and indeed, there is no society that does not have religion. We perceive as individuals a force greater than ourselves, which is our social life, and give that perception a supernatural face. We then express ourselves religiously in groups, which for Durkheim makes the symbolic power greater. Religion is an expression of our collective consciousness, which is the fusion of all of our individual consciousnesses, which then creates a reality of its own. It follows, then, that less complex societies, such as the Australian aborigines, have less complex religious systems, involving totems associated with particular clans. The more complex the society, the more complex the religious system. As societies come in contact with other societies, there is a tendency for religious systems to emphasize universalism to a greater and greater extent. However, as the division of labor makes the individual seem more important (a subject that Durkheim treats extensively in his famous *Division of Labor in Society*), religious systems increasingly focus on individual salvation and conscience.

Durkheim's definition of religion, from *Elementary Forms*, is as follows: "A religion is a unified system of beliefs and practices relative to sacred things, that is to say, things set apart and forbidden – beliefs and practices which unite into one single moral community called a Church, all those who adhere to them." (Marx, introduction) This is a functional definition of religion, meaning that it explains what religion does in social life: essentially, it unites societies. Durkheim defined religion as a clear distinction between the sacred and the profane, in effect this can be paralleled with the distinction between God and humans.

This definition also does not stipulate what exactly may be considered sacred. Thus later sociologists of religion (notably Robert Bellah) have extended Durkheimian insights to talk about notions of civil religion, or the religion of a state. American civil religion, for example, might be said to have its own set of sacred "things": the Flag of the United States, Abraham Lincoln, Martin Luther King Jr., etc. Other sociologists have taken Durkheim's concept of what religion is in the direction of the religion of professional sports, the military, or of rock music.

Max Weber

In his sociology, Weber uses the German term "Verstehen" to describe his method of interpretation of the intention and context of human action. Weber is not a positivist – in the sense that he does not believe we can find out "facts" in sociology that can be causally linked. Although he believes some generalized statements about social life can be made, he is not interested in hard positivist claims, but instead in linkages and sequences, in historical narratives and particular cases.

Weber argues for making sense of religious action on its own terms. A religious group or individual is influenced by all kinds of things, he says, but if they claim to be acting in the name of religion, we should attempt to understand their perspective on religious grounds first. Weber gives religion credit for shaping a person's image of the world, and this image of the world can affect their view of their interests, and ultimately how they decide to take action.

For Weber, religion is best understood as it responds to the human need for theodicy and soteriology. Human beings are troubled, he says, with the question of theodicy – the question of how the extraordinary power of a divine god may be reconciled with the imperfection of the world that he has created and rules over. People need to know, for example, why there is undeserved good fortune and suffering in the world. Religion offers people soteriological answers, or answers that provide opportunities for salvation – relief from suffering, and reassuring meaning. The pursuit of salvation, like the pursuit of wealth, becomes a part of human motivation.

Because religion helps to define motivation, Weber believed that religion (and specifically Protestant Calvinism) actually helped to give rise to modern capitalism, as he asserted in his most famous and controversial work, *The Protestant Ethic and the Spirit of Capitalism*. In *The Protestant Ethic*, Weber argues that capitalism arose in Europe in part because of how the belief in predestination was interpreted by everyday English Puritans. Puritan theology was based on the Calvinist notion that not everyone would be saved; there was only a specific number of the elect who would avoid damnation, and this was based sheerly on God's predetermined will and not on any action you could perform in this life. Official doctrine held that one could not ever really know whether one was among the elect.

Practically, Weber noted, this was difficult psychologically: people were (understandably) anxious to know whether they would be eternally damned or not. Thus Puritan leaders began assuring members that if they began doing well financially in their businesses, this would be one unofficial sign they had God's approval and were among the saved – but only if they used the fruits of their labor well. This along with the rationalism implied by monotheism led to the development of rational bookkeeping and the calculated pursuit of financial success beyond what one needed simply to live – and this is the "spirit of capitalism." Over time, the habits associated with the spirit of capitalism lost their religious significance, and rational pursuit of profit became its own aim.

The Protestant Ethic thesis has been much critiqued, refined, and disputed, but is still a lively source of theoretical debate in sociology of religion. Weber also did considerable work in world religions, including Hinduism and Buddhism.

Secularisation and Civil Religion

In relation to the processes of rationalisation associated with the development of modernity, it was predicted in the works of many classical sociologists that religion would decline. Despite the claims of many classical theorists and sociologists immediately after World War II, many contemporary theorists have critiqued secularisation thesis, arguing that religion has continued to play a vital role in the lives of individuals worldwide. In the United States, in particular, church attendance has remained relatively stable in the past 40 years. In Africa, the emergence of Christianity has occurred at a startling rate. While Africa could claim roughly 10 million

Christians in 1900, recent estimates put that number closer to 200 million. The rise of Islam as a major world religion, especially its new-found influence in the West, is another significant development. Furthermore, arguments may be presented regarding the concept of civil religion and new world belief systems. In short, presupposed secularization as a decline in religiosity might seem to be a myth, depending on its definition and the definition of its scope. For instance, some sociologists have argued that steady church attendance and personal religious belief may coexist with a decline in the influence of religious authorities on social or political issues.

Religious Belief

Religious belief usually relates to the existence, nature, and worship of a deity or deities and divine involvement in the universe and human life. Alternately, it may also relate to values and practices transmitted by a spiritual leader. In some religions, like the Abrahamic religions, it is held that most of the core beliefs have been divinely revealed.

Different religions attach differing degrees of importance to belief. Christianity puts more emphasis on belief than other religions. The Church has throughout its history set out Creeds that define correct belief for Christians and identify heresy. Luke Timothy Johnson in his book on the Christian Creed says that "Most religions put more emphasis on orthopraxy (right practice) than on orthodoxy (right belief). Judaism and Islam have each created sophisticated systems of law to guide behaviour, but have allowed an astonishing freedom of conviction and intellectual expression.

Both have been able to get along with comparatively short statements of belief. Buddhism and Hinduism concentrate on the practices of ritual and transformation rather than on uniformity of belief, and tribal religions express their view of reality through a variety of myths, not a 'rule of faith' for their members." Christianity by contrast places a peculiar emphasis on belief and has created ever more elaborate and official statements in its Creeds. Some Christian denominations, especially those formed since the Reformation, do not have creeds, and some, for example the Jehovah's Witnesses, explicitly reject them.

Whether Judaism entails belief or not has been a point of some controversy. Some say it is does not, some have suggested that belief is relatively unimportant for Jews. "To be a Jew," says de Lange, "means first and foremost to belong to a group, the Jewish people, and the religious beliefs are secondary." Others say that the Shema prayer, recited in the morning and evening services, expresses a Jewish creed: "Hear O Israel, the Lord is our God, the Lord is One." Maimonides's Thirteen Principles of the Faith are often taken as the statement of Judaism' fundamental beliefs. They may be summarised as follows:

- *God is the Creator.*
- *God is a unity.*
- *God is incorporeal.*
- *God is the first and the last.*
- *It is right to pray to God and to no other.*
- *The words of the prophets are true.*
- *The prophecy of Moses was true.*
- *The Torah was given to Moses.*
- *The Torah will never change.*
- *God knows all the deeds of human beings and all their thoughts.*
- *God rewards those who keep His commandments and punishes those that transgress them.*
- *The Messiah will come.*
- *The dead will be resurrected.*

Muslims declare the shahada, or testimony: "I bear witness that there is nothing worthy of worship except Allah, and I bear witness that Muhammad is the slave and messenger of Allah."

Religious Movements

In the 19th and 20th centuries, the academic practice of comparative religion divided religious belief into philosophically defined categories called "world religions." However, some recent scholarship has argued that not all types of religion are necessarily separated by mutually exclusive philosophies, and furthermore that the utility of ascribing a practice to a certain philosophy, or even calling a given practice religious, rather than cultural, political, or social in nature, is limited. The current state of psychological study about the nature of religiousness suggests that it is better to refer to religion as a largely invariant phenomenon that should be distinguished from cultural norms (i.e. "religions"). The list of religious movements given here is therefore an attempt to summarize the most important regional and philosophical influences on local communities, but it is by no means a complete description of every religious community, nor does it explain the most important elements of individual religiousness.

The four largest religious groups by population, estimated to account for between 5 and 6 billion people, are Christianity, Islam, Buddhism and Hinduism.

- Abrahamic religions are monotheistic religions which believe they descend from the Jewish patriarch Abraham.
- Judaism is the oldest Abrahamic religion, originating in the people of ancient Israel and Judea. Judaism is based primarily on the Torah, a text which Jews believe was handed down to the people of Israel through the prophet Moses in 1,400 BCE. This along with the rest of the Hebrew Bible and the Talmud are the central texts of Judaism. The Jewish people were scattered after the destruction of the Temple in Jerusalem in 70 CE. Judaism today is practiced by about 13 million people, with about 40 per cent living in Israel and 40 per cent in the United States.
- Christianity is based on the life and teachings of Jesus of Nazareth (1st century) as presented in the New Testament. The Christian faith is essentially faith in Jesus as the Christ, the Son of God, and as Savior and Lord. Almost all Christians believe in the Trinity, which teaches the unity of Father, Son (Jesus Christ), and Holy Spirit as three persons in one Godhead. Most Christians can describe their faith with the Nicene Creed. As the religion of Byzantine Empire in the first millennium and of Western Europe during the time of colonization, Christianity has been propagated throughout the world. The main divisions of Christianity are, according to the number of adherents:

- o Catholic Church, headed by the Pope in Rome, is a communion of the Western church and 22 Eastern Catholic churches.
- o Protestantism, separated from the Catholic Church in the 16th-century Reformation and split in many denominations,
- o Eastern Christianity which include Eastern Orthodoxy, Oriental Orthodoxy and the Church of the East.

- Islam refers to the religion taught by the Islamic prophet Muhammad, a major political and religious figure of the 7th century CE. Islam is the dominant religion of northern Africa, the Middle East, and South Asia. As with Christianity, there is no single orthodoxy in Islam but a multitude of traditions which are generally categorized as Sunni and Shia, although there are other minor groups as well. Wahhabi is the dominant Muslim sect in the Kingdom of Saudi Arabia. There are also several Islamic republics, including Iran, which is run by a Shia Supreme Leader.
- The Bahá'í Faith was founded in the 19th century in Iran and since then has spread worldwide. It teaches unity of all religious philosophies and accepts all of the prophets of Judaism, Christianity, and Islam as well as additional prophets including its founder Bahá'u'lláh.
- American religions are often derived from Christian tradition. They include the Latter Day Saint movement, Jehovah's Witnesses among hundreds of smaller groups.
- Smaller Abrahamic groups that are not heterodox versions of the four major groupings include Samaritanism, the Druze, and the Rastafari movement.
- Indian religions are practiced or were founded in the Indian subcontinent. Concepts most of them share in common include dharma, karma, reincarnation, mantras, yantras, and darœana.
  - o Hinduism is a synecdoche describing the similar philosophies of Vaishnavism, Shaivism, and related groups practiced or founded in the Indian subcontinent. Concepts most of them share in

common include karma, caste, reincarnation, mantras, yantras, and darœana. Hinduism is not a monolithic religion in the Romanic sense but a religious category containing dozens of separate philosophies amalgamated as Sanatana Dharma.

- Jainism, taught primarily by Parsva (9th century BCE) and Mahavira (6th century BCE), is an ancient Indian religion that prescribes a path of non-violence for all forms of living beings in this world. Jains are found mostly in India.
- Buddhism was founded by Siddhattha Gotama in the 6th century BCE. Buddhists generally agree that Gotama aimed to help sentient beings end their suffering by understanding the true nature of phenomena, thereby escaping the cycle of suffering and rebirth (saCsara), that is, achieving Nirvana.
  - Theravada Buddhism, which is practiced mainly in Sri Lanka and Southeast Asia alongside folk religion, shares some characteristics of Indian religions. It is based in a large collection of texts called the Pali Canon.
  - Under the heading of Mahayana (the "Great Vehicle") fall a multitude of doctrines which began their development in China and are still relevant in Vietnam, in Korea, in Japan, and to a lesser extent in Europe and the United States. Mahayana Buddhism includes such disparate teachings as Zen, Pure Land, and Soka Gakkai.
  - Vajrayana Buddhism, sometimes considered a form of Mahayana, was developed in Tibet and is still most prominent there and in surrounding regions.
  - Two notable new Buddhist sects are Hòa H£o and the Dalit Buddhist movement, which were developed separately in the 20th century.
- Sikhism is a monotheistic religion founded on the teachings of Guru Nanak and ten successive Sikh

Gurus in 15th century Punjab. Sikhs are found mostly in India.

- o There are dozens of new religious movements within Indian religions and Hindu reform movements, such as Ayyavazhi and Swaminarayan Faith.

- Iranian religions are ancient religions which roots predate the Islamization of the Greater Iran. Nowadays these religions are practiced only by minorities.
  - o Zoroastrianism is a religion and philosophy based on the teachings of prophet Zoroaster in the 6th century BC. The Zoroastrians worship the Creator Ahura Mazda. In Zoroastrianism good and evil have distinct sources, with evil trying to destroy the creation of Mazda, and good trying to sustain it.
  - o Mandaeism is a monotheistic religion with a strongly dualistic worldview. Mandaeans are sometime labelled as the "Last Gnostics".
  - o Kurdish religions include the traditional beliefs of the Yazidi, Alevi, and Ahl-e Haqq. Sometimes these are labelled Yazdanism.
- Folk religion is a term applied loosely and vaguely to less-organized local practices. It is also called paganism, shamanism, animism, ancestor worship, and totemism, although not all of these elements are necessarily present in local belief systems. The category of "folk religion" can generally include anything that is not part of an organization. The modern neopagan movement draws on folk religion for inspiration.
  - o African traditional religion is a category including any type of religion practiced in Africa before the arrival of Islam and Christianity, such as Yoruba religion or San religion. There are many varieties of religions developed by Africans in the Americas derived from African beliefs, including Santería, Candomblé, Umbanda, Vodou, and Oyotunji.
  - o Folk religions of the Americas include Aztec religion, Inca religion, Maya religion, and modern Catholic beliefs such as the Virgin of Guadalupe. Native

American religion is practiced across the continent of North America.

- Australian Aboriginal culture contains a mythology and sacred practices characteristic of folk religion.
- Chinese folk religion, practiced by Chinese people around the world, is a primarily social practice including popular elements of Confucianism and Taoism, with some remnants of Mahayana Buddhism. Most Chinese do not identify as religious due to the strong Maoist influence on the country in recent history, but adherence to religious ceremonies remains common. New religious movements include Falun Gong and I-Kuan Tao.
- Traditional Korean religion was a syncretic mixture of Mahayana Buddhism and Korean shamanism. Unlike Japanese Shinto, Korean shamanism was never codified and Buddhism was never made a social necessity. In some areas these traditions remain prevalent, but Korean-influenced Christianity is far more influential in society and politics.
- Traditional Japanese religion is a mixture of Mahayana Buddhism and ancient indigenous practices which were codified as Shinto in the 19th century. Japanese people retain nominal attachment to both Buddhism and Shinto through social ceremonies, but irreligion is common.

- A variety of new religious movements still practiced today have been founded in many other countries besides Japan and the United States, including:
  - Shinshûkyô is a general category for a wide variety of religious movements founded in Japan since the 19th century. These movements share almost nothing in common except the place of their founding. The largest religious movements centred in Japan include Soka Gakkai, Tenrikyo, and Seicho-No-I.e among hundreds of smaller groups.
  - Cao Đài is a syncretistic, monotheistic religion, established in Vietnam in 1926.

- o Unitarian Universalism is a religion characterized by support for a "free and responsible search for truth and meaning."

Sociological classifications of religious movements suggest that within any given religious group, a community can resemble various types of structures, including "churches", "denominations", "sects", "cults", and "institutions".

Mysticism and Esotericism

Mysticism focuses on methods other than logic, but (in the case of esoteric mysticism) not necessarily excluding it, for gaining enlightenment. Rather, meditative and contemplative practices such as Vipassana and yoga, physical disciplines such as stringent fasting and whirling (in the case of the Sufi dervishes), or the use of psychoactive drugs such as LSD, lead to altered states of consciousness that logic can never hope to grasp. However, regarding the latter topic, mysticism prevalent in the 'great' religions (monotheisms, henotheisms, which are perhaps relatively recent, and which the word 'mysticism' is more recent than,) includes systems of discipline that forbid drugs that can damage the body, including the nervous system.

Mysticism (to initiate) is the pursuit of communion with, or conscious awareness of ultimate reality, the divine, spiritual truth, or Deity through direct, personal experience (intuition or insight) rather than rational thought. Mystics speak of the existence of realities behind external perception or intellectual apprehension that are central to being and directly accessible through personal experience. They say that such experience is a genuine and important source of knowledge.

Esotericism is often spiritual (thus religious) but can be non-religious/-spiritual, and it uses intellectual understanding and reasoning, intuition and inspiration (higher noetic and spiritual reasoning,) but not necessarily faith (except often as a virtue,) and it is philosophical in its emphasis on techniques of psycho-spiritual transformation (esoteric cosmology). Esotericism refers to "hidden" knowledge available only to the advanced, privileged, or initiated, as opposed to exoteric knowledge, which is public. All religions are probably somewhat exoteric, but most ones of ancient civilizations such as Yoga of India, and the mystery religions of ancient Egypt, Israel

(Kabbalah), and Greece are examples of ones that are also esoteric.

Types of Religion

Some scholars classify religions as either *universal religions* that seek worldwide acceptance and actively look for new converts, or *ethnic religions* that are identified with a particular ethnic group and do not seek converts. Others reject the distinction, pointing out that all religious practices, whatever their philosophical origin, are ethnic because they come from a particular culture.

Modern Issues in Religion

Interfaith Cooperation

Because religion continues to be recognized in Western thought as a universal impulse, many religious practitioners have aimed to band together in interfaith dialogue and cooperation. The first major dialogue was the Parliament of the World's Religions at the 1893 Chicago World's Fair, which remains notable even today both in affirming "universal values" and recognition of the diversity of practices among different cultures. The 20th century has been especially fruitful in use of interfaith dialogue as a means of solving ethnic, political, or even religious conflict, with Christian-Jewish reconciliation representing a complete reverse in the attitudes of many Christian communities towards Jews.

Secularism and Irreligion

As religion became a more personal matter in western culture, discussions of society found a new focus on political and scientific meaning, and religious attitudes (dominantly Christian) were increasingly seen as irrelevant for the needs of the European world. On the political side, Ludwig Feuerbach recast Christian beliefs in light of humanism, paving the way for Karl Marx's famous characterization of religion as "the opium of the people". Meanwhile, in the scientific community, T.H. Huxley in 1869 coined the term "agnostic," a term—subsequently adopted by such figures as Robert Ingersoll—that, while directly conflicting with and novel to Christian tradition, is accepted and even embraced in some other religions.

Later, Bertrand Russell told the world *Why I Am Not a Christian*, which influenced several later authors to discuss their breakaway from their own religious uprbringings from Islam to Hinduism.

The terms "atheist" (lack of belief in any gods) and "agnostic" (belief in the unknowability of the existence of gods), though specifically contrary to theistic (e.g. Christian, Jewish, and Muslim) religious teachings, do not by definition mean the opposite of "religious". There are religions (including Buddhism and Taoism), in fact, that classify some of their followers as agnostic, atheistic, or nontheistic.

The true opposite of "religious" is the word "irreligious". Irreligion describes an absence of any religion; antireligion describes an active opposition or aversion toward religions in general.

Critics of religious systems as well as of personal faith have posed a variety of arguments against religion. Some modern-day critics hold that religion lacks utility in human society; they may regard religion as irrational. Some assert that dogmatic religions are morally deficient, elevating as they do to moral status ancient, arbitrary, and ill-informed rules.

Related Forms of Thought

Religion and Philosophy

Religion and philosophy meet in several areas — notably in the study of metaphysics and cosmology. In particular, a distinct set of religious beliefs will often entail a specific metaphysics and cosmology. That is, a religion will generally offer answers to metaphysical and cosmological questions about the nature of being, of the universe, humanity, and the divine.

Religion and Superstition

Superstition may be said to be belief in non-causal links between unconnected things. Religions is more complex and includes social institutions and morality. But religions may include superstitions or make use of magical thinking. Members of one religion often think other religions as superstitious. Some atheists, agnostics, deists, and skeptics regard religious belief as superstition. Religious practices are likely to be labelled "superstitious" when they include belief in miracles or extraordinary events, supernatural interventions, apparitions, charms, omens, incantations, an afterlife or the efficacy of prayer..

Greek and Roman pagans, who saw their relations with the gods in political and social terms, scorned the man who constantly trembled with fear at the thought of the gods (*deisidaimonia*), as a slave might fear a cruel and capricious master. The Romans called such fear of the gods *superstitio*. Early Christianity was outlawed as a *superstitio Iudaica*, a "Jewish superstition", by Domitian in the 80s AD. In AD 425, when Rome had become Christian, Theodosius II outlawed pagan traditions as superstitious.

The Roman Catholic Church considers superstition to be sinful in the sense that it denotes a lack of trust in the divine providence of God and, as such, is a violation of the first of the Ten Commandments. The Catechism of the Catholic Church states that superstition "in some sense represents a perverse excess of religion". "Superstition," it says, "is a deviation of religious feeling and of the practices this feeling imposes. It can even affect the worship we offer the true God, e.g., when one attributes an importance in some way magical to certain practices otherwise lawful or necessary.

Myth

The word *myth* has several meanings.

1. A traditional story of ostensibly historical events that serves to unfold part of the world view of a people or explain a practice, belief, or natural phenomenon;
2. A person or thing having only an imaginary or unverifiable existence; or
3. A metaphor for the spiritual potentiality in the human being.

Ancient polytheistic religions, such as those of Greece, Rome, and Scandinavia, are usually categorized under the heading of mythology. Religions of pre-industrial peoples, or cultures in development, are similarly called "myths" in the anthropology of religion. The term "myth" can be used pejoratively by both religious and non-religious people. By defining another person's religious stories and beliefs as mythology, one implies that they are less real or true than one's own religious stories and beliefs. Joseph Campbell remarked, "Mythology is often thought of as *other people's* religions, and religion can be defined as mis-interpreted mythology."

In sociology, however, the term *myth* has a non-pejorative meaning. There, *myth* is defined as a story that is important for the group whether or not it is objectively or provably true. Examples include the death and resurrection of Jesus, which, to Christians, explains the means by which they are freed from sin and is also ostensibly a historical event. But from a mythological outlook, whether or not the event actually occurred is unimportant. Instead, the symbolism of the death of an old "life" and the start of a new "life" is what is most significant. Religious believers may or may not accept such symbolic interpretations.

Bibliography

Bedi, M.S. : *Social Development and Social Work* , Himanshu, Delhi, 1994.

Bhalla, S.K. : *Social Work With Lawbreakers of Society,* MD Pub, Mumbai, 2008.

Bhattacharya, Sanjay : *Social Work : An Integrated Approach*, Deep and Deep, Delhi, 2003.

Bose, N. K.: *The Scheduled Castes and Tribes and Their Present Conditions*, Calcutta, University of Calcutta, 1969.

Chaklader, Snehamoy : *Sociolinguistics: A Guide to Language Problems in India*, New Delhi, Mittal, 1990.

Chaturvedi, Pratima : *Social Work : Theories and Practices,* Book Enclave, Delhi, 2005.

Das, D.K. Lal : *Practice of Social Research : Social Work* Perspective, Rawat, 2000.

Devi, Ranjna K. : *Social Work, Philosophy, Concepts and Dimensions*, Omega, Delhi, 2009.

Dumont, Louis: *The Caste System and Its Implications*, London, Granada Pub. Ltd., 1970.

Gorhe, Neelam: *Social Development and Dalit Women*, Gyan Pub. House, New Delhi, 1995.

Iqbal, Shaikh Azhar : *Problems of Social Welfare and Social Work*, Sublime, Delhi, 2005.

James, Silverberg: *Social Mobility in the Caste System in India*, Mouton Publishers, The Hague, 1968.

Joseph, Benjamin: *Scheduled Castes in Indian Politics and Society*, New Delhi, Ess Ess Publications, 1989.

Joseph, Sherry : *Social Work Practice and Men Who Have Sex With Men*, Sage, Delhi, 2005

Katare, Prakash M : *Social Work and Folk Culture*, Arise Pub, Delhi, 2006.

Khan, M A : *Social Work and Social Policy, Concepts and Methods*, Book Enclave, Delhi, 2007.

Kohli, A S : *Human Rights and Social Work, Issues, Challenges and Response*, Kanishka, Delhi, 2004.

Kumar, Hajira : *Social Work, Social Development and Sustainable Development*, Regency, Delhi, 1997.

Lakshmanna, C.: *Caste Dynamics in Village India*, Nachiketa Publications, Bombay, 1973.

Mathur, Raj Bala : *Modernisation of Social Work, Planning and Administration*, Book Enclave, Delhi, 2007.

Mishra, Brijesh : *Glimpses of Social Welfare in India : Problems and Perspectives*, ABD Pub, Delhi, 2006.

Nagpaul, Hana: *Social Work in Urban India*, Rawat, Delhi, 1996.

Naqi, Mohammad : *Social Work for Weaker Sections*, Anmol, Delhi, 2005.

Parmar, P.M. : *Social Work and Social Welfare in India*, Sublime, Delhi, 2002.

Reamer, G. : *Social Work Values and Ethics,* Rawat, Delhi, 2005.

Ritter, Gerhard A.: *Social Welfare in Germany and Britain: Origins and Development,* Kim Traynor, New York, 1986.

Rizwi, A K : *Social Policy and Social Work*, Mohit Pub, Delhi, 2008.

Sen, S K : *Social Work Practices*, Book Enclave, Delhi, 2007.

Shirley, Dennis : *Community Organizing for Urban School Reform,* Austin, University of Texas Press, 1997.

Shrivastava Raju: *Gerontological Social Work in India : Some Issues and Perspectives*, B.R., Delhi, 2000.

Sinha, Debotosh : *Aspects of Industry and Occupational Social Work*, Abhijeet Pub, Delhi, 2007.

Sundar, I. : *Social Work Practices in Health and Medical Profession*, Sarup Book Pub, Delhi, 2009.

Vijai, Abha: *Voluntary Organisations and Social Welfare*, ABD, Delhi, 2000.

Index

□□□